In Praise of *A Sacred Walk*

"Reading *A Sacred Walk* was like having an intimate conversation with a close friend, one who cares enough to risk sharing lessons from her life in order to help others. It particularly spoke to my heart at this time because my brother and I have the responsibility of making certain my mother has the loving care she needs. Anyone would find encouragement from this book, whether they are fully devoted Christ-followers or not."

Camilla L. Seabolt,
CEO/Executive Director, Community Bible Study, Colorado Springs, CO

"*A Sacred Walk* takes a unique approach to dealing with death and dying. As might be expected, it is filled with helpful, practical ideas and insights for caregivers. But this book is different in that it also focuses on lessons the living can learn from the dying."

Kenneth C. Haugk, PhD,
Founder and Executive Director of Stephen Ministries, Inc., St. Louis, MO,
Author of *Don't Sing Songs to a Heavy Heart*, and *Christian Caregiving: A Way of Life*

"We all must prepare for our sacred walk through the valley of the shadow of death, and this amazing resource and personal story will help many face the fear and process of dying. Authers has captured the essence of something we don't want to talk about. The heartfelt honesty, the experience drawn, and the helpful teaching will be a valuable fountain for all those facing the death of a loved one. This book will help you heal the fear and issues that surround "the ultimate healing." Read it and reap as you weep. This book will touch your soul."

The Rev. Nigel Mumford, Director
Christ the King Spiritual Life Center, Greenwich, NY
Author of *The Forgotten Touch* and *Hand to Hand: From Combat to Healing*

"Authers writes clearly, compellingly and with compassion. She demystifies the practical and legal details of getting one's affairs in order and motivates readers to take action with interesting stories and anecdotes that bring the chapter on estate planning alive…Excellent!"

Kimberlee A. Barrett-Johnson, CFP
Barrrett-Johnson & Associates, Ameriprise Financial, Charlottesville, VA

A Sacred Walk

Dispelling the Fear of Death and Caring for the Dying

Peace,
Donna Authers

Donna M. Authers

A&A Publishing
Charlottesville, Virginia

Quotations from the Bible are taken from
the New International Version if no other translation is mentioned.

To respect confidentiality, names of individuals in this book
have been changed where appropriate.

Fourth printing 2012

www.asacredwalk.com

ISBN 978-0-615-24585-0

Printed in the United States of America

A&A Publishing
Charlottesville, Virginia

Your love has given me great joy and encouragement.
(Philemon 1:7)

With eternal gratitude to

Anna
my mother, who taught me how to live
and how to die with no regrets

Angelina
my grandmother, who broke my fear of death

Sister Therese
my spiritual mother, who shared her spiritual tool kit

The Holy Spirit
who continues to comfort, guide, correct, and inspire

Acknowledgments

There is no such thing as a self-made man or woman. We are the sum total of all our experiences and everyone has been given a helping hand at one time or another. I've had many. This book is dedicated to the caregivers of this world and the people who have taught me how to live life to the full, particularly my mentoring mothers, other family members and the special friends with whom I have shared a sacred walk.

My thanks go to the many psychologists, social workers, doctors, pastors, lawyers, estate planners, hospice nurses, and administrators in assisted living facilities who have complemented and enhanced my training as a caregiver to friends in crisis, especially the dying and their families.

The task of writing a book about the lessons learned from my mentors and care receivers over the years could not have been undertaken without the encouragement of many people. I am particularly indebted to my close friends who patiently read the initial manuscript and urged me to complete this labor of love, including memoir-writing coaches Kevin Quirk and Stephen Pfleiderer.

It is no surprise that the inspiration needed to complete this project came chiefly from my husband Roger. I am blessed to have his unconditional love, his God-given patience, his support through good times and bad, and his keen, critical eye.

Donna M. Authers

Contents

Part I—The Fear of Death: How Do We Face It?

Part II—Preparing to Die: How Best to Help

Part III—Experiencing Death: A Sacred Time

Part I

The Fear of Death: How Do We Face It?

In the Beginning

Start by doing what is necessary; then do what's possible; and suddenly you are doing the impossible.
(Saint Francis of Assisi)

Monday, April 9

Mom had summoned me the day before. She was dying. I packed for Florida, and went to bed wondering if I would have the strength to make this trip without my husband by my side. Roger would be home in less than a week fresh from a Habitat work site.

After a fitful night's sleep, my eyes opened to the brightness of the digital clock which read 4:55 a.m. I leapt out of bed and shouted, "My God! The limo will be here at 5:00!"

No human had ever moved as fast as I did that morning. Into my jeans and shirt I jumped, disengaged the security system, ran downstairs, and peered into the darkness. Just as I thought, the limo had arrived and the driver decided to wait in the driveway. *Why in God's name didn't he ring the bell when he saw the house was dark?*

"Quick! Take my suitcase while I get my other bag. My alarm didn't go off." Taking two steps at a time, I returned upstairs to the bathroom, threw my make-up in my carry-on, grabbed my shoes, and dashed downstairs again. Sitting on the bottom step, I stuffed my feet into my Reeboks, reset the house alarm, locked the door, and ran to the waiting car—heart racing! They were boarding the plane when I arrived at the gate.

By contrast on the Tampa end, the limo driver was late. *Where is he? Mom is waiting for me!* After calling the company, I was told, "Stay at baggage claim, he will be there soon." Another 15 minutes passed—the longest 15 minutes of my life. Precious minutes with my mother lost!

Once he arrived, we made it to her house in less than an hour. Mom opened the door, greeted me with a smile—but one that looked as if she had pulled it up from her toes. Throwing her arms around my neck, she held on tightly and whispered in my ear, "Thank God you're here."

For me, that was how the last nine days of my mother's life began. I promise I won't leave you hanging on what happened next, but before I tell the complete story of her final days, there is so much I want to share with you—things like how to face our own fear of death, the practical considerations after coming to terms with our mortality, and how to help someone you love through the dying process.

Have you already faced this situation? Are you in the middle of it now? Do you anticipate it happening soon? Are you dreading the prospect? One of the most testing times in anyone's life is when you must cope with a life threatening illness—yours or someone close to you—especially as the end draws near. If you don't know what this feels like, I will give you the full, rich account of my experience with my mother, not because it is the perfect model, but because it's the greatest gift I have to pass onto you. Good comes out of grief when we are able to learn from it, grow as a result of it, and experience the depth and breadth of our faith in ways we never expected.

This is an important topic because, thanks to technology and advances in medical science, far fewer people die suddenly. Most of us and our loved ones will live with chronic, life threatening illnesses with varying degrees of comfort and support at home, in assisted living facilities, nursing homes, or hospitals. Consequently, the grieving process can begin long before a person actually dies.

My familiarity with grief and the dying process comes from experiencing multiple deaths within my own family as well as from being a caregiver to the dying and their families for nearly two decades. Statistically speaking, I'm more than three quarters of the way through my own life, and I want to tell you what I've learned about how to find meaning and joy on this road in spite of the bumps—potholes, even—we may encounter along the way.

Faith, with its accompanying doubts and questions, is the backdrop of my story and, it was faith that called me into action. It is an integral component to grieving well and the reason I have been able to be present with others during the most profound crisis in their lives. The concept of "good grief" had always been an oxymoron to me, and embracing death was the farthest thing from my mind for the majority of my life.

Born in 1942, my earliest memories are of sickness, accidents, and wars. I always had a gnawing fear—terror, really—not only of life but of death. Can you relate to that? Like many youngsters today, I remember saying, "What's the point of life if we're just going to die anyhow?" Today things are different, and the story of the men and women who have inspired me with their lessons of how to live and die without fear, is…well…it's their story. But it's also mine—and I want to share it with you, especially the miraculous story of how my fear of death was broken thanks to Grandma. It no longer throws me into a black hole, but still I don't look forward to dying. Not even suicidal people want to die. They just want things to be different.

Have you received worrisome news about your health? Maybe a member of your family has an illness with no known cure. Are you wondering what practical things you should do to help prepare for the inevitable, or are you a reluctant caregiver, perhaps just a friend who is uncomfortable talking to someone who has been diagnosed with a life threatening illness? It is also possible that you are a professional who gives end-of-life advice such as an estate planner, an insurance broker, or someone in the health care industry. And if you are an ordained minister or part of a lay caring ministry with a heart's desire to comfort those who grieve—to all of you I say—please take my hand and come with me as we explore this sacred writing.

It's sacred because I didn't write this book alone. It was written on my heart by others who are no longer with us, but their spirits linger. You will meet some of them and my mentoring mothers to whom I've dedicated this book. They may remind you of your own mentors. As I walked them part way home, my perspective on life changed. Their stories will motivate you to get your affairs in order, help you cope more easily with the surprises in your own life, and provide useful suggestions if you are called to action when someone you know or love needs tender loving care.

Before the first draft of this book was completed, I had to put some of the lessons I learned to immediate use when, out of the blue, I was diagnosed with breast cancer. Facing a life threatening disease or being told you have to accommodate a chronic illness for the rest of your life is a very scary thing.

Part of my recovery program from surgery and cancer treatments included a self-imposed change in diet along with exercise and supplements to build my immune system—a permanent change of lifestyle. The combination was so successful that we traveled to see a group of friends who had been praying for me. Bob, one of our close friends, had called my husband regularly during the ordeal to ask over and over again, "Is she all right, reeeeeally?"

At one point during the festive reunion, Bob was uncharacteristically quiet as he watched from across the room. I meandered over and asked, "Why do you keep staring at me? Can't you see that I'm fine?"

He said, "Yes, and maybe that's the problem. You look so great that I'm beginning to think nothing ever happened to you."

With my hand tugging gently on one side of my sweater, I jokingly said, "Oh, it happened all right; would you like to see the scar?" He didn't.

As you read on, you will most likely recall the mental snapshots of pain and joy, laughter and tears during the trials and triumphs of your own life. Think about the good that came out of those experiences and share your insights with others. The lessons learned from many of my special friends, especially those who have died, are more than a gift. They are a legacy, and I feel compelled to pass them on to you.

This book also includes an intimate account of the last nine days of my mother's life. Including this was not an easy decision. But you may find value in seeing how the lessons learned from my previous care receivers and their families came together for us. It may sound strange, I know, but embracing the reality of death is a life-affirming, life-enhancing process! And when we no longer fear the dying process, life takes on new meaning.

While I don't think of myself as a "religious" person or someone who wishes to be identified with a particular denomination, I am a person of faith—distinctively Christian faith. I make no apologies for that. However, it saddens me to think there are people searching for a place to discover the purpose and meaning of life who may look at members of organized religion and ask themselves, *"Why would I want to become one of them?"* When church politics or claims of having the "right" theology prevail, even God must sometimes want to shy away.

Faith is not about religion, it is about a relationship. When a relationship with God is combined with emotional openness and honesty between us and others, it is powerful. This faith facilitates healing of body, mind, and spirit, and prompts us to care for one another.

It was faith that prompted me to write this book – a faith not only in the relationships of my past and the lessons learned, but my faith in

God and in you. Let me explain. In the beginning, I questioned whether or not to tackle this life and death project, and wondered if you would actually read and share this book with others since it is not about well-known celebrities or persons of notoriety.

A friend with the gift of encouragement spurred me to action when he said, "If you feel you are being called to do this, then you really have no choice. Just write what comes out of you—from your heart—and let God worry about who's going to read it."

Well, here it is, and I truly hope you will be able to embrace life more fully after reading the vivid vignettes about the real-life people you will meet on the pages of this book. They are a diverse group—funny, courageous, and full of human emotions and faults. The value of their lives will be extended if you come a few steps closer to achieving what I have come to think of as the ultimate goal of life: to live and die with no regrets.

Honor your father and your mother, so that you may live long in the land the Lord your God is giving you.
(Exodus 20:12)

No Stranger to Death

Blessed are those who mourn, for they will be comforted.
(Matthew 5:4)

My early experiences of sudden, untimely deaths in our family formed the basis of my near paralyzing fear of death. As I grew into adulthood, I continued to hug the walls of funeral parlors when obligated to pay my respects. Television had not yet begun to desensitize us to violence, and wars were not brought "live" into our living rooms. Kids, however, did compose ghoulish rhymes about what happens when you die. *"The worms crawl in, the worms crawl out; your teeth decay and your eyes fall out."* The dozens of times I visualized my coffin being lowered, I made my mother promise to never put me in the ground. It was a mausoleum for me!

Fear began to take hold of me soon after my father was killed in World War II when I was a small child. Army PFC Joseph Michael Del Sardo died in Luzon, a Philippine island, on January 20, 1945. The sounds and images of my grieving mother and relatives must have been etched into my two-year-old subconscious mind. I cherished the stories and pictures of my father, but Mom saved the details of where and how she was notified of his death until I had the adult curiosity and courage to ask her about it. She also waited until I was old enough to understand and appreciate the letters Daddy wrote his little daughter from the front lines. His death forever changed our lives on so many levels.

Mom was only 24 when Daddy died, so she remarried and eventually gave birth to another daughter. But after only seven months, my new baby sister Lorraine died of spinal meningitis some time after midnight on my fifth birthday. The day of her death is one of my first conscious memories. I remember waking up to tearful wails and a house already filled with relatives and a doctor. The only birthday present for me that day was being protected from this contagious disease. I wriggled and screamed to escape the examining hands of the doctor and others who were holding me down while my mother frantically gathered Lorraine's clothes to burn as a precaution.

Later, when I was a young teen, Grandpa committed suicide. Reluctantly, I entered the funeral home where I would see for the last time the man who sheltered and cared for me and Mom when we moved in with him and Grandma after Daddy died. Now he lay silent with a hole in his head, plugged and powdered at the bullet's point of entry. Walking into the funeral home felt like an out-of-body experience, and it also triggered my first feeling of true anger as I stood in a corner observing all the people coming and going. *Why is everyone talking, smiling and some laughing? Shut up! Have you no respect? Doesn't anyone feel my pain?* From a distance I looked at the casket and silently cried, *Grandpa, wake up. Why did you do that? Everybody loves you! What's going to happen to us now?*

This memory registers an important point. Special care and attention should be taken with young people when they experience death, especially of a loved one, for the first time. It is a very frightening and confusing time in their young lives. If death is not discussed with our tenderhearted children who long to know what is on the other side of this life, some develop an unhealthy curiosity about death, or they can live with unnecessary fear for many years.

Talk to your children about how people will behave when they grieve and about life after death, even if you have doubts. If you don't believe in an afterlife, they should know that others do and be encouraged to ask questions and talk about their fears. You will then have no regrets when the loss of someone dear to them occurs.

Nearly six years after Grandpa's death, my Uncle Bennie was killed in an automobile accident, a victim of a drunk driver. He was only 24 and I was 20. Since we were so close in age, he was more of a big brother than an uncle. We grew up together and were confidantes. Our plan was that he would walk me down the aisle on my wedding day. Bennie loved children, but would never see his own beautiful daughter, yet to be born. The casket was closed because they were unable to put him back together. The point of impact with the telephone pole was the front passenger seat where he was riding.

Pictures of Ben adorned the funeral parlor and the casket appeared to float in a field of flowers. People stood in line for blocks including

Army buddies who flew across the country to grieve for our "golden boy," a nickname he acquired as a fair-haired child who tanned so easily in summer. But his best friend John broke through the crowd straight from a hunting trip and rocked the casket when he threw his body across it in shock. His denial of the news of Bennie's death evaporated as his cries and sobs shook every bone in his body. Later at the church service, I can still remember feeling the vibration of my internal scream when I saw his casket being carried into church, *Bennie's in that box!* I now know that he wasn't; it was only his body.

Only a few years later, Aunt Bessie, my grandmother's youngest daughter, also died prematurely crying in her mother's arms, "Mama, save me; I'm dying." At 38 she was drowning as fluid filled her lungs, the result of an undiagnosed condition. Aunt Bessie left a husband and three young children, her mother, a remaining brother and three sisters who were beginning to think our family was cursed—my worst fear for years. Aunt Bessie's physical problems worsened after the psychological trauma she suffered when Grandpa died. He had shown her the gun the night before the morning he killed himself. She didn't believe anyone could do such a thing, let alone her own father.

So you see, exposure to death came early and a little too fast for me, long before I was able to learn the meaning of life or know how to deal with loss. However, these experiences were eventually put to good use. After retiring from a business career, I was drawn to a ministry, Stephen Ministry, which extends pastoral care to those in crisis, many of whom were grieving. To my surprise, my history of personal loss had value.

Helping others express their feelings and consider how to cope with various physical, emotional, and spiritual problems was like being on familiar territory. Sadly, some of my special friends have died, but not before talking about their regrets and the resulting lessons learned. It was apparent that once they were able to embrace the reality of their own mortality, they were able to reflect on those things that affirm and enhance life. For many of them, the quality of their last days, even years, was the best they had experienced. Relationships were strengthened or restored, and they spent time doing whatever made them feel happy and fulfilled.

Embracing the reality of death is a life-affirming, life-enhancing process.

Whatever your belief system—God or no God, life after death or nothing—one thing is certain, death is inevitable. There is no way to know precisely when death will enter your life. You cannot fight it. You have no control over it. Modern medicine and healing prayers may delay it, but death will come, sooner or later. So what do we do?

One perspective comes from the noted spiritual author Henri Nouwen. In his book *A Meditation on Dying and Caring*, he said that over time he came to think of Death as his friend, not the enemy. He viewed death as merely something that helped him make the transition from this life to the next.

Previously, my fear of death was so terrifying I could hardly talk about it, let alone think of death as a friend. Today, it's difficult to describe adequately the exhilarating feeling of having complete freedom from that fear. It was my grandmother who helped me experience "good grief" for the first time in my life and who proved to me that life does not end at death.

The Spirit himself intercedes for us with groans too deep for words.
(Romans 8:26)

Grandma's Final Gift

But perfect love casts out fear.
(1 John 4:18)

Just telling you that I no longer fear death is not enough. You really must know how my transformation took place. Prepare yourself for a real treat, maybe a little laughter, too, as I share Grandma's final gift with you. Perhaps she will make you think of your own grandmother. If not, for any reason, then feel free to adopt mine, and let her speak directly to you through one of my favorite Grandma stories.

Her name was Angelina Melodia, and just like a melody, that beautiful, lyrical name will sing in my heart forever. She knew sorrow at a very early age, seeing what death and starvation did to her country following the ravages of World War I. Within the first year of their marriage, she and Grandpa emigrated from the island of Sicily in Italy to America not long after learning they were to have a child—my mother. Grandma was only 18 years old.

In spite of their desire to build a safe and secure future in this "brave new world," the grief of leaving her parents an ocean—a continent—away was a burden that weighed heavily on Grandma for many years. She never saw her parents again. Her children gave new meaning to her life. Because of them, six in all, she learned to call America home. Even though she did not have much of a formal education and spoke no English when she arrived in the United States, Grandma fully immersed herself in the American way of life. But it was a lonely struggle because her entire support system was back in her small home town of Alcamo.

Hearing Grandma tell the rich stories of her village and of the people they met on their nearly three-week Atlantic crossing, as well as how she adapted to her new country, gave me a glimpse into the courage, creativity and fortitude of this amazing woman.

Without emotional crises, there is no growth.

As I matured, I marveled at how she was able to work through the grief of continued losses—her parents whom she never saw again, her husband, her youngest son, and her youngest daughter. She stoically carried the emotional scars of these painful experiences for the rest of her life, and because of our close family ties, she also helped shoulder the personal pain of her children and grandchildren through the years. She was the one who taught us how to cope, one loss at a time. Crying with her through sad times and watching her gradually get back into life inspired everyone else to do the same. She seemed to grow stronger with each blow she endured, and even laughed in the face of her own death.

Granddaughters and grandmothers often share a special relationship, and ours was no exception. Perhaps because she had promised my father that she would take care of me and Mom when he went to war, our bond was never broken. She loved Daddy as if he were her own son; and after her death in 1983, we found his picture in her wallet along with his obituary she had clipped from the newspaper in 1945.

Grandma was the one constant in everyone's life. She was most comfortable in the kitchen, cooking and baking Sicilian specialties for her family and guests. After Grandpa died, her role of mother and homemaker was renewed. She now had the time and the heart to visit frequently so she could help her working daughter raise two children alone. Often when we came home from school, Grandma would be standing at the ironing board after washing our clothes; and the smells of our favorite sauces and soups to replenish the freezer filled our home. Not given to a show of partiality, her practical gifts, offered in love, were spread equally throughout her family. Everyone enjoyed spending time with Grandma.

As a child I remember climbing onto her lap and laying my head on what she used to call her "pillows." I used to stuff Kleenex in my training bras, and while other relatives made fun of the uneven lumps in my sweater, Grandma did not. She was always looking for practical solutions to a problem. Advising us with extra syllables that colored her speech, she'd say, "Dolly, if I could give-a you some of mine, I would. I have-a too much."

Grandma not only had a great sense of humor, she had the "memory of an elephant." After her mastectomy at the age of 80, she remembered the awkward years of my youth and said, "Isn't it ironical that afa-ta all those years of trying to give 'em away, now I have-a to wear a falsie!"

As a child, Grandma kept me amused by allowing me to play beauty shop with her, and even gave me permission to sit on the little stool in front of her vanity so I could apply her make-up, powder and lipstick. When she grew old, one of the younger grandchildren gave her wrinkle cream for a present, and I remember her saying, "Dolly, it's-a too late!" Grandma took pride in her appearance, but one day as she passed a mirror, she did a double-take, peered into it and said, "Whos-a dat?" Shaking her head, she explained that she felt exactly the same on the inside as when she was a young girl.

Grandma never wanted anyone in or out of the family to see her unless she was perfectly dressed. She never understood why men were placed in a coffin wearing a business suit, but funeral directors dressed women in a negligee. "Don't-a you dare let 'em do that to me! Nobody's gonna see me in a night-a-gown. When I die, I wanna be dressed up-a!"

Unfortunately, the inevitable happened. Grandma's cancer spread to her brain during the summer before she died causing seizures. She moved into my mother's home for a couple of months until she had to be rushed to the hospital with a series of convulsions that lasted six and a half hours. I lived out of town, so when Mom called to tell me Grandma was close to death, I drove like a madwoman from my home in Ohio to get to the Pittsburgh hospital in time.

When I arrived, Cousin Kathy and I relieved other family members who had been waiting for her to be transferred to a regular room. Finally! Grandma, now paralyzed on one side of her body, rested while Kathy and I spoke in whispers, waiting for her body to recover after this ordeal. Soon, she managed to say hello, with a heavy slur, to show she recognized us.

In a while, it was lunchtime and Grandma loved to eat—especially at smorgasbords dispelling the theory that your appetite gets smaller as you age. Kathy and I wondered if she would ever be the same again. When the food cart arrived with Jell-O and bouillon, Grandma heard the noise, opened her eyes, and just as we were about to tell them to take the tray away, she spoke.

Leaning closer to interpret her impaired speech, we knew she would be with us for a while longer when she said with characteristic humor, "Shovel it in and cancel the l'undertaker; you'll know I'm dead when I can't-a eat!" Laughing through our tears, Kathy spooned in the soup, and I shoveled in the Jell-O.

We are most comical when we take ourselves too seriously.

Since she now needed round-the-clock professional care, Grandma was transferred to a residential hospice.

Grandma was always hot. Even in winter, she slept with only a sheet covering her and kept one leg out. Things were no different now; she kicked off the blanket even in the hospice. It's true what they say—when you get older you never change; you just get "more so."

Grandma's hospice room was one of eight, four on either side of a common area where relatives could gather. Each room had a large picture window overlooking this "living room" so the patients could see the overflow of relatives. The nurse thought she would convince Grandma to keep herself covered by saying, "Angelina, there's a man across the way, and he can see right into your room; so quit kicking off the covers!"

She giggled and replied, "You mean to tell-a me, there's a man in a place-a like-a this, who wants to look-a me? If that's-a true, take it all off and give-a him his last thrill!"

Like many strong women, Grandma was fiercely independent, so after selling the family home, she had moved into a senior apartment building where she could still cook and have her own space. She didn't want to be a burden on any of her children. Since she never drove a car, it would have been much easier for my mother if Grandma had moved in with her at that point, but Mom gladly did the double shopping and other errands to honor Grandma's desire to live alone for as long as she was able. In the summer of 1983, before the seizures began, Grandma was told she had only four to six months to live.

One day the phone rang, and when I answered, it was surprising to hear Grandma's voice. "Donna, it's-a me. I need to talk-a to you about my children! I'm-a dying, and you're the only one I can talk-a to." I swallowed the lump in my throat, and decided to take a week's vacation so I could bring her home for a long visit. Just like old times, I had her all to myself, and it gave my mother a well-deserved break.

During our time together, Grandma wanted to talk about everything. She retold the story about coming to America, and she filled in a lot of gaps about the many things I didn't understand as a child. She explained what it was like to grow up in another culture, her courtship with Grandpa, and how World War I affected her and those she loved. As I soaked up the vignettes about the 1920 ocean passage with Grandpa, being processed at Ellis Island, and the heartwarming stories of their transition years when she learned to adapt to her new life, I knew Grandma would get around to the main reason she wanted to see me.

After days of reminiscing, the time had come for her to get right to the point by clearly stating that she wanted to talk about her feelings and views not only of life but of death. She made me promise to deliver these messages to her children and other grandchildren when she died.

One of the hardest things in life is to look into the eyes of someone you love and acknowledge, let alone talk about, their death. I wanted to change the subject as my mother, aunts, and uncles had done—but this week was not about me. Grandma needed to express her feelings before it was too late.

As we neared the end of our week together, I was struck with the fact that she was not dying. She was living! Yes, there was cancer in her body, but she was still filled with life and love and stories and laughter and wisdom to share. All I had to do was listen and in return I was given priceless memories and lessons that will now last beyond my lifetime.

Pain of any kind is usually eased when we focus on others.

An integral part of this particular Grandma story is your knowing that, when I was young, she and Grandpa owned a restaurant. They were known as Mama and Papa Melodia and their neon sign called everyone in for "Hot Sausage, Spaghetti, and Pizza," and so much more. I memorized every song on the multicolored, bubbling, floor model jukebox and sang along with the 45's that customers played almost nonstop.

As a special treat during the week we spent together, I took Grandma to a Marie Osmond concert since she had always enjoyed the "Donny and Marie" television show. On the drive home I learned that, absent the magic of special effects, she judged this live performance to be somewhat disappointing. Her grandmother's prejudice soon revealed itself. "I think-a your voice is better. Sing-a to me like you did in the restaurant." Fortunately, I remembered the lyrics of those popular songs so I could comply—but not without difficulty.

It wasn't easy to pitch the notes and form the words knowing it might be the last time I would sing for her. If she liked the song, she clapped with both hands. If it was just so-so, she clapped with one hand by slapping it on her leg. If she didn't like it at all, she kept silent. Grandma never lied, and was often brutally honest. I laughed to myself and launched into another number, singing one song after another. The next day, on my back deck, Grandma had another request, but one of a different kind.

She asked me to pray that she would not linger because she didn't want to be a burden. Our consummate caregiver did not want to reverse roles. I don't know where the voice came from, but I heard myself saying, "No! Who do you think you are?"

She considered the question, and before she could respond, the voice continued. "God may not be through using you. Why should I pray for Him to cut your life short? You're the strong one in this family, Grandma, and some of us aren't ready to let you go. Maybe God will allow you to linger for a while so we can get used to the idea. I'd rather pray 'Thy will be done' and pray hard even harder that you have no pain. Is that alright with you?"

She looked at me thoughtfully, then nodded her head in agreement. "Okay," she said. "From now on it's 'Thy will-a be done'." In the following weeks whenever I asked her how she was feeling, she would simply give me a cheerful, "Thy will-a be done!"

On the last evening of her visit, she wanted to know if I had any other questions, so I mustered up the courage and said, "Yes, I have two. The first is this: After living in two different cultures on two different continents, suffering through two world wars and all our family tragedies, how would you describe life?"

I'll never forget her grin and giggle when she answered, "Life is a bigga surprise! You never know what's going to happen even to the finale." Quickly, she added, "Thank God we don't, because we couldn't cope-a. I would've lost my mind or died of a heart attack long ago."

I remember hugging her and telling her that her answer was wonderful before tentatively asking the second question. "This second one is a little more difficult under the circumstances. Now that you are nearing the end, Grandma, what is the meaning of life? Why are we here?"

Without hesitation this time, she said, "Oh, this one is easier! We're here to help each other get through it—one day at a time if that's what it takes. And this is another thing I want you to tell everyone. Celebrate the love we shared and the opportunity we had to help each other. You know, to give each other a little push-a in life when we need to keep going."

Life is a big surprise, and we are meant to help each other get through it.

She went on to say, "I'm-a gonna be the first in our family to die in old age, so *my* death will not be a tragedy. Remind my children that I've lived a long time. Tell them I was tired and ready to go. Save your tears for the untimely losses of our spouses and children, for the sicknesses, accidents and wars. Remember the love we shared and, above all, look forward to the day when we see each other again."

We talked about where she thought she was going and who she thought she would see again, and I reminded her of what Jesus said after His resurrection. He promised to prepare a place for us in His Father's house of many mansions.

She sighed longingly, and then began to chuckle—no, cackled. Her laugh was more of a cackle, very distinctive. "A mansion! What I'm-a gonna do with a whole mansion? If I thought I could have a little, little corner of a room, I'll be happy."

Then, as if she sensed my fear of losing her—in spite of all my bravado—she leaned forward, took my hands in hers, looked directly into my face and said, "Dolly, remember you too will be where I am some day. Dying is part of life. Don't-a be scared." I listened, but more than words were needed to help break the chains of my fear of death.

Just three months later in November, I stayed in the hospice with Grandma as she lay in a coma for the last six days of her life. In the evening when all other visitors went home, the nurses encouraged me to talk to her since the sense of hearing is the last to go. When I could think of nothing more to say, I decided to sing to her once more. To my surprise, I could not think of a single lyric. The only song that came to mind, *Be Not Afraid,* was never on her juke box. Over and over again I sang it, hummed it, and la-la'ed it. *"Be not afraid. I go before you always. Come follow me and I will give you rest."* Later, I understood why I could think of nothing else.

At her funeral service, I delivered Grandma's eulogy, incorporating all she had asked me to tell her children. As I passed the casket in the center aisle, I tapped it and said, "I did it, Grandma!" The priest surprised me a few minutes later by dragging me out of the pew just before Holy Communion, ignoring my protestations. In spite of the fact that he knew I had not been to church in years, he said, "You are meant to be here with me." With that, he gave me the quickest lesson in how to be a Chalice Bearer: "You offer the cup saying 'The blood of Christ' and when they take a sip, you wipe off the rim and give it to the next guy."

As I nervously waited for the first person to receive the cup of wine, Grandma began to sing. *"Be Not Afraid. I go before you always. Come follow me and I will give you rest."* I was sure it was her! Through the organist, she was singing "our song" back to me from a world we have yet to see. There was no question in my mind that it was her way of telling me she heard the tribute and the message she gave me three months earlier.

Coincidence? Some people may think so, but what happened two months later will give them pause to think otherwise. My mother was shopping and ran into a lady who said, "Ann, I haven't seen you since your mother's funeral. Your niece did such a beautiful job with her eulogy."

Mom replied, "That wasn't my niece; that was my daughter."

"Oh! You're reminding me that my daughter was there, too. In fact, she played the organ. The strangest thing happened to her at communion. After your daughter spoke, she was unable to play and sing what she had rehearsed. She said her hands froze, and not knowing what to do, she quickly rifled through a stack of sheet music and *was told* to play "Be Not Afraid."

My mother could hardly believe her ears and called me as soon as she came home—but I didn't need confirmation. In my mind's eye, I once again saw Grandma's smiling face and, as if we were still in my backyard, I heard her whisper, *"I told-a you. I'm-a gonna see you again."*

The fear of death had actually left me the moment I watched Grandma take her last breath. That's when I finally and silently said, "It's okay to go, Grandma; because I will be where you are someday." Amazingly, when we entered the funeral home two days later, I was able to walk right over to the casket—without fear or hesitation! Our family flowers were not typical of funerals. They were symbolic of spring—a time to celebrate love and new life.

Her body was clothed in a beautiful pink dress with pleated sleeves and pearls which Mom, Cousin Kathy, and I had purchased two days before she died—no nightgown for her! Using pictures of Grandma as a guide, the undertaker made her appearance match as closely as possible to the way she looked sitting on my deck in August. But it was not my grandmother. It was only "the house" she used to live in.

Standing next to her casket, I thought to myself, *So this is what good grief feels like.* I was filled with gratitude and joy mixed with sadness for not having her in the flesh any longer. Grandma left me with a legacy of lessons and one final gift—she broke my fear of death and confirmed through a precious song that I will see her again.

There is life after death. Believe and live with faith, hope and love so you will have no regrets as you near the end of your own life.

Grandma's faith strengthened my own, and there is no doubt in my mind that she is living in more than a little corner of a room in heaven.

In my Father's house there are many mansions; if this were not so I would have told you. I am going there to prepare a place for you. (John 14:2)

Living Libraries

Whoever walks with the wise will become wise;
whoever walks with fools will suffer harm.
(Proverbs 13:20)

I've heard it said, "When an old person dies, another library burns down." Grandma was a living library whose wisdom and practical advice rivaled the content of many self-help guides on the shelves of any bookstore. She taught me that birth and death are the bookends of life. In between we are free to write our own story as we move and grow, one chapter at a time. If only we could tap into each other's personal encyclopedias to capitalize on our collective experiences.

Experience is great, but it takes too long to get it.

Experience may be the best teacher, but it takes much too long to get it. If one is willing to take the time to delve into the stories of another person, it just might save a lot of time and heartbreak. The apple doesn't fall far from the tree, so it will not surprise you to learn that my mother Anna was my favorite library. I call Mom, Grandma, and Sister Therese, a remarkable teacher of mine, my "mentoring mothers." A mentor is defined as an "experienced and trusted adviser." That title also fits others who have crossed my path.

Think of the mentors in your own life, and I know you have them. They may not be your mother, grandmother or even a close relative, but your living library may be a friend, neighbor, teacher, or the greatest boss you ever had. I'm referring to the people who made you feel as if you could do anything, the special individuals who encouraged you and gave the precious gift of time when you needed a friend. Perhaps you are thinking of someone who helped you make it through just one more day a long time ago.

If you've never had a mentor or you have lost contact with them for one reason or another, look around you. You will be amazed to find that we are surrounded by living libraries in our neighborhoods, churches, and social clubs. Many are tucked away in retirement communities, rehabilitation centers and nursing homes all over this country, bursting to share their wisdom and advice.

Families today are separated physically or even emotionally as a result of lifestyle, career, or other relationship issues. Our transient society makes it difficult to seek advice or comfort from traditional sources. If you've lost touch with your treasure troves of wisdom, whom will you call the day you want to ask, "What do I do now?" Visit a living library today or begin the search for one. You won't be sorry. Everybody has a story to tell; just listen and develop a relationship with a new living library or two. They will help you navigate more easily through the uncharted waters of this imperfect world.

A consistent piece of advice I received over the years was to set goals for myself. While this is fundamental to growing in a positive direction, my Living Libraries stressed the fact that life's goals should not be focused solely on material things. If we only pursue those things that give us instant gratification or add to our wealth and notoriety, there is danger in losing sight of the fact that this game of life will end one day. It is sad, indeed, to listen to a friend or loved one recount their regrets when there is little time to recapture the "could've, would've, should've" opportunities that passed them by.

People with few regrets inspire others. They tend to have different priorities than those set by society. Rather than being self-centered, their goals are focused on enhancing the quality of their relationships, and their desire to "give back" is put into action. Too many of us talk about volunteer work for the betterment of others but tend to put it off until it's too late. Life happens and it can be over in a twinkling of an eye.

I've learned that it is best not to wait until retirement or the children are grown to make memories out of our dreams or long-term goals. If you want to bequeath a lasting legacy, consider that people are remembered far longer for how they make us feel when we are with them rather than for "the stuff" they will leave behind.

My mentoring mothers were big on making memories and telling stories, and they never shielded me from the highs and lows of life. That played a large role in the development of my core values and my spiritual DNA. Let me give you a snapshot of our relationships.

Take the time to make memories that will live on in those who knew and loved you.

For now, you already know something about Grandma and her final gift to me, and you know that she immigrated to America with Grandpa along with many others. But not everyone had the distinction of arriving on the 4th of July. The year was 1920; Grandma was only 18 years old and pregnant with my mother.

When I think of my mother years after she passed away, the wind still blows through the hole in my heart. Anna Melodia was everything to me—mother, father, sister and best friend—quite a job! Filling multiple roles in life is hard work, but for her there was no choice. After Daddy was killed in World War II, Mom soon remarried so her little girl could have a father. Mom and Pete, my stepfather, had two additional children. You know my sister Lorraine died when she was only seven months old, and my brother was born two years later. Unfortunately, when Larry was four and I was eleven, my mother's second marriage ended in divorce.

We were the original latchkey kids, and Mom struggled to raise us alone without having had a formal education. Being the oldest child, she dropped out of school to work in a candy factory at the age of 13 to help Grandma and Grandpa who by then had five children. Her first paycheck went to buy Grandma, her sister Angie, and herself new winter coats.

Without child support payments, my mother worked long, hard hours in the retail trade, buying and selling ladies' clothing. My job was to watch Larry after school and stay in contact with her by phone so she could instruct me on how to start dinner. Saturday was cleaning day, but Sunday was cooking class. Soups, stews, sauces, meatloaf, pot roast and the like were stored in the Frigidaire for the week. No TV dinners for us! After my second year of college, Mom enrolled in a business school to ultimately secure employment with regular hours in credit and apartment management that did not require her to work weekends. Happily, nobody checked her non-existent high school transcript.

After Larry and I were old enough to leave home, she married for the third and last time. Within the first year of their marriage, Mom discovered that John had deep-seated emotional problems stemming from his childhood, a fact that had been hidden from her. Mom's gifts of love and compassion accounted for her determination to try and make up for the years of abuse and neglect he suffered as a young person. When John was eventually diagnosed with Alzheimer's Disease, Mom continued to care for him until the week before she died.

Anyone with a relative who has psychological problems or abnormal social behavior of any kind knows the enormous challenges faced by the rest of the family. Everyone is affected and sometimes it feels as if, unlike cancer or heart disease, mental illness is contagious. In spite of the challenges presented by John's behavior, my mother was able to maintain a cheerful outlook on life, and she loved making memories for everyone near and dear to her heart, including her care-receiving husband.

Mom always said Life is the best teacher, but to learn well, you have to keep coming to class. She never missed a day, no matter how hard the curriculum, and she never gave up. Even though she suffered the consequences of her poor choices in life, she transferred the lessons she learned from one situation to another and was convinced that every mistake would somehow pave the way for a brighter tomorrow. One of the best lessons she taught us was to look to the future with great expectations, no matter what happens. I still try today, but she was the queen of optimism!

Never give up on life. The best is yet to come.

As a child, I resented her guidance whenever it seemed to conflict with her own behavior. Her usual reply was, "Listen to what I say, not what I do." That did not appease me then, but now I understand she was telling me to obey and trust her wisdom to avoid future problems of my own making. She knew her children needed a code of conduct if, unlike herself, they were to have no regrets later in life.

The faculty in the school of "My Life" was superb, but in spite of their example, I had to take some classes over again. Call me stubborn. It took a long time to realize that Hindsight and Experience are much harder teachers than Mom. If you know what I'm talking about, you most likely agree it would have been so much easier to have listened in the first place.

The person I count as my third most significant mentor is Sister Therese. She was the spiritual mother of my youth, my confidante during the turbulent teens. She was humble, creative, intuitive, and was the first to teach me that relationships and forgiveness should be at the top of our priority list throughout life. We met when Mom enrolled me in Mt. Assisi Academy, a convent and day school for girls, just a short walk from home.

One morning, Mom telephoned Sister Therese to tell her that I had run out of the house without my lunch ticket after an argument. She asked her to make sure I ate a good meal at noon so she could go to work without worrying about me. Sister Therese did more than that. After giving the rest of the class study time, she took me outdoors for some private tutoring. As we walked through the academy gardens, this gentle Franciscan nun persuaded me to go home and apologize to my mother—with instructions to make my bed before coming back to school!

Over forty years later, Sister Therese would help me assemble the spiritual tool kit I needed to help my mother die in peace. In a later chapter, you will read the story of how we were reunited on a mountaintop in Arizona, and I'll share a very powerful tool she gave me to use when you feel you may be losing control of your life.

My three mentoring mothers are still my favorite Living Libraries. While they were very different individuals, each in their own way worked diligently to channel their emotional energies into positive pathways to healing and reconciliation. I don't know about you, but I've squandered some of my energy on harbored feelings of anger, guilt, bitterness and debilitating grief over relationships lost. How these remarkable women had the endurance to sustain themselves through very difficult times was a mystery to me. Later I learned that God played a pivotal role, and over time their faith in his plans and promises grew stronger when confronted with yet another one of life's surprises.

Most people learn about God and his promises through the best selling publication of all time—The Bible. However, our family never read it at home as I was growing up, and it never occurred to me to read it for myself. How about you?

I developed an interest in reading Scripture after I began working as a Stephen Minister. This title was given to volunteer lay caregivers in my church after completing a comprehensive training program over a period of several months. You will learn more about this remarkable ministry in a later chapter. For now, let me confess that, prior to accepting my first assignment, I felt very insecure. My discomfort stemmed not from befriending someone in the throes of an unpleasant life situation. After all, I had experienced many of life's surprises and I was well trained on how to provide Christian care. No, I was concerned about the fact that my new friends might ask me what the Bible had to say about their circumstances.

After decades of work in the business world, it was becoming increasingly obvious to me that my former career was nothing more than a training ground to prepare me for the privileged work I was being called to do. At this stage in my life, I needed a new and different type of training program because I felt totally out of my depth. Still, I was reluctant to reveal my lack of Bible knowledge.

It is embarrassing to admit to knowing so little about the greatest book ever written, especially if one claims to have a foundation in Judeo-Christian teaching. Oh, I had a Bible, but it was given to me when I graduated from high school—a large red leather-bound copy that was very difficult to read, and to tell the truth, at the age of fifty, I still had not cracked the binding! It never occurred to me to read the Bible for myself. Isn't that what church is for on Sundays? Many people have that view. Do you? And where is that old Bible lying around your house, anyway?

Deciding to enter this new world of discovery caused a dilemma. Because I don't like getting information second-hand, I discounted reading books *about* the Bible. I wanted to go right to the source and not use someone else's filter, and time was of the essence. However, there was the added problem of stilted language in my old, red-leather book, and I also wondered if I could trust the translation of this ancient document to reveal the answers to questions of life today?

Then one day a colleague invited me to attend Community Bible Study, a lay-led class with people from a variety of faith traditions. I happily learned that there are modern translations taken directly from the original Greek and Hebrew writings, and promptly bought a new, easy-to-read edition. As for believing what I read, I did my research and discovered that over the centuries scholars have proven that the Bible is more reliable than much older manuscripts we accept as truth; and many who have tried to disprove its authenticity have become believers in the process. With that, I enrolled in my first ecumenical Community Bible Study class on Thursday mornings.

To my amazement it consisted of approximately 150 women drawn from every denomination as well as others who did not go to church at all. Sharing our respective insights on a weekly basis was fascinating, and I began to see how this Good Book could be used as a source of inspiration and hope that would bring comfort to my special friends.

Have you ever been hooked on a good book—one you couldn't

put down or wait to read over again? Well, that's what happened to me when I began my journey through the pages of what is called "the greatest book" ever written.

For some, B-I-B-L-E is an acronym standing for **B**asic **I**nstructions **B**efore **L**eaving **E**arth because it contains sound advice and better guidelines for daily living than can be provided by any present-day mentor.

Mentors can teach us just so much, but the Bible trumps any advice you can glean from another human being. It not only contains God's guidelines for daily living but also stories of our spiritual ancestors who faced every type of human experience, illustrating exactly how to overcome any life or death crisis. Because of that, the Bible has become for me a most cherished Living Library, an indispensable resource.

Mom and Grandma never read the Bible until late in life. They came to believe in God by walking a different path and learned how to embrace life and death experientially. When they finally did delve into the promises of God as found in Scripture, they were filled with more hope, joy, and anticipation about life after life than they ever dreamed possible.

Choose to believe in a loving God, to forgive the hurts of the past, and to love unconditionally.

Believing in God and His promise of eternal life is a choice. I learned from my mentoring mothers that to have a life worth living we must make wise choices. My choice to believe in a God of love resulted from my learning how to forgive the hurts of the past and to love unconditionally—a formula for peace in our war-torn world.

Establishing and having confidence in one's belief system is a spiritual process. Exactly how it's done is something we must discover in our own time and at our own pace. I was a slow learner. Are you? Don't wait too long to discover the truth of the lessons contained in your Living Libraries.

Pay attention, my child, to what I say; listen carefully.
Don't lose sight of my words. Let them penetrate deep within your heart,
for they bring life and radiant health to anyone
who discovers their meaning.
(Proverbs 4:20-27)

The Great Scapegoat

Does it please you to oppress me, to spurn the work of your hands, while you smile on the schemes of the wicked?
Your hands shaped me and made me. Will you now turn and destroy me?
(Job 10:3, 8)

Have you ever blamed or questioned God about the things in your life that have gone wrong? You are not alone. Generally speaking, nobody gets more blame than God. He's The Great Scapegoat. For years, my own mother was part of the throng that blamed God for everything bad that happened in her life. Why, we even call natural disasters "Acts of God."

Think about the parent whose small child has cancer, the person watching a loved one slowly waste away with diseases of the mind or body, and the man or woman who has a surprise recurrence of cancer just when their life was beginning to return to normal. Some people even view illness or lost dreams as punishment from God. When we are confronted with the unexplainable, the uncontrollable, it is not uncommon to turn to God and cry, "Why? Why are you doing this? Why are you allowing this to happen? What did I do to deserve this?"

When he was at the peak of his career, comedian Flip Wilson didn't blame God. The line in his act that always got a laugh was, "The Devil made me do it." There is truth in humor; however, blaming God, the devil, our parents, the system, or society for our misfortune can keep us stuck in a bad situation. The real truth is accidents happen, we make bad choices, and sometimes we become victims of the bad decisions made by individuals, governments, or industry for the sake of the almighty dollar. Yet, man has been using God as a scapegoat for centuries. Take our ancient friend Job.

Historians and theologians estimate that the Book of Job was written 1800 to 2000 years before Christ was born. As the story goes, Satan caused Job to lose his health, his family, position, and all his material possessions so he would turn his back on God. But Job refused to "curse God and die" as his wife suggested. His friends joined the fray and suggested that the relationship between him and God was broken because of something Job must have done to anger God. They begged Job to repent, but he knew he had done nothing wrong. Because Job remained steadfast, God restored his health, blessed him with a new family and twice the wealth he had before his time of testing began.

The question for us is this: Will we use the unfortunate circumstances of life as opportunities to learn and draw closer to God or will we move farther away? Is it possible to be like Job whose faith never wavered? Discussing these questions with those who knew they would soon die provided me with revealing insights and prompted new questions into God's role in suffering. While many felt they had a lot in common with Job, one of their recurring questions was, "How does blaming God square with man's inhumanity to man?"

Are we not the ones—as environmental scientists claim—destroying our planet and the earth's atmosphere? Could blaming a Higher Power for my disease and natural disasters like Hurricane Katrina be another example of how we avoid accepting responsibility in our personal lives or in partnership with the rest of the world? Why is there such a rise in the incidence of cancer, autism in children, and Alzheimer's disease, for example? Should we blame God for dictators and their military regimes that live like kings as their people starve or refuse help from the rest of the civilized world?

Every one of these discussions ended with agreement that we will never have all the answers here on earth because our puny brains cannot comprehend the mind of God. For some of my friends, it was too painful to consider that anyone else but God caused their misfortune, but many others decided that the relationship between God and suffering has to do with one of the greatest gifts we have as human beings—free will. But our freedom to choose is a double-edged sword. We must live with the consequences of our actions. A bad choice either causes personal pain or results in someone else's suffering, maybe both.

Of course, there are people who do take responsibility for their actions, and one of them was my friend Sally. I didn't know her for very long because when her son introduced us she was just weeks away from death. Her body was deteriorating from lung cancer that had spread to her bones and brain. On one of my visits with Sally, she was lying still and must have been processing her thoughts on this subject when, with eyes still closed, she began to speak.

"You know, this has nothing to do with the tobacco companies or God.

I don't need a scapegoat. I did this to myself. This is my fault. Even though it's been years since I stopped, I'm suffering the consequences of my choice to smoke." She turned to look at me and gently delivered her sound advice, "Don't ever blame God."

Two days before she died Sally rallied and asked me for a favor. She was very weak but managed to say these words: "Donna, I have lung cancer of the brain, so before I am unable to communicate, I want you to know that I've forgiven myself and I've asked God to forgive me for not living out the plans he had for my life. But there is one last good thing I can do, but I need your help."

"Anything, Sally. What is it?"

Gasping for each breath, she said, "I want you to put me in a wheelchair and wheel me outside where people can see me as they pass by—especially the young people—and hang a sign around my neck."

"And what should I write on the sign, Sally?"

Running her fingers across her chest where the sign would lay, she answered. "Do Not Smoke!" Her breathing was much labored, but she continued. "Too late for me. Not for them. Tell them. Tell them for me." She then slowly slipped into a medically induced sleep.

Through Sally, I was able to see that our life has value right up to the day we take our last breath. Even on her death bed, God was using her to teach us the lesson she learned the hard way and to show us the power of faith. She was not afraid and she was given the peace that surpasses understanding.

Pain is not in vain if it helps repair and strengthen our relationship with God.

Another story involves a very healthy woman who was being interviewed not long after her husband and three children were killed in an automobile accident. The reporter knew she was a woman of faith, so he asked her how she could believe in a God who destroyed her life by taking her entire family away from her. She tenderly replied, "Oh, no! God is not to blame for the deaths of my husband and children. My family was the victim of someone else's choice to drink and drive. God is the one who is helping me get through this time of sorrow. He is my model of forgiveness, and He is the one who will help restore meaning and purpose to my life."

On some level we have come to expect the unanticipated deaths by accident or even disease, but when the World Trade Center was destroyed on September 11, 2001, everything changed. People all over America and around the world flocked to churches that day and in the weeks and months that followed, hoping to find answers and comfort in their grief. They were not seeking the God terrorists misguidedly used as the scapegoat for their actions. They were seeking a God of love, compassion, mercy, and justice. We were caught completely off-guard in an incomprehensible situation, and no human could satisfy our longings in the aftermath of the unthinkable. Since then and because of the ensuing war on terror, we all have a heightened awareness of our mortality.

When people are confronted by death, sudden or not, most of us want to believe there is something more than the world in which we now live—and that God will have the last word. It matters not if we lose a loved one in an accident, a national disaster, in a hospital, or at home. Life-altering events often prompt us to revisit the question "Is this all there is?"

Judging from the popularity of all things "spiritual" including the occult, many millions of dollars are spent trying to find the answer to that question in self-help books or the writings and seminars of modern-day gurus. In some circles, it seems the thinking about God has evolved from being a scapegoat to being a figment of man's imagination. There is a view that faith in a Divine Being is nothing more than a misguided theory or a faulty crutch that has no place in an enlightened society. Only you can decide whether or not to believe in God. It's a choice.

Absent this belief, vulnerable people welcome a more scientific approach or philosophy that offers a formula for *self* empowerment with the hope of becoming "one with the universe." Recently, the BBC reported that in England 1,000 people a day consult a spiritualist of one kind or another. I wonder what the number would be in America. It seems as if many people think they have grown beyond the basic teachings of the Bible, but still continue to search for someone or something to help them make sense out of life.

However, when you spend time at the bedside of a person who is dying, you will discover they want nothing more than to believe they are going to transition into the arms of a loving God who promises eternal life, the One who created the universe. People who have reported near-death experiences speak not only of a bright light but also the peace and joy they felt when they were briefly reunited with loved ones who have gone before. While I miss my mentoring mothers, I'm grateful that I can call upon their timeless advice and the indelible marks they left on my life whenever I begin to doubt the existence or gracious nature of God. Who are you missing right now?

Faith is a gift. And once I accepted it, life has never been the same. And I've learned that directing our anger and blame toward God is not very productive. Relationships among individuals or nations can't develop or be restored when people walk away from the table, and the same is true with our relationship with God. He never walks away. We do. Our stories and those of our spiritual ancestors contained in the Bible can attest to that.

Where do you stand on these important questions? Are you willing to gamble on another person's belief system or their interpretation of the Bible? Will you choose to accept what someone else thinks about the nature and character of God? Have you ever even thought about the fact that many people base their beliefs on second- or third-hand information that might be casual or misguided thinking? We wouldn't do that if our business depended on it, and it's much more important to have first-hand knowledge about God when life and death hang in the balance.

God is not my scapegoat any longer but a parent, a Heavenly Father, who gives me the freedom to make my own decisions and to live with the consequences. And like any loving parent, if we do turn our backs on him, God longs for us to return by way of that same free will. It's never too late, and he always waits for us with open arms.

Behave as if you believe; God will handle your doubts.

Somewhere along the bumpy ride of indecision and spiritual conflict most of us experience, I was told not to worry when I doubted the existence of God or his loving nature. The best advice I ever received was to just keep behaving as if I believed, and God would handle my doubts, my anger, and even my blame. Exactly how my faith became personal is a story I want to share with you. Its ripple effect changed the course of my mother's life.

For I know the plans I have for you," declares the LORD, "plans to prosper you and not to harm you, plans to give you hope and a future." (Jeremiah 29:10-12)

A Divine Relationship

I no longer call you servants…I have called you friends.
(John 15:15)

When I began to seek the truth about God, my view of a vengeful God who could wreak havoc on his creation from time to time was transformed. I now know that he wants to be in relationship with humanity in general and with each of us specifically.

Talking to people near the end of their lives about these issues challenged me to ask myself some questions: Just why do I believe in God? Is God really my God or the God of my mentoring mothers and other special friends?

I found my answers not so much from studying the magnificent order of the universe and nature, nor solely from what I was taught or the scholarly writings of theologians. No. When my life seemed to be falling apart and there was no place else to turn, I cried out in desperation, and God was there. It is personal. Over the years, I experienced and witnessed what can only be called miracles including healings in body, mind and spirit—too many to be called coincidence.

Having faith is crucial to being in a position some day to embrace death, but it's important to honor and remember how we came to faith. For many people, hearing others talk about a relationship with God is like waving a red flag in front of a bull. I've seen people roll their eyes and think of nothing but fundamentalists in the worst sense of the word—someone who imposes their religious views on others. Being asked about my relationship can make me feel uncomfortable as well, but only when it feels as if the question is part of an approval process, like I'm being vetted for entrance into an exclusive club.

I actually love to tell the story of how my divine relationship with

Christ began and how God used this experience to draw my mother back into his loving arms. I want to hear your story one day, but now telling mine may give you a fresh perspective on the phrase "personal relationship with God" and illustrate why I believe faith is not about religion, it's about a relationship.

Grandma never talked about the origins of her faith, she just lived it; and as for Mom, well, she was angry with God for the great majority of her life. She stopped talking to Him in 1945 when he allowed my father to be killed in the war. Oh, she believed he existed and made my brother and me go to church every Sunday, but she refused to come with us. Besides, so much harm has been done over the centuries in the name of religion. However, a study of Scripture reveals that Christ himself did not come to establish a religion, but to restore our relationship with God.

My rebellion against religion had more to do with the leadership of the modern-day church than it did with God. Personality conflicts, leadership issues, doctrinal differences, and church politics can be a big turnoff. Many years passed before I recognized pastors and clergy for what they are: imperfect human beings called to serve in a specific capacity—just as we all are. I now honor the position they hold and respect their service, but no longer place them on a pedestal. Their presence in a pulpit does not make them any more or less human than the rest of us. The unfortunate thing is that most people equate God with organized religion, and too often when a person walks away from church, they walk away from God. I was not much different.

For many years I did not actively participate in church, but it was impossible for me to deny the existence of God given the order of the universe and my strong belief that God loves us whether we go to church or not. However, I believed that God helps those who help themselves. My concept of a relationship with God was this: He's the one who gives us talents and abilities which we are to develop, and on Judgment Day we'll find out how well we did. Surely, he was too busy to be involved in my life!

Seeing how my mother struggled first as a widow and later as a divorcee, I decided to be the first in my family to go to college. Call it negative motivation, but my degree would be the insurance policy I needed to take care of myself even if I married and stayed home to raise a family. You never know what's going to happen to you. Upon graduation, I went to work for IBM in a marketing support role. I thought life would be smooth sailing. However, within a year, I married someone who was not only an atheist, but an alcoholic.

For nearly ten years, I suffered in silence as my marriage failed, but I dreaded the prospect of divorce. My career compensated for what was lacking at home. Having reached the top of my game in a management position traditionally held by females, I changed direction and became one of the first women to work in a commissioned sales position. This move promised significant financial rewards and opportunities if I succeeded. But then it happened—my marriage ended.

I was devastated and felt as broken and hopeless as Humpty Dumpty. By the grace of God, my new job was still intact, but I began to see that self-sufficiency and success did not bring me happiness. That was the lowest point in my life. I felt so alone. Grieving the loss of a dream is one of the saddest deaths of all.

Just in time, my friend Marilyn was bold enough to buy me a little book entitled *God Calling*. It's a daily devotional that reads like Jesus is writing you personal notes as a "friend." And it changed my life forever. I knew about Jesus and his position as Son of God and Savior of the world, but how could Jesus be my friend? As I read through this book, I learned that it was not much different than developing an earthly relationship. I learned there were incredible benefits to having Jesus as a friend here and now. Through the book, Jesus reasoned, "If you had a friend in need, wouldn't you do anything in your power to help? Well, think about it, if we become friends, I'm God and I can do anything!"

Gradually, my understanding about being self-sufficient was being corrected. One evening I read that God wanted me to depend on him for everything and learned that it was okay to pray for myself. Jesus said on the pages of this book that when I prayed, I should be specific because that's how I would know when to give thanks.

I decided to give this "friendship thing" a try, especially since it had nothing to do with religion. It was mid-November, and my biggest problem was making my annual sales quota. The pressure to make my numbers intensified during the divorce proceedings, because I feared losing my job along with my marriage. Without either, I felt I had no value, and my future looked like a black hole.

My only hope—back then—was in IBM and a sales contest called "Double Dip" which doubled the value of every order closed but only during the month of November. Interestingly enough, doubling every order on my prospect list would qualify me for the 100% Club—a prestigious national recognition event for "winners."

I looked at the ceiling (I thought God was "up" there) and started explaining "Double Dip" to Jesus in great detail—as if he didn't know! I remember saying, "Okay, Lord, if you really want to be friends, I would appreciate your help by softening the hearts of my prospects so that every single order I have worked on is signed no later than November 30." I knew that was a statistical impossibility, but with God all things are possible. So off we went!

During the week, Jesus and I made one closing call after another, and guess what happened—absolutely nothing! Nobody ordered anything! Oh, I continued talking to him but my conversation took on a different tone. I was having a little trouble with this "friendship thing" and asked Him for a sign to prove he heard me. He was silent. So I resigned myself to failure.

Then the phone rang. It was a sales rep from another division who needed a product I sold to fill a gap in a system he was proposing—but it was for the following year. Since I had nothing to lose and nothing better to do, I agreed to make what I thought was a casual call. Instead, I was ushered into a conference room where the entire Executive Board of this company had assembled, and all eyes were on me.

While surprised and unprepared for this audience, I relaxed into my "self-sufficiency" using the talents God gave me. I actually had fun flowcharting on their chalkboard how my multi-purpose product would fit into their future system. Surprisingly, I easily handled their complex questions and objections.

Suddenly, the President interrupted and asked to see a demonstration. The only date he had free was November 30 and the only time the demo room was available was also November 30. What a coincidence! The scales fell from my eyes when—as our office was closing—the customer signed an order so large that it not only put me in the 100% Club, it also made me Regional Sales Rep of the Year! Needless to say, my relationship with my new Best Friend was off and running!

Loving Relationships matter, not Religion.

On November 30, 1978, I heard Jesus speak to my inner most being, *"Precious child, trust me. My timing and my ways may be different from yours. But I am true to my word; just keep talking to me, and know that it's not what* you *do, but what* I *can do through you that matters. You will never be alone."*

The moral of this story is this: Having a true relationship with someone requires spending time with them. It's no different with God, but no matter what faith tradition a person has, everyone must decide for themselves whether or not they want to have this divine intimate relationship.

After reconnecting with God for the first time as an adult, it occurred to me that, as with any friendship, a relationship needs to be developed. So when I was invited to attend a weekend retreat called Life in the Spirit, I agreed. The divorce process was nearing its end, and I thought it would be a refreshing change. I never anticipated the chain of events that followed.

During the retreat, I used the free time to process my understanding about God and "my new Best Friend." The formal sessions then began to open my eyes to the reality of the Holy Spirit, the Comforter whom Jesus promised to leave with us. It was an encouragement for my future. The concept of self-sufficiency that I had adopted was gradually being transformed.

Many tears were shed as I reflected on the poor "solo" choices I made in my life. As anxiety about the future was gradually replaced with peace, my countenance began to change. I knew I was forgiven for the years I ignored God, and I was able to forgive myself and my soon-to-be ex-husband for our respective roles in a failed marriage. The sting of bad memories was being washed away. I looked forward to a fresh start in my life, and it felt as if I was being "born again."

For if you forgive men when they sin against you, your heavenly Father will also forgive you. But if you do not forgive men their sins, your Father will not forgive your sins.
(Matthew 6:14)

While at the retreat, my thoughts turned to my mother, and I cried on her behalf. She carried so much anger, guilt and frustration because of the physical, emotional and spiritual pain she had suffered over the years. Mom did not have a positive view of God, let alone a relationship with Him, so I took my small group into my confidence and asked them to join me in two specific prayers for my mother—freedom from pain and insomnia. The doctors were unable to diagnose the source of her physical discomfort, and she had not been able to sleep through the night in over a year.

When I arrived home late Sunday evening, I called Mom, and found she wanted to know everything about the retreat. It was hard to describe an experience with God, so all I could say was it was powerful, enlightening, and that I felt good about it. I chose to leave out the part about praying for her. Then she said, much to my surprise, "I want to go."

I was shocked and quickly added, "Mom, you couldn't handle it. I cried all weekend." Mom only cried at funerals.

"Maybe it's time for *me* to cry. I really want to go."

Nervously I enrolled her in the next available retreat, but given her history with God and religion, I didn't know how she would react.

While my mother had a strong will and considered herself a survivor, she was about to discover the source of her strength after nearly sixty years. I later learned just how angry she was with God. She remained single for a long time after divorcing her second husband and our bonds strengthen. When she learned someone had told Larry and me that we were only half-brother and sister, she fiercely objected. "Don't you let anybody tell you that ever again. You both came from my womb and you are 100% brother and sister!" She drew us close to her and said, "This is the only brother you are ever going to have and this is the only sister you are ever going to have. We are "The Team" and we need to take care of each other.

It was not until we moved away from home that she married for the third time. She did not know then that her new partner John had, among other emotional problems, an obsessive personality disorder. Several years before Mom's upcoming retreat, he learned about God's saving grace through Christ and religion became his obsession.

He read the Bible constantly, lectured to Mom and anyone within earshot, listened to teachings on television, radio and on tape night and day. He was driving my mother crazy and alienated family and friends with his single-mindedness. To protect his pride, Mom never told anyone he was receiving psychiatric care, and constantly tried to cover for him. There was a stigma associated with mental illness, which sadly persists today in many ways.

Not long before she was to come to Ohio for the weekend retreat, Mom fractured her spine. She lay in the hospital for days undergoing diagnostic testing which showed an advanced stage of osteoporosis. At 58, Mom was told that she had the skeletal frame of a 90-year-old woman. The rapid deterioration of her bones may have been due to the fact that she had no medical treatment during menopause ten years earlier.

Whatever the reason, she was told that because she had such a frail and fragile frame she should never bend to make a bed, wash the bathtub, or push a vacuum cleaner. She was warned not to make any quick movements. The doctor sent her home in a body brace with instructions to lay flat on her bed so the fracture could heal. Hydroculators under her back for moist heat gave her some relief if she remained motionless. When Mom told me all of this, I said, "I'll cancel the retreat."

To my surprise, she screamed, "No! No you won't. I want to go."

I pleaded, "But, Mom, you shouldn't sit in a car for two and a half hours driving to my house, let alone go through the motions and emotional stress of the retreat. There will be others; wait until you heal and then we can reschedule."

"No! I want to go—now!" I now know Mom's insistence was because she had waited long enough to actively seek answers to the questions about God that had built up over the years. Why did he not protect my husband when he went to war? Was our family under a curse? How else can you explain the other tragic losses of my infant child, my brother and sister and father? Why am I being punished? Are you laughing as I contend with a man who talks about nothing but God? Where are you when bad things happened? Do I really matter to you at all?

So the next day, Friday, she and John drove from Pittsburgh to Ohio, and that very evening we took her to the St. Joseph Christian Life Center in Cleveland. Wanting to protect the coach of our "team," I spoke privately to a staff member about her condition, and even suggested the kind of people that would be a good match for her. I wanted her small group experience to be a good one.

Bob, the lay minister leading the retreat with his wife Juta, finally looked at me and said, "You know, it's time for you to leave. God is the one who puts the small groups together. I'm sure he knows exactly what your mother needs. Quit worrying. Just leave and come to the service on Sunday evening."

Nervously we left for home, but through my restless night I wondered how she was adjusting to the environment. Saturday went by slowly with no word from her, and we were instructed not to call. Toward the end of the day, the phone rang, "Hi! It's me!" Talking a mile a minute, she said, "It's wonderful! I have so much to tell you! I want you to meet some people! You are going to be here tomorrow for the service, aren't you? I can't wait to see you. Gotta run! But I just wanted to make sure you knew what time to be here! It's unbelievable! I love you! Bye!"

My heart leapt in response to her excitement. In my mind's eye, I could see her beaming face and could hardly contain myself. On Sunday, family and friends were ushered into the pews of the chapel where we waited for the participants of the retreat to take their places on either side of the altar. How long I had waited to see my mother in church! I was nervous as I watched her respond to the start of the service. As we began the first hymn, I looked up and saw my mother singing. Singing!

But Mom can't sing, I said to myself, and nearly laughed as I recalled her feeble attempts at Christmas and New Year's Eve gatherings—and she never remembered any of the words. In her younger days, she occasionally called me from a party if no one knew the lyrics of a particular song. "Hey, Don, how does it go?" She would try to sing a few lines or hum the melody, usually out of tune, expecting me to fill in the blanks. Now, here—in a church, no less—my mother was singing! And, she knew the words.

As I stood there watching, she lifted her arms. My eyes filled with tears of happiness as I said aloud, "That's my Mom, the one with her hands raised! That's my Mom!" The story of how Mom reconciled with God began to unfold after the service when we found each other in the crowd.

It's okay to be angry with God, but get over it as quickly as you can.

When the retreat began, Mom was assigned to a small group. Each person was asked to introduce themselves and comment on why they were there and what they hoped to gain from the weekend. Mom was first, but she folded her arms saying, "I'm here to audit the course. You see, I'm married to a religious nut, and I want to see what all the fuss is about."

The leader was gracious and said, "That's fine, Anna. Thank you for your honesty."

After one of the main speakers talked about the power of prayer, her small group reconvened, and they were offered an opportunity to ask for personal prayer. Again, Mom was asked to participate. "Anna, do you have any prayer requests?"

Mom replied, "Absolutely not." Her reason was clear. "I'm not going to discuss my personal problems with you. That's private. It isn't right to talk about things outside your family. My conversation with God is my business and I don't want to share it with strangers."

The leader gracefully responded, "Okay, but if you don't mind, let's see if anyone else would like prayer." Later I was told that they thought my mother was either "of the Devil" and put there to break up the group, or this woman needed the Holy Spirit very badly. They prayed for her anyhow, but silently. What happened next is incredible, and supported Bob's claim that God himself organized the group.

The first person who asked for prayer from the group was grieving the loss of her daughter of seven months, the same age Mom lost my sister to spinal meningitis. The next person's father committed suicide—Grandpa! The next had a brother who was killed in an automobile accident like Uncle Bennie, and another was grieving the death of her husband who left her to raise a two-year-old child alone. And so it went. By the time they had gone full circle, my mother was sobbing, drowning in her tears.

Years of fear, anger, self-pity, and resentment were too much for my mother to bear. She finally cracked and soon this broken vessel would be mended and filled with new life. As soon as Mom laid the last brick in the wall she had been building between herself and God, it began to crumble. The destruction, while painful, was necessary. Many of us build walls between ourselves and God when we are confronted with death, but tearing them down is the only way we can see and hear the truth about our relationship with him.

When they had gone full circle, she finally spoke through gut-wrenching tears, "Everything you said all happened to me!" The pent-up questions came tumbling out and the love of God that flowed through the people in her small group covered her like soothing balm. She was lifted up and out of the pit as the years of pain and sorrow drained from her heart.

In that moment, my mother was having her first real experience of good grief. This was her first lesson on how much we can actually learn through death—and it laid the foundation on how she would later handle her own.

During the retreat's quiet times, her small group leader, a sweet lady with snow white hair, spent time with Mom. She listened intently, and after hearing Mom's story, she opened the Bible to the Book of Isaiah, and began reading the first three verses of Chapter 43, substituting Mom's name for Jacob and Israel. The scales fell from her eyes, and for the first time in Mom's life she heard the truth about where God had been when all those bad things happened to her.

Isaiah 43:1-3 says, *"But now, thus says the Lord who created you, Anna, and who formed you, O Anna: 'Fear not, for I have redeemed you, I have called you by name; you are mine. When you pass through the waters I will be with you; and through the rivers they shall not overflow you; when you walk through the fire you shall not be burned, the flames will not set you ablaze. For I am the Holy One of Israel, your Savior'."*

In hindsight, Mom was able to see that God did not leave her or forsake her during times of trouble. It was because he was with her that she survived. When she reflected on the heavy burdens of her past, she wondered why she had not died of a broken heart. She finally had the answer. God carried her through. That's how she survived. He was the one who kept her from drowning in troubled waters, from dying in the desert of despair, loneliness, frustration and fear of the future, and who gave her the strength to raise her children alone.

Mom once revealed that when we were young, there were many nights she drove home hungry, tired, sick, and very lonely after standing on her feet working 12 to 16 hour days in the retail industry. Often she doubted herself and wondered how she would be able to make ends meet and care for all of us. As a young woman the burden was so overwhelming that she thought how easy it would be to just turn the wheel of the car and drive over one of the hills in Pittsburgh. *How easy, and then it would be over.* But she remembered her children and grew more determined to clear her mind of self-destructive thoughts and take good care of us.

Yes, God gave her the gift of children to give her life meaning and purpose. Every challenge she was able to overcome made her stronger, and more creative. Today I still marvel at how she was able to send us to private schools, take a vacation every year, and manage to pay the mortgage and bills on her meager salary. She was in training and she passed her lessons of life onto us.

My mother never even considered asking God for help, thinking he had given up on her. She now had to face the fact that she had given up on him and made the decision to go it alone. Sometimes we are inspired by God even when we don't acknowledge him or have the words to ask for help. Over the years, she rightly made the intentional decision not to focus on her anger with God, but to focus on what she had left, not what she had lost. At the Life in the Spirit retreat, Mom finally was introduced to the source of her strength.

Mom spent the next two days of the retreat not only asking questions but confronting those who used such Christian jargon such as "God spoke to me." She asked, "Are you crazy? What do you mean God spoke to you—did you hear him with your ear, or what?" Her mind and heart were open at last and she was transformed. After learning that she had been forgiven by and reconciled to God, she was now able to forgive others, including herself. She was free. She was spiritually and emotionally healed. Best of all, one of my prayers was answered.

Her group finally did pray for her and she left the retreat carrying her back brace and no longer had any pain! The bone scans proved it. God had healed her fractured spine and she never had a problem with osteoporosis again. Her bone scans were normal until her death at eighty years of age. A miraculous healing!

Why? I don't know why she was healed and others are not. No one can presume to comprehend the mind of God. What I do know is that even Lazarus who was raised from the dead eventually died, but on occasion Jesus gives us a glimpse into why healing takes place when we read his words in the Bible.

I do these things so that you know who I am…
Your faith has healed you."
(Matthew 9:22)

Do we really need to see a miracle with our own eyes to believe in the power of God? Prayer for healing is a normal part of Christian worship, but some churches have a special place set aside for prayer and spiritual consolation. Those who work in Christian Healing Centers tell me that, while not everyone is cured, everyone is healed by having a renewed sense of peace and hope. Believe and be blessed.

Because you have seen me, you have believed;
blessed are they who have not seen and still believe.
(Mark 16:14)

Being cured of osteoporosis strengthened the gift of faith she willingly received at the retreat and from that moment on she put her faith and trust in Christ. In the years that followed, rather than being angry with God when bad things happened, she thanked Him for the opportunity to put her faith into action.

After the retreat, inner healing continued to take place as Mom, John, and I forgave ourselves and each other for the hurt we caused one another. Deep down we knew the rest of life's journey somehow would never be the same.

Recognizing our need to be forgiven is the first step in our ability to forgive others.

Mom and John returned to Pittsburgh with her hydroculators and back brace in the trunk of the car. The next morning my second prayer for Mom was answered. This is her story as told to me later that day.

Exhausted and emotionally drained after the long weekend, Mom went to bed early. Because of her insomnia, she knew sleep would not last long. However, when she awoke and thought it was around 1:00 a.m., the clock said 5:30 a.m. She shook it, thinking it was broken. As she stared at it in disbelief, a strange sensation came upon her. She felt someone's arms around her, but it wasn't John. He was sound asleep with his back to her on the other side of the bed. At first the touch startled her, but then she felt warm and comforted, like she was being cuddled and rocked back to sleep. Within her spirit she heard someone say, *"Shhh. It's all right. Go back to sleep."*

"Then," Mom said, "I saw the face of a baby—a beautiful baby with large dark eyes. Such beautiful, soft brown eyes. Knowing eyes. Eyes that looked into my soul. Eyes full of compassion and understanding. He looked deeply into mine and seemed to say, *'I know you. I love you.'*" The shush was heard again, and she was lulled back to sleep and awoke at 9:00 a.m. saying, "I will never forget those eyes."

Having a Divine Relationship with God helped Mom face her future as John's caregiver, as well as future deaths in our family and her own—without fear.

All things work together for good for those who love God
and are called according to His purpose.
(Romans 8:28)

A Mountaintop Experience

But with God all things are possible.
(Matthew 19:26)

During my childhood Mom did not participate in mother-daughter church related activities, mostly because of her work. Sister Therese filled the role of my spiritual mentoring mother through high school. When Mom reconciled with God many years later, she resumed her rightful role and prayed me through my final divorce proceedings and beyond.

For well over a decade more, she asked God to send me a man after his own heart with the hope of my remarrying. Her mother's prayer was answered when I met Roger on a business trip in Paris. He was from England, and since both of us traveled extensively, we had a long-distance telephone courtship. It was quite obvious that God had brought us together. When we decided to get married, we wanted to be part of a faith community but didn't know how to go about choosing a church since we came from different religious traditions.

After thirty years, my thoughts ran to Sister Therese. On one of the pilgrimages into our past, we visited the convent of the Sisters of St. Francis in Pittsburgh and discovered Sister Therese had been transferred to Arizona for health reasons and was told she was then the director of a hermitage. I called to arrange a meeting.

"Good morning, Our Lady of Solitude House of Prayer," the voice answered.

"Good morning, may I speak to Sister Therese?"

"This is Sister Therese."

The next voice I heard was that of a 12 year old girl squealing in delight, "Sister Therese, Sister Therese! This is Donna Del Sardo. Oh, you probably don't remember me after thirty years."

"You mean St. Francis?" I could hardly believe my ears. She actually remembered me and the fact that she had asked me to be the lead role of St. Francis in one of our high school plays. "How's your mother and your brother, Larry?"

After a few minutes, I wasted no time asking if Roger and I could visit. "But, Donna, this is a hermitage. We don't talk here. I only speak when the people staying here need spiritual counsel."

"That's exactly why I'm calling, Sister Therese. We need your advice on how to connect with God as a couple, given our different religious upbringings." She agreed to set aside two hours to meet with us if we were willing to make the effort to come to her. So rather than flying home at the end of our respective work weeks in different parts of the country, Roger and I met in Phoenix, rented a car, and drove north to Black Canyon City. We found her waiting for us at the appointed hour atop her desert mountain, with signs along the winding uphill road that read, *"No Smoking Except for Fire of Prayer"* and *"No Hunting Except for Peace and God."* She still had a sense of humor.

She greeted us warmly, and though she no longer wore the Franciscan habit, I recognized her delicate facial features and her loving eyes. With her hug, I felt her thin fingers that had grown strong over the years of piano and organ playing. In my mind's eye, I could see us walking and talking on the grounds of Mount Assisi during high school. I recalled the day my mother had phoned her to let her know I had left without my lunch card after an argument. I couldn't wait to see Sister Therese again, and had so many questions for her.

After introducing Roger, I asked him to get the camera out of the car and turned to Sister Therese. "Quick! Before Roger comes back, tell me how old you are?"

I was always curious and, surprisingly, learned we were only about a dozen years apart. She was undoubtedly in her early 20's when we first met, but endowed with spiritual gifts and wisdom beyond her years that God wanted her to use. As the three of us settled into our visit, we asked to hear her story. We wanted to know why she gave up music and teaching to live the life of a hermit in the desert.

"I always wanted to become a cloistered nun. It had been my heart's desire since I was very young. I wanted to devote my life to God, to be with him, and intercede for others through a life of prayer. However, the Carmelites turned me down. I was angry because I wanted to be the one in control of my vocation. 'I'll show them,' I thought, so I became a Franciscan and majored in English and music so I could teach those subjects.

"However, I was miserable because I was not doing what I truly wanted to do. One winter day, I ran outside in frustration—in the middle of a snow storm. I shook my fist at heaven and said, 'Father, you know I hate it here, so I need to know if this is the work you would have called me to do. If so, I'll go right back and gladly do it without ever complaining again, but I need a sign and I want it now!'

"As soon as I said that, in the middle of a snow squall, a red cardinal flew out of nowhere and landed on my shoulder! I got so scared; I ran back into the convent and never opened my mouth again. For years I taught, and led two all-girl choruses. We performed concerts and made recordings so the proceeds could go for the care of the Sisters. After I developed severe arthritis, they sent me here to Arizona."

"The cardinal story is amazing, Sister Therese," I said. "I've never heard of a bird flying in the middle of a snow storm, let alone landing on your shoulder."

She added with a chuckle, "Cardinals have become very special to me; and the funny thing is, the day I arrived in Phoenix, the headline on the front page of the newspaper read, *The Cardinals Arrive in Phoenix*, the winter home of that baseball club. I wrote to the team's manager to tell him my story, and he sent me tickets to the games. We still keep in touch."

God always answers prayer, but his timing might be different or he may have a better plan.

After telling Sister Therese how God brought us together, we shared our spiritual dilemma with her. "We want to join a church and learn to pray together so the next 50 years will be different than the last. Since I was raised Catholic and Roger a nonconformist Protestant in England, we don't know how to begin."

She turned her head and sweetly said, "That's easy. Shop around and let the Holy Spirit be your guide. He'll tell you where to go."

"Shop around? What do you mean? How will He tell us?"

"I don't know how, but I know you will know. Just pray and go to different churches and ask God if this is where he wants you to be. When you involve God in all your decisions, you won't regret it. He always answers prayer, even if He says 'no' or 'not now.' Just trust Him."

As our time on her mountain was coming to an end, she offered to show us around the grounds and tell us the story about how she came to live atop her beloved mesa. Not long after being transferred to Arizona, her arthritis improved. This new health coincided with a parishioner dying and leaving the mountaintop—house, pool and stock portfolio—to the diocese. Sister Therese's earlier vision of leading a life of prayer and solitude returned, and she had the courage to ask the bishop for the property to build a house of prayer. Much to her surprise and delight, the bishop was inspired to agree.

In this way, God rewarded her for all her years of faithful obedience. Now it was time to give her a new mission—one that matched her heart's desire.

If we are willing, God will use us all to work out his purpose during every phase of our lives. Sister Therese inspires us to trust in God's perfect timing, without regret. We never lost touch with her again, and I was able to tap into her spiritual tool kit when I needed it most.

Delight in the Lord and he will give you the desires of your heart.
(Psalm 37:4)

The Prayer of Abandonment

Father, into your hands I commend my Spirit.
(Luke 23:46)

As Grandma said, life is a big surprise. The news of an unexpected terminal illness or sudden death is one of those not-so-good surprises. Fear, shock, and strong gut-wrenching emotions can emerge and bring you to your knees at times like these. I will never forget the phone call from my mother in December 1998.

"Donna, I have cancer." Those words hung in the air and threatened to absorb all of the oxygen in the room. I sat stunned for what seemed an eternity, and then shook my head as I tried to control the many questions that raced through my mind. How can they be sure? How large is the tumor? Has it spread?

I wanted to turn into a sponge and absorb the fear and anxiety I heard in her voice, but I was instantly thrust into a whirlwind of emotions of my own. Visions of her suffering and in pain entered my head. I stifled my feelings and fought to stay strong and clearheaded. How is she going to tolerate the pain since she is allergic to pain medicine? Will they recommend chemotherapy? *"Stop it!"* I said to myself. *"First things first!"*

After calming my mother and telling her I would be on a plane the next morning, I called other family members to tell them so Mom would not have to go through the ordeal of spreading the news. It's amazing what you can do when you have to. Next, I made calls to specialists in my area to gather information, learn a new vocabulary, and equip myself with the right questions to ask Mom's doctors. I packed, then made an appointment to get a haircut. I was prepared and in control! But not for long.

Driving home from the salon, I began to cry—the first tears shed. They surprised me, but I couldn't stop. With blurred vision, I slowly made my way home. Fortunately, Roger was not home, so I was able to let my feelings freely flow. Wailing, I paced in circles throughout the house and finally cried aloud to God.

"Why? Why? Don't let this happen to her. Let it be a mistake. Not cancer!" I began shouting orders. "You either heal her or take her! There is no in-between here! Don't you dare let her suffer! You can't let her suffer. You were supposed to suffer for all of us." In my hysteria, I cried, "Who did you forget that she has now to suffer instead of you? Can you hear me? Are you listening?" I yelled.

Feeling completely powerless and needing some top-down support, I called on reinforcements. Loud enough to be heard in heaven with tears streaming down my face I pleaded, "Daddy, Grandma! I could use a little help down here. Please talk to him. You're right there. Tug on his sleeve. I need you! Tell him his little girl, Anna, needs him. Help!"

I begged, "Please, God, if you can hear me, I need a sign. If you're listening, give me a sign." Then it came to me, "Sister Therese!" I ran to the phone. In hindsight, she was the answer to my prayer. Why else would she have popped into my mind the split second I asked for a sign. Perhaps that was another reason God inspired us to be reunited when Roger and I sought her counsel five years earlier.

I dialed the number, fully expecting an answering machine. After all, it was a hermitage and she was in prayer most of the day. I'll leave a message. She'll call me back. But, no, she answered! "Sister Therese," I cried. "It's Donna. My mother has just been diagnosed with cancer. I've been screaming and crying and yelling at God for the longest time. I'm awful." I relayed all the news in between sobs and told her how I had been ordering God around as I helplessly paced throughout the house. Expecting sympathy, all I heard was laughter. "Why are you laughing?"

"Precious child," she said, "I'm not laughing at you. I'm delighting in what a wonderful relationship you have with God! To think you feel comfortable enough to raise your voice in all your passion and insist on communicating with Him is just terrific. It's rather like the very personal and intimate relationship you have with Roger. If you argue and yell at him, does that mean you don't love him? Of course not; Roger knows you love him, and certainly God knows you love Him. After all, He's the one who gave you emotions. God is right there with you, and He hears you."

I later realized that through Sister Therese, I was talking to God. She was God with skin on. We discussed my fears and concerns about dealing with the doctors, the surgery, recovery period, the complications presented by John's mental condition, and the strain on us with the distance between New York and Florida. After I had regained some composure, she knew I was ready to receive something special from her spiritual tool kit.

She said, "I'm going to give you a prayer to take with you to Florida. I want to read it to you and I want you to listen very carefully. It's something that helped me when my father died." As an introduction, Sister Therese addressed the heart of the matter. "You are feeling out of control because you are not in control, and you need to abandon yourself into God's hands. Slowly, with meaning, she began to read:

Prayer of Abandonment

Father, I abandon myself into your hands.
Do with me what you will.
Whatever you may do, I thank you.
I am ready for all. I accept all.
Let only Your will be done in me, and in all
your creatures.
I wish no more than this, O Lord.
Into your hands I commend my soul;
I offer it to you with all the love of my heart,
For I love you, Lord, and so need to give myself,
To surrender myself into your Hands,
Without reserve, and with boundless confidence,
for you are my Father.
Amen.

A peace began to come over me and I thanked her. But she continued, "Wait a minute, I'm not finished. That is only one way to pray that prayer, Donna. There are really three ways to pray it. The second is like this, and you can say it silently with me if you like." She began to pray, pausing between each phrase so the words would sink in:

"Father, I abandon* my mother *into your hands." The shock of those simple words nearly knocked me over. Abandon my mother into your hands? How could I do that? I began to cry again.

The prayer continued, ***"Do with* her *what you will."*** What? I can't hand her over. My daddy asked *me* to take care of her. It's my job! Do I really believe God loves her enough to care for her the way I would? She's my mother. She has gone through so much. How could I abandon her?

Let only your will be done in* her *and in all your creatures. I wish no more than this, O Lord. I have prayed "Thy will be done" a million times in my life, but these were scary words now. Did I trust God enough to give up my will for her to live? Could I accept his will which may mean giving her up to death? Could I trust Him to take care of her if I couldn't be with her?

Into your hands I commend* her *soul. I offer it to you with all the love of my heart. A great calm began to envelop me as I was reminded through this prayer that we are spirit. We are God's creatures who are "in the world," but are not "of it." Our home is in heaven with God. He will take us back, but we must leave our earthly body here. It is only the house we live in after all. Will he not protect and cherish the soul he created? I began to relax and see the light at the end of the tunnel. Yes, Lord, I do commend her soul into your hands.

For I love you, Lord, and so need to give* my mother, *to surrender* my mother *into your hands. I do love you, Lord, and you are the only one I trust. I can give her to you because I know that I am in over my head. I can do nothing, and I know the doctors are only mortals who make mistakes. You are her only safe haven on earth and in heaven.

Without reserve, and with boundless confidence, for you are* her *Father. Yes, Lord. I have no reservations. She is yours and I do have boundless confidence! You are the only one I can turn to, unreservedly. You are the Great Physician and Savior. You can save her from this disease if she has more work to do, or you can save her from the fear and sting of death by giving her your gift of eternal life and the peace to accept it in your time. You are her Father and my Father. We are sisters in Christ and I know that you have no grandchildren. We are equally dependent on you to guide and protect us now and through eternity. ***Amen.***

As I let the words sink into my heart, the boulder that was lying on my heart gradually and miraculously was lifted. The physical pressure was gone. My shoulders relaxed, and I breathed a deep sigh of relief. The tears on my cheeks were dry. Sister Therese stayed silent, giving me time to reflect, but there was more. As if to reinforce God's love for me, she continued. "The third way to read this prayer is as if God is praying it to you."

Donna, *I abandon myself into your hands. Do with me what you*

will. Whatever you may do, I thank you. What? How can God do that? Does he know what he's doing? How can he thank me for whatever I may do to him? Now this is what I call a responsibility. I can take care of my family and friends, but how can I be trusted to take care of God?

***I am ready for all. I accept all. Let only your will be done in me, and in all your creatures. I wish no more than this,* Donna.** Such trust has never been given to me. It is too awesome for me to comprehend. Does he really trust me that much? Is this a subtle reminder that I have something to do with how others view God?

Into your hands I commend my soul; I offer it to you with all the love of my heart, For I love you,* Donna, *and so need to give myself, to surrender myself into your hands, without reserve, and with boundless confidence. I was being reminded that he already gave himself to me without reserve, no strings attached. Yes, he does love me, and he proved it by dying on the cross for me. He came to earth in the person of Christ to teach me how to live, and especially how to die. Because he was raised from the dead himself, I can trust that I, too, will have eternal life just as He promised. By the power of the Holy Spirit I now understand why he can surrender himself into my hands. He knows I love him and that he will equip me to share his truths with others, especially Mom and my family so they can trust and love him. He has confidence in me.

For you are* my daughter. *Amen. Yes, he is the Father who placed me in my mother's womb. (Psalm 139)

After walking through the prayer as Sister Therese guided me, I was miraculously released from paralyzing tension and panic. I had clarity of thought. I knew what my role was opposite God's in this life and death situation. Abandoning myself and my mother into God's hands was the safest thing to do.

When you surrender yourself to God, you gain a Powerful Partner worthy of trust.

The experience of reciting the Prayer of Abandonment was like adding mortar to the cracks in the foundation of my faith. Life has a way of doing that, creating hairline cracks in the rock on which we say we stand. That prayer, especially because of the way Sister Therese presented it to me, was the turning point so early in this family crisis. It heightened my awareness that God would indeed protect Mom. He would be able to do immeasurably more than I could humanly do for her.

Suddenly, I knew what I had to do. Now my emotions could be used for good when I got to Florida. My fears dissipated and my confidence in the future was suddenly boosted, and my heart filled with peace and anticipation. The emotions were still a part of me, but they were not flailing, nor controlling my behavior any longer. I still did not know *how* things were going to work out, but I knew that we would be able to get through this latest "surprise of life."

I would do the practical things, be her advocate and remind my mother of all she knew about the promises of God. My prayer was that she would continue to have peace, freedom from pain, strength to endure the surgery, and be given more opportunities to create memories. How wonderful it was to be free of gripping emotional turmoil, to be energized and feel renewed. I could not wait to help her through this ordeal.

Sister Therese reminded me that I wasn't going to Florida alone. God would be with me. In fact, he always goes before and clears the way, waiting with open arms—wide enough for my mother and me—and you, too. She faxed the Prayer of Abandonment to me so I could carry it with me and share it with my mother as soon as I arrived. Indeed, Mom prayed that prayer every day for the rest of her life, and she had supernatural peace.

There will be some who may find it difficult to pray this prayer. I did. It was chilling at first and contrary to all I had been taught. The Prayer of Abandonment acknowledges our failure to succeed in controlling the events of our lives. Consider how often we have glibly given others the advice to "let go and let God." However, when faced with a life changing crisis or the death of a loved one, this advice is not so simple. No, it takes spiritual maturity to grasp its enormity, and to give our burdens to a God who may seem very far away. If I'm completely honest, there were times when abandoning my mother into God's hands felt as if I was giving up the hope of a cure.

The phrase in the prayer that says we have "boundless confidence" can also stick in our throats because when we are vulnerable, our faith can be shaken. There was another man who had shaky faith. He brought his son to Jesus and asked if he could heal him. When Jesus told him that it was possible if he believed, the man responded with what has become one of my favorite prayers in the Bible, *"I do believe; help me overcome my unbelief!"* (Mark 9:24)

While we may be anxious when we tell God its okay to do whatever he wants to do with us, it's reassuring to know that we are not alone. Most of us call upon him when we have run out of options—when we do not have answers or control over the situation. When my hope seemed thin, I was reminded of the words of Jesus quoted in Matthew 7 and in Luke 11: *"Which of you, if his son asks for bread, will give him a stone? Or if he asks for a fish would give him a snake? If you then, though you are evil, know how to give good gifts to your children, how much more will your Father in heaven give good gifts to those who ask him?"*

Deuteronomy 4:40 says we are to trust and obey so *"it will go well with you and your children."* Mom trusted God and did her best to obey the call he had on her life since her experience at the Life in the Spirit Retreat. Her faith and her relationship with God deepened because she worked at it. Consequently, things did go well for Mom for nearly three years. She enjoyed quality of life in spite of the cancer and was able to deal with the good and the bad by focusing on life not death until her last days.

Bless the Lord, O my soul, and all that is within me, bless his holy name.
(Psalm 103:1)

Part II

Preparing to Die:
How Best to Help

The Practical Side of Death

Listen to advice and accept instruction, and in the end you will be wise. (Proverbs 19:20)

I was on the brink of facing one of my most dreaded fears—losing my mother. She lived for more than two years after her diagnosis but there was no way of knowing that. We had to be prepared for the worst and I wanted someone to tell me what I had to do when she was finally gone. So many questions filled my waking hours. How would I be able to provide ongoing support for her when I lived so far away? Were her affairs in order? Would she survive the surgery? What if she became incapacitated, and what would we do about John? What if…what if…what if…?

There were so many things to do and consider. Drawing on what I learned from others in similar situations was a blessing now that it was my turn to confront the death of someone dear to me. I needed all the advice and reminders I could get, and now I'd like to return the favor by sharing what I learned about how to prepare yourself, and how best to help your friends and loved ones when faced with a life threatening illness. If you learn nothing else from these stories I hope it is the importance of getting your personal affairs in order without delay, even if you are young and enjoying robust health.

Mom and John did not have their affairs in order, and I can tell you that visiting an attorney when you are in the middle of a family health crisis adds an enormous amount of emotional stress and strain on everyone involved. Matters can be significantly more complicated and contentious if there is any question about a person's mental acuity as was the case with my mother's husband. Don't wait for an untimely illness or an accident to spur you to action. We will have no regrets if we take care of these practical details when we are able to think clearly and rationally.

There are many professionals to help, and books abound on the subject. Most people dislike paperwork, dealing with lawyers, or taking care of business that relates to facing the end of life. We tend to push it to the back burner even though we know we aren't going to live forever. Our unwillingness to tackle this task may stem from thinking that doing so demonstrates a lack of faith or hope in being restored to health. Or perhaps we're just procrastinators, knowing full well what we must do—but not today.

Regardless of the reasons or excuses, we need to face the fact that illness can strike at any time, even when you don't feel sick. Accidents happen and people die suddenly during routine procedures in a hospital. Today we are very much aware of the possibility of becoming a victim of a violent crime or international terrorism. The reality of death should not be ignored.

If any of these things happen, your family members may find themselves locked in disputes as they try to guess what you or your loved ones would have wanted with regard to end-of-life care, or how to disperse all the "stuff" accumulated during your lifetime. You probably have stories of your own to illustrate the point, and regularly we are made aware of family disputes following the death of a celebrity or another high profiled individual.

Now is the time to consider the following checklist, and weigh the benefits of having these documents in place for yourself, whether or not you have children or close relatives, regardless of your age or state of health. It's simply a smart thing to do.

Last Will and Testament

A will is the expression of your final intent. Assuming you care about others in your life, or how your worldly goods will be disbursed when you die, you need to have a Last Will and Testament. It will help your heirs or beneficiaries avoid a thoroughly unpleasant experience with the court system. Otherwise, the process of sorting out your affairs can take months, even years, and many families are torn apart as they argue about how you may have wanted to divide your estate.

It is wise to review your will every five years or more often if circumstances change such as a move to another state. Your net worth will have changed, and you may wish to alter the bequests you originally documented. Relationships evolve over the years and the people you wished to remember in your will may have already died. Others more recently may have enriched your life so much that you would like to include them to show your appreciation for their friendship. Also, a charitable organization may have grown out of favor due to poor management or worse, and others have emerged whose cause better matches your passion.

Charitable bequests are viewed by many as giving to another loved one, a charity child. Bequests of this nature can do so much good. If that is your desire, your wishes should be well documented while you are of sound mind. You may find Louisa Mae Hitchcock's story interesting.

Ms. Hitchcock was a philanthropic soul, but she never reviewed her Will. Her estate was divided among individuals and charities according to her original instructions. One entity that would benefit from her estate was the church. Comparatively speaking, this bequest was a modest sum. She, apparently, had a falling out with the pastor so the money went to establish a Parishioners Fund with instructions that not one penny was to be used for church operations or property. I had the privilege of serving on the three-member Board of Trustees charged with disbursing funds to specific members of the church who were "sick or in need or want." Her will stated that if any residual monies were left in her estate when it was settled, the amount should be added to the Parishioners' Fund.

By the time she died, she had outlived most of the people slated to receive her bequests and her stock portfolio had improved significantly. It was not her intention, but the church ultimately received over one million dollars! This was a very different distribution than she had originally intended. Unfortunately for the church, the trust was so tightly worded that the trustees were unable to use the money for the greater good of the community even when it grew into multiple millions. Individuals Ms. Hitchcock never knew continue to benefit from her Will.

Make a Last Will and Testament and review it periodically; consider using percentages rather than making specific monetary bequests.

Another occasion to redraft a will is in the case of a second marriage. The experience of my friend Joan punctuates this point. The grief and rancor within the family that was caused by her second husband's procrastination cannot be underestimated. It was traumatic for everyone when he was diagnosed with an advanced stage of cancer not long after their honeymoon. His condition deteriorated so rapidly that he had to be roused on his death bed so the lawyer could help him leave his house to his new wife. Following this sad death, years of court battles ensued between her and the children from her husband's first marriage.

If you plan to exclude someone from your will, your reasons should be well documented. Not doing so or dividing your estate unequally among family members without explanation almost certainly results in litigation. It is disheartening when relatives argue over who should have not only the money but every last item of jewelry, artwork, furniture, even knickknacks.

Make an Addendum to Your Will

One way to avoid family squabbles is to write out your wishes for how your property is to be distributed. Consider making a specific list of people and what "treasure" you want them to have and attach it as an addendum to your will. Even someone assuming ownership of the family photo album after a death can cause family resentments.

Grandma was not a woman of great wealth. Mom handled her finances at the end of her life and kept track of every penny spent. She shared with her brother and sisters a detailed account of what Grandma owned at the time of her death. As a result, there was no discord, and there was just enough money left to give five thousand dollars to each of her surviving children. Leaving some money to her children was very important to Grandma, but what gave her great pleasure was supervising the orderly disbursement of all her other worldly possessions while she was still alive.

Toward the end of her life but before hospice, Grandma sat in bed at Mom's house like a queen holding court and said, "Mary Ann, I want-a you to have my new sweater; it's a good color for you. Sharon, you take-a my pots and pans, and Larry, you can have my original passport and rosary I brought from Italy. What do you want, Donna?"

A novel idea from my Uncle Mario is worth considering. He had the contents of his house appraised then wrote the name and value of every item on 3 x 5 cards and called his three children to a meeting. He laid them out on the dining room table and, based on the total value of everything, gave them each an equal amount of play money. He and my aunt watched them negotiate with one another on what they would have when they would die one day. "It was fascinating to watch my children bargain and compromise with one another; I highly recommend it," he said. The siblings could not leave until my uncle and aunt were each satisfied that dueling children would not be added to his legacy and harmony would reign long after they were gone.

After documenting and verifying their choices, the list was attached to their Last Will and Testaments. That was over 15 years ago and my uncle is still alive and dancing. Some items have already gone to their new homes when he downsized recently, but there are no regrets.

Insurance and beneficiaries

If you have insurance of any kind, whole life or term, these are other documents that should be reviewed periodically along with your will. Make sure you are still satisfied with the beneficiaries as stated. You may not have an estate like Ms. Hitchcock, but most people carry some form of insurance, if only to handle rising funeral expenses.

Thinking about individual insurance beyond a house or car is difficult for many people, even savvy small business owners. Even when the owner knows who will run their business when they die or are incapacitated, formalizing a succession plan is a good idea. My friend Murray, an expert in this field, tells me there is one aspect of insurance that is often overlooked. Small business owners should make sure their policy is sufficient to cover the federal tax due, or else their heirs may be forced to sell part or all of the business prematurely.

Murray offered this additional observation: "I don't ever recall anyone refusing to embrace the reality of death and make a Will once the financial issues and matters of business succession were clearly presented. In fact, they were relieved when the owner's life insurance was at least equal to the expected tax, bringing peace of mind to all family members." There is no shortage of professional help available to determine your needs.

Another problem that can occur when settling an estate is identifying the organization responsible for redemption. When I tried to cash in my mother's policy, I discovered that the insurance company that originally wrote it years before had changed hands many times. It took much time and effort to discover the name of the current corporate owner so that I could redeem the policy.

Keep important policies and documents in one place so your executor has all the information needed to process administrative details.

My late friend Florence did not plan to live as long as she did, so she had no financial resources to care for herself in old age. She had no family, and without investments or a long-term care policy, she lived out her greatest nightmare, residing in a nursing home on Medicaid.

During an exciting career in journalism, Florence traveled widely as a reporter, editor, and author in her own right. When her various medical conditions impaired her mobility, she was confined to a wheelchair for ten years. Her multiple degenerative diseases resulted in her being completely bedridden in a home for over three years. Because she was mentally alert and did not have a terminal diagnosis, she never recovered from the grief of losing her independence.

She did, however, have the forethought of purchasing a prepaid insurance policy to have a say in what would happen to her body after death. Florence left instructions for her cremation and disposition of her ashes, and wrote her own obituary—gifts welcomed by her Executrix.

Power of Attorney

A Power of Attorney (POA) is a document giving legal authority for another individual to make administrative decisions and sign your name to documents when you are not able. Having this important instrument in place means you do not have to worry about paperwork if you ever become too weak, too stressed, or are too medicated to handle your affairs.

Consequently, the person to whom you assign your POA should be chosen carefully—one who is trustworthy, responsible, and dependable so they will fulfill their duties on a timely basis. Examples of what a POA might do for you include paying your bills, balancing your checkbook, completing forms, and signing your name to paperwork associated with doctors, medical facilities, Social Security, Medicare or Medicaid, or financial institutions.

There is one caveat, however. A straight Power of Attorney does not apply when a person is incapacitated, so the instrument attorneys will most commonly recommend is a Durable Power of Attorney (DPOA). Both the POA and the DPOA are void at the moment of death.

This is an important fact, particularly in the case of husbands and wives who have separate bank accounts, and the like. The surviving spouse will be unable to access the account or retrieve documents unless it is a joint account. Consulting with an attorney or estate planner will avoid any inconvenience. After death, the Executor or Executrix named in the Last Will and Testament will be responsible for seeing that your wishes are carried out.

Health Care Agent

Complementary to the POA, each of us should identify someone willing to interface with the medical system, or intervene if needed, just in case we are in no condition to assert ourselves. A Health Care Agent may be the same person you choose as POA, or different, but establishing one is a separate undertaking. Depending on the state in which you live, the title Health Care Agent may have a different name. This person will be your "advocate" or "surrogate" in the medical system. Because of privacy laws, this is an essential legal document so doctors and medical staff are able to consult with the person you deem to be your agent if you are unable to speak for yourself.

Here are two examples of what a Health Care Agent or Surrogate can do. As my mother's Health Care Surrogate in Florida and Florence's Health Care Agent in Connecticut, I was able to review their medications and communicate with the medical staff responsible for their care. But I soon learned there are no guarantees.

When Mom entered the hospital for surgery, I prepared a list of drugs to be avoided and made sure it was kept with her chart. It was also taped to her bed and the door of her hospital room. Unfortunately, those measures did not guarantee the staff would read the list. The day after her first surgery, Mom's primary care doctor found her to be in extreme pain when he was making his rounds. He mumbled something to the nurse who produced a syringe. As they were about to give her a shot, I asked what drug they were using. It was Demerol, and I lost control.

"Demerol! You are her primary care doctor and you can't remember she's allergic to Demerol!" Pointing to the list on her headboard, "Why did I bother? Look at her chart! Can't you read? You're going to kill her!"

Turning to Mom, he said, "Anna, what happens when you take Demerol?"

Through gritted teeth, she whispered, "My tongue swells up and throat closes; eyes enlarge and bug out of my head—can't breathe. They took me to the ER."

"Oh," he said, then looked at me. We stepped into the corridor and reviewed the options and every traditional pain medication that was on Mom's to-avoid list. The doctor shrugged and said, "I don't know what else to do."

"If this were your mother, would you shrug your shoulders and say, 'Oh, well, I can't think of anything else and walk away? Think! What you would do if this was your mother?"

"I guess I would consult with a Pain Specialist."

"Then what are you waiting for? You should have consulted with her surgeon and a specialist in pain management before surgery and anticipated this. Pick up the phone and get him here immediately."

Thankfully, the specialist was able to give Mom two days of relief, but if she had taken the drug any longer, it would have caused severe internal bleeding. Mom endured the pain of her surgeries, and the only relief she received was from God. I sat with her for two weeks reading the Psalms and praying with her throughout the night. Later, when I faced shoulder surgery of my own, I wanted her advice and asked how she got through the pain. She said, "The best advice I can give you is not to run from the pain. Relax into it. My mantra those two weeks was 'I'm in the pain, I'm in the pain; thank you, Jesus, for being with me in the pain.' So, sweetheart, that's my advice: don't ever run from the pain because that's where the Lord meets you—in the pain."

Don't run from pain because that's where the Lord meets you—in the pain.

Elderly people in any type of health care institution should have a Health Care Agent. My friend Florence was weak and distressed and after many falls at home and a hospital stay, she was unable to return to an independent living environment. She needed someone to explain her complex medical history to the staff at a local nursing home, handle the admissions paperwork and subsequent Medicaid application. Because of the many places she lived and life threatening surgeries she had in other countries, she had special dietary requirements and allergies that had to be taken into consideration. An allergy to bleach required them to wash her sheets separately to avoid a severe, itchy rash on her thin, frail body.

People in nursing homes have typically lost their youth, their health, probably many friendships, and Florence feared institutional living would rob her of some very basic rights. She wasn't completely wrong. When entering a care facility, they must adjust, much too quickly, to the institution's procedures, including a drastic change in what and when they eat. This was extremely difficult for Florence since her mind was still intact. For most of her life she adhered to a rigid vegetarian diet and used supplements to maintain her immune system. She asked me, as her Health Care Agent, to fight for her right to take vitamins and minerals which the nurses had taken from her. To add to the indignity, they insisted she use the laxatives they would give her, not the ones that worked for her. She felt like a prisoner.

Once things were sorted with one nurse supervisor and the aides, the process had to be repeated due to changing shifts, understaffing, high turnover rates and poor communication. Choosing a trustworthy and committed relative or close friend who is willing to assume the position of Health Care Agent is something you will not regret.

Living Will

Much has been written about the importance of having a Living Will or an Advanced Directive as it is sometimes called. Worldwide attention was given to Terri Schiavo and her family as they struggled with conflicting medical views on whether or not she was brain dead. Terri did not have a living will. The ensuing family feud, accompanied by such strong emotions, was a spectacle that could have been avoided.

However, drawing up a Living Will can be tricky business. You need to be specific regarding the wording without room for interpreting your true wishes. Geraldine's Living Will said that she did not want to be kept alive if she were brain dead. Undocumented conversations with friends about her deteriorating condition indicated she wanted to die a natural death without being placed on a feeding tube when she could no longer swallow. However, that was not specified in her Living Will and when she was unable to communicate, a feeding tube was installed. Her family did not want to be responsible for what they perceived as starving her to death. She received excellent care in a nursing home bed for four years before she passed away.

Not everyone wants to have a Living Will; it's a personal choice, so there should never be any pressure to prepare one. Some people have expressed discomfort with the thought for fear that the medical system might hasten their death, particularly if they have chosen to be an organ donor. Others have said they may change their minds if they prepare one when they are healthy. The desire to live, to survive, is a basic instinct and may preclude previous thinking on the matter. Having a Health Care Agent who knows your wishes and is willing to carry them out is all you may need.

When making a Living Will, be specific and periodically review it to ensure it reflects your current wishes.

DNR Order

The first I heard of a "Do Not Resuscitate" document was when I discussed my mother's Living Will with the oncology nurses caring for her. I was told that unless a patient had a DNR Order, the doctors would use all measures to keep them alive, even if the Living Will is kept with their chart. This is encouraging from one standpoint, but depending on the condition and wishes of the patient, a DNR Order is something to consider.

Since the function of the medical system is to treat and cure people, a person needs a DNR Order to prevent being resuscitated if their heart stops or from being involuntarily hooked up to a ventilator or feeding tube. Many people do not wish to be kept alive by artificial means because it may prolong suffering for them and their families.

The signed DNR Order must be kept with your doctor and attached to your medical chart along with your Living Will. It is a very difficult document to sign, but there are those who view it as insurance that "man" will not interfere with God's timing and their desire to die a natural death, at home if possible.

Burial and Funeral Wishes

If you care what happens to your body after you leave this world, document your wishes or others will have to decide what to do. Conflicts may arise if more than one person has an opinion on the matter. This is especially important in blended families. It would be helpful if there is no ambiguity over whether or not you wish to be cremated or buried, for example. If cremated, do you want your ashes scattered and where, or just laid to rest in a special place?

It made me uncomfortable at the time my mother gave me instructions, but when she died, I was grateful that I knew she wanted to be buried near her parents' grave and what clothes she wanted to be buried in. After sharing her wishes with her husband, she left a note covering all the details including the fact that she wanted her maiden name, not her married name, to be on her headstone. Mom's children were fathered by different men and she did not want to show partiality to any of them saying, "I have been faithful to three husbands during my lifetime, but I was born a Melodia and I will die a Melodia." That's the name engraved on her tombstone along with Isaiah 43, the scripture that opened her eyes and heart to God and helped to re-established their relationship on her Life in the Spirit Retreat.

Because the practical details were finalized six months before Mom passed away, all we had to do the morning of her death was make one phone call to activate the system we put in place. Our family was able to spend time reflecting on her life, rather than scurrying around to select the casket and make arrangements to ship her body back to Pittsburgh.

I've known people who have written their own obituaries, chosen their pall bearers and hymns for their service along with the Bible passages or poems to be read. Any or all of these things can reassure the family that they are doing everything in line with your wishes.

Getting your affairs in order, taking care of practical details long before you need to, is a valuable gift that allows your family to grieve well, without regrets, and to celebrate the memories you made together.

For where your treasure is, there your heart will be also.
(Matthew 6:21, Luke 12:34)

The Compatibility of Faith and Grief

Do not grieve as others who have no hope.
(1 Thessalonians 4:13)

"Good grief" does not mean we won't experience sorrow and pain. It hurts to lose someone we love, and God knows that all too well. The Gospel account of the story of the death and resurrection of Lazarus is a good example. When his sister Martha saw Jesus coming toward her village days after her brother died, she ran to meet him saying these gut wrenching words, "Lord…if you had been here, my brother would not have died." Then, as if to exemplify for us the compatibility of faith and grief, Martha continued, "But I know that even now God will give you whatever you ask." Even Jesus wept.

Overcoming our fears about death and dying and grieving well requires emotional and spiritual muscles. If we develop them by tapping into our faith, we will be able to say with boldness and confidence as did Paul in 1 Corinthians 15:55, *Where, Oh Death, is your sting?*

The sting usually comes from our concern for those we may one day leave behind, or from the pain and emptiness left by the loss of a loved one. The sting comes from not understanding the grieving process that can serve us well. The sting lingers when we are unable to express our grief. The sting begins to dissipate when we acknowledge our humanity and our vulnerability. This is a good thing. Learning how others have come through the grieving process helps us realize we are not alone, and may prevent us from getting stuck in our grief.

We actually become acquainted with the grieving process in gentler ways throughout life, such as when we make a major move and grieve the loss of our friends and familiar lifestyle. Losing a job, a beloved family pet, or our health for a period of time are other situations that cause us grief. Being caught in the undertow of divorce is like a death. It's the death of a dream of living happily ever after.

Grieving the loss of a marriage through divorce does not usually attract the same level of consolation and support as the loss of a spouse through a physical death. Depending on the circumstances, it can be worse. Consumed by feelings of regret, rejection, confusion, fear, loneliness when I was going through a divorce, I felt that life would never be the same again. My mother shed light on this very dark mood one day when she reminded me that she had survived both divorce and the death of a spouse. In her wisdom she said, "You're right. Things will be different from now on, but different doesn't mean it won't be better." That simple statement watered a dormant seed of hope, and she fertilized it by adding that living alone doesn't mean we have to be lonely.

After life changing events, things will be different, but different doesn't mean it won't be better.

Whatever the reason for grief, you can't give it short shrift. Experts tell us that after the initial shock of loss, grief comes in stages: denial, anger, depression and acceptance, and then a time of gradual rebuilding. One thing to remember, though, is that these stages do not always happen sequentially—sometimes they happen simultaneously. No two people grieve the same way. Grief has no timetable to mollify the sadness one feels, the deep seated yearning for a relationship lost.

It is not uncommon for grief to shake our trust in God, even for those with great faith. When confronted with the bare medical facts that she only had six months to live, my faith-filled mother, suddenly needed reassurance. She also felt guilty that she would be leaving us! Talking openly about her feelings eased the sting of grief for both of us.

Weeping may remain for a night, but rejoicing comes in the morning. (Psalm 30:5b)

We developed a little ritual on my monthly visits to her. Nighttime was when the reality that she was dying would hit me, not during the busyness of the day. I usually drifted off to sleep on my tear-stained pillow. Before I knew it, Mom would knock on my bedroom door. Softly, she would say, "Good morning; are you awake?" *Thank you, Lord! You've given us another day together.*

After I had propped up a pillow for her, she would climb into bed with me. I curled up against her, put my head on her chest and threw my leg over hers. It was time to settle in for some serious mother-daughter pillow talk. One day she whispered, "What questions do you have? Is there anything you want to know?"

"I can't think of anything, Mom."

To this she replied, "You're right, we have no secrets." We would reminisce and talk about the good times we had, especially the good that came out of the bad. One morning it was as if she could read my mind. She knew I couldn't bear the thought of losing her, my most loyal supporter and best friend, so she said, "And don't think just because I'm gone you're going to be rid of me, because I'm going to be sitting right here." She tapped me on the shoulder with her little arthritic index finger. "I'll be whispering in your ear every day of your life!"

Jokingly, I cringed and said with a feigned laugh, "Oh, no! Not every day." During moments like this I would pull the sheet up under my chin or over my cheek so my tears would not penetrate her night gown.

She rarely saw me cry, but when she did, her voice would crack and say, "Don't start because, if you do, I will and I'm afraid I won't be able to stop."

One morning, she was the one who choked back tears, and finally found the words to say what was on her mind. "Do you know what really makes me sad? Wondering who's going to be with you when you die."

In a flash—as if to put my finger in the dike before the dam breaks—I said, "Why, you will, of course!" I wondered where the words came from, but continued, "I don't know where I'll be, but I know that, even if it appears that I will be in a room all alone, you will be there, comforting me, and welcoming me home. Remember when Grandma was in the hospice and you told me you heard her talking to her mother?" She remembered.

"Well, you will be with me, along with lots and lots of angels like the ones who are here right now filling this bedroom, waiting to guide you to heaven. They may be the same ones who have surrounded you every day of your life." As if to reassure myself and to remind her, I said questioningly, "You do believe that when you leave, Mom, we will only be apart for a short time, don't you?" She nodded her head, pressed the sheet to her eyes, and I'm sure our tears mingled in the fibers. "Besides, didn't you tell me you will always be sitting on my shoulder, whispering in my ear?" I finally made her smile.

After Mom's diagnosis, we would occasionally exchange notes or letters when it was easier to write the things we wanted to say to one another. She must have known I was trying to be strong when I said I wasn't crying, and she worried about how I was going to handle her death. A few days after one of my visits, I received yet another lesson in the mail from her—one that would help prepare me to handle her passing.

Dearest Donna,

God help you, but you have inherited many of your mama's bad faults. My mother had a saying, "If anything bad happens in this family, let it happen to Anna; she can cope with it." But I didn't want to cope with it. I wanted sympathy and pity and tears—the whole schmeer the world wasn't giving me. Okay. What to do? What to do? Ah, well! Work! Work harder! Do better! Who needed sympathy? I did! But I had to put up a brave front. Tough, that's me!

The lesson is: When you are vulnerable—show it! People—friends and family—are all afraid of us because of our exterior. They believe they are intruding. Darling girl, it's a lesson I'm still learning. Don't wait till you go to learn. I love you so strongly, more than my life. Kiss Roger and tell him he is going to have his hands full, so let him and others in.

Mom

On this point, I was not a quick learner. I soon discovered that when we try to stifle grief or hurry it along, its sting will reappear to confuse and confound. This longing for someone you love can pop up at the most unexpected moments for months and even years after the loss when something triggers the memory of a loved one. At some level I was still in denial even after my mother passed away and, unconsciously, did not allow myself to fully grieve.

There was so much to do. How could I take the time to cry when there were two memorial services to plan as an accommodation to friends and relatives in different states, sort through all the clothes and household goods, select a realtor, and help John settle into the assisted living facility? But the sting of grief eventually caught up with me.

Nearly a year after she died, I was at home dusting, and picked up a small picture frame holding a photo of my mother's smiling face taken at her last Christmas party. I studied it and noticed her hair. For the first time, the realization hit me that I would never see her or be able to touch her hair again. The memories of all the years I set and styled her hair came flooding back, and the dam I built to control my emotions was breaking. I felt the texture of the strands of her hair between my fingers. I could smell her familiar scent mingled with the fragrance of the styling gel and hear her say, "Looks better than going to the beauty shop!" I started to cry and talk to her picture.

"Mom, I miss you so much. I'm never going to be able to do your hair again!" My sobs seemed to come from the core of my very being, and I was frightened. The sound coming out of me triggered the memory of what I heard coming from the bedroom of a mother whose son had committed suicide many years earlier. Keening, it's called—crying that results from the piercingly cold pain of acute, bitter sorrow. It was my turn.

All of our senses are involved in the grieving process, and any of them are able to trigger new levels of grief at unexpected times. Remember my admonition from Mom. Don't be too busy to grieve because emotions demand attention. If you don't express them when they rise up, you may be driving down the road five years from now and burst into tears, not knowing why. Love your tears; they are a blessing.

Grieve well and don't be afraid to show your vulnerability.

Some people are thrown into the grieving process without warning. "Shock and awe" are terms not limited to war. When a loved one dies suddenly, it feels like an internal tsunami that brings you to your knees, or an earthquake with aftershocks rocking the entire nervous system for days. Another way for a person to relate to the grief, shock and helplessness felt in a sudden death is to recall what it was like to watch the Twin Towers implode, or a Humvee explode in Iraq for the first time. Words like "there's been an accident" or "your test results are positive" cause shock waves to bounce off the walls of your heart. All of these reactions are normal. It's a human response and has nothing to do with faith.

Grief manifests itself in different ways. For some it is an outward expression and for others, very private. Depending on our cultural backgrounds and past experiences, everyone grieves differently, but even well-meaning friends and acquaintances can forget this truth.

Judge not lest you be judged.
(Matthew 7:1)

Even if you are more than a casual acquaintance to someone who has recently lost a loved one, do not assume you know what's going on in their life. Appearance can be deceiving and you may not know everything about their past experiences. Nobody knows the full range of another person's thoughts and feelings—hopes, dreams lost, anger, guilt, or fear of the future.

One of my special friends is a beautiful woman who met and married a widower with three boys. She then had two more of her own, and God was at the center of their lives. Their Bible had been read so much, it was falling apart. When her husband died suddenly, I was there when she had to tell her six-year-old son that the Daddy he adored died at work. No one can presume to know the depth of grief she and her three older stepsons felt when she had to tell them they had now lost their father as well.

This brave young woman not only had the responsibilities of being the sole parent but also running their family-owned business. Unfortunately, her husband had not insured himself or the company, thinking he was still too young. She would have lost everything if she had not risen to the occasion. "What a brick she is," people would say. "Look how she bounces back—she's fine now."

Yet, others criticized her for not grieving "properly." What people didn't see or hear were the tears at three o'clock in the morning, or the middle-of-the-night telephone calls and visits from a close friend. For the sake of her children, the dark and silent hours provided the only time for her to have the luxury of healing tears.

However and whenever we grieve the many types of losses in life, we need to do it well. Good grief involves expressing your emotions. Identify them. Accept them. Explore them with a close friend or counselor. Maintaining a "stiff upper lip" can lead to isolation, a prolonged healing process, and feelings of being helpless and hopeless. Denying our emotions can have long-term negative effects on us. A note from Cindy shows how God used her family pet as the catalyst she needed to begin a long awaited healing process. She had just taken her dog Kate to the animal hospital when she wrote:

There is nothing the vet can do for our family pet and friend. The cancer is growing so fast that even if he amputates, it will reappear within the month. Maybe it won't heal at all and we would still have to put her down. We decided to bring her home and keep her as comfortable as possible until she begins to suffer and then we will put her to sleep. We are so very sad—but somehow God, in His wisdom, has even allowed this to happen. As I prayed today, I felt that grieving our pet's impending death will allow us to grieve more actively every loss we have experienced in the past two years.

My husband and I have many, many tears to shed, but since we have been avoiding or trying to diffuse our feelings at each time of crisis, those tears have not come easily. I think God knows we must cry and release all our grief to Him, and losing Kate will make it very real. But now, I just feel very, very tired and just very unmotivated to do anything. Even simple activities of daily living seem like such an ordeal.

My friend again reinforces the one way to move forward with your grief is to talk about it. Don't ignore your feelings and try to understand the reason for the depth of your sadness. By the way, at the time of this writing Kate is still with Cindy and she is much more cheerful.

Faith and grief are compatible, but don't be surprised by the many faces of grief we wear throughout the grieving process.

Grief is good, and if we go through our unique grieving process with healthy support, we will be able to embrace deeper relationships with God and others. Good Grief stands on the promises of God with confidence, and it will strengthen our faith and help us embrace life once more with a renewed sense of purpose.

So with you: Now is your time for grief, but I will see you again and you will rejoice, and no one will take away your joy. (John 16:22)

The Luxury of Receiving Care

Never will I leave you; never will I forsake you.
(Hebrews 13:5)

Receiving care is not just a luxury, it is a necessity. Nonetheless, expectations often dictate that we strive to appear strong and in control of every aspect of our lives. Most of us derive a great sense of satisfaction when we help someone in need. It feels good, even noble, to be perceived as a caregiver rather than a care receiver. The reality is that one day we will ask ourselves this question: "Why should I have all the fun?"

Being fully human as well as divine, even Jesus allowed himself to receive care from others. We're not meant to carry our burdens alone, but on whom can we call? Family, friends, neighbors, trained caregivers, and medical professionals can all play valuable roles in helping us through difficult times, but usually the first words heard when a crisis strikes are, "Oh, my God!" If only it were more than a meaningless exclamation. Let's take a closer look at these various sources of care.

God

It seems many of us tend to cry out to God when we have lost complete control and are unable to rise above difficult circumstances. I believe he will answer our sincere cry for help, but I've also learned that it's much easier to seek help from someone we know very well. If we want that person to be God, we should be developing a relationship with him during good times. Calling on a good friend, especially God, can be a stabilizing influence and their very presence in times of trouble will comfort us and remind us of the faith, hope and trust we have in that friendship. We will know for certain that when we cry, "Oh, my God," he will be there.

Compared to other friends, God alone understands the depth of our emotions during a life changing event, and he wants us to call on him. Sometimes when we are particularly distraught, it may feel as if God has not heard us. Even people who usually sense his presence have said it felt as if God had abandoned them. Remember, Jesus cried out as he hung on the cross, "My God, my God, why have you forsaken me?" (Matthew 27:46) He did not, and throughout both the Old and New Testaments in the Bible God has promised that he will never leave us or forsake us.

My Living Libraries have solidified the fact that God did not create us to be independent, self-sufficient people. He wants us to live in community, to be in relationship first with him and then with one another. But we are a stubborn lot. During my divorce, I remember feeling so alone and vulnerable after leaving my brave face at the office. I was too proud and depressed to ask for help, not even from God. And yet, some evenings I would look at the telephone and cry, "Why don't you ring? Doesn't anybody care how much I'm hurting?" My attempts to handle things alone were unraveling. In hindsight I can see how God uses troubled times to remind us of our need to be connected with him and our fellow humans in meaningful ways.

There are countless stories in the Bible that show how most of God's promises involve interaction—our doing something before he does something. Moses had to stretch out his hand before the Red Sea parted (Exodus 14:25). Forty years later, the Israelites had to step into the Jordan River when it was at flood stage before God made a path through it so they could cross over into the Promised Land (Joshua 13-16). Jesus commanded, "Stretch out your hand," to the man with the shriveled arm before it was completely restored (Mark 3:3-5). And we are told that *if* we keep God's commands, *then* it will "go well with you and your children after you" (Deuteronomy 4:40).

During Jesus' life and ministry, people had direct access to God, and when he ascended into heaven, Jesus promised to send his Spirit to live in those who believed in him. It is by the power of God's Spirit in us that we are able to not only give, but be open to receiving his love, care and comfort. It is unlikely that we would refuse help from Jesus if he were here in the flesh, so we should enjoy the luxury of receiving care from him through his ambassadors to strengthen us emotionally, spiritually and physically. Traditionally, our parents, siblings, and extended family members have been our primary sources of support.

Family and Friends

When I was young and someone died, the care our family received truly was a luxury. A steady stream of people came to our home to mourn with us, and as if by magic, food appeared on our table and chores were done. We were able to comfort one another by recalling the now cherished memories of our loved one. For weeks, even months, friends and neighbors were never far away. They showered us with visits, phone calls, cards and letters, and more food. The intense pain of grief is more bearable when it's shared.

Things are different today with our changing lifestyles and our mobile society. Often we must look beyond our traditional support system for consistent, sustained help when we need it most—in the months or years that follow a memorial service. With the technology we have at our fingertips, it takes little effort to stay in touch, but the reality is that we have to get quickly back into life. And that can mean we are miles away from each other in a matter of a week or two.

Even family members who live in close proximity to one another can't always be there as we work through our crisis. Our normal routines at work, home, and in the community take precedence, and there is pressure to get through the grieving process in a hurry. Whether it's real or self-imposed pressure, a person may have difficulty adjusting in the aftermath of loss. This reality often lays heavy on the heart.

In the Garden of Gethsemane, Jesus also had difficulty getting the kind of support and comfort he desired in his hour of need—and his friends were actually with him! On three different occasions, Jesus asked his closest disciples, "Can't you even stay with me for one hour?" It's disappointing and hurtful when people don't live up to our expectations. But earlier Jesus had received the luxury of care when Mary anointed him with expensive perfume at the Last Supper. Did the fragrance linger on his skin during his trial and crucifixion to remind him that he was loved?

No matter how close we are to our family and friends, they may not be the right people to help us regain our balance after a traumatic event in our lives. They may be too emotionally involved to be effective caregivers and miss the clues that tell them of our needs. And some families just drift apart over the years for a variety of reasons.

Like Mom, many retired persons move to warmer climates fearing a premature loss of independence caused by winter accidents. They dread being a burden to anyone, and instead decide to live their retirement dreams in an area where their children and grandchildren would want to visit frequently. While it made good sense at the time, the decision may come back to haunt them. "You were the one who moved!" is the angry mantra of some adult children, perhaps overcompensating for their guilt at not being able to spend quality time with their parents after they relocate.

Also, careers have taken younger family members away from home base first, causing them to be separated from the voices of experience in their lives. Distance may not be the only thing that widens the gap between us and our traditional support group. Even if we live in the same town with our relatives, the pressure of growing responsibilities and an adult social life can distance us from one another. New relationships are built outside the family unit, and maintaining contact becomes an effort—even a burden on an already overloaded schedule. Communication begins to feel like obligation, and guilt can be masked by defensive attitudes.

We have also lost the art of letter writing, and many senior citizens still find the use of a computer daunting. When available, e-mails and the ability to view still and motion pictures of our loved ones from afar helps us stay connected, but it plays a distant second to personal contact. Is it possible for a person to have the luxury of receiving care in our fast-paced society? The answer is yes, but it may be necessary to receive care from those beyond our inner circle.

Focus on the relationships you have, not the ones you've lost.

Natural Caregivers, Stephen Ministers, Professionals

If you have natural caregivers in your inner circle, cherish them. They are the ones who know how to listen patiently as we learn how to cope with a problem that's not going to go away. It takes time to think through the pros and cons of alternative solutions and to decide how and when to take new steps to recovery. But some family members and close friends may not be natural caregivers. They may be problem solvers, fixers, who are inclined to give unsolicited advice. Others may smother us with so much attention that we can't sort out our own thoughts.

While we all need quiet time when we go through a crisis, isolation can lead to depression. Our inability to answer recurring questions about our past or future can haunt us, and may persist without help.

To experience the luxury of receiving care, we need to set aside our pride and the notion that we don't need anybody. Many cultures teach the value of remaining stoic and independent, in control of our emotions and our life, but the saying "God helps those who help themselves" has no theological basis. We are meant to be interdependent people. In truth, a special caring friend made in an hour of need will never replace our long-standing relationships, but their listening ear will add value to our lives.

People who know us best want to stop our hurting and may pressure us into moving forward with our lives before we are ready. They also tend to over-relate or talk about similar problems they had in the past. When you are the one in crisis, listening to stories of somebody else's past pain does not ease yours. You need someone who is there just for you.

Maybe that's why many people turn to prayer. When we talk to God, he truly listens and gives us time to work things out for ourselves with his gentle nudges of inspiration. Prayer is a powerful tool, especially when we use it in conjunction with someone who has God-given gifts of compassion and a listening heart. Unexpressed and unexplored fear, anxiety, anger, sadness, guilt, and grief can be toxic to our body as well as our spirit. Students of philosophy and human behavior have discovered that confronting our feelings can be a catalyst for enormous emotional and spiritual growth.

While some natural caregivers are drawn to caregiving professions, others instinctively support neighbors and friends out of the goodness of their hearts. Some volunteer through various caring organizations or church ministries. One such ministry began when Dr. Kenneth Haugk, a pastor and clinical psychologist, trained a few selected natural caregivers, members of his congregation, to help him extend pastoral care to others beyond the limited hours he had available. They were so well received that in 1975 Dr. Haugk established a non-profit organization and Stephen Ministry was born.

Under his leadership, Stephen Ministries, Inc. has developed a comprehensive system of preparing, recruiting, training, and supervising lay people to provide distinctively Christian care to those in need. The name of the ministry was derived from the Bible in The Book of Acts, Chapter 6. Here we find the disciples facing a similar dilemma that all pastors and clergy have within their congregations. The apostles were attempting to care for a growing number of followers, and it began to impact the time they had available to fulfill their callings—to teach and preach the Word of God. Needing others to help, Acts 6:5 says in part, "They chose Stephen, a man full of faith and of the Holy Spirit."

At the time of this writing, Stephen Ministries, Inc., a non-profit organization, has trained and equipped over 55,000 leaders who, in turn, have trained over one-half million caregivers as Stephen Ministers in the United States and abroad. Stephen Ministry has been an active caregiving ministry available to every Christian denomination for decades. After undergoing a screening process, selected men and women work under supervision to develop their caregiving skills in an intensive training and ongoing education program. Once commissioned, a Stephen Minister is matched with someone who needs encouragement as they learn to cope with one of life's many surprises, and a new friendship develops.

The special relationship that grows is largely due to the Stephen Minister's empathy, trustworthiness, and ability to be a good listener. Confidentiality is the cornerstone of this ministry. Stephen Ministers do not give advice, but they ask good questions and act as a sounding board so their care receivers can make their own decisions. If a person needs professional help, Stephen Ministers are familiar with community resources and can make referrals. Their motto is "Stephen Ministers care, but God cures." It is a ministry of presence where a dependable, non-judgmental friend shows up when needed most.

Having worked in this ministry for over a decade, I encouraged my own mother to include Stephen Ministry in her network of support when she was diagnosed with ovarian cancer. Her church did not have a Stephen Ministry, but knowing that some congregations make Stephen Ministers available to nonmembers, I told her about it. Her initial reaction was typical.

"I don't need a Stephen Minister; I have you. You're my best friend, and we talk every day. Beside I don't want to bring a stranger into my home at this stage."

The suggestion of confiding in a person she didn't even know made her uncomfortable. She was vulnerable and did not want anyone to disturb the dynamics of our relationship. So, I explained.

"Of course you have me, Mom," I said. "But I live so far away; and when we talk, haven't you noticed how we instinctively protect each other? You don't tell me exactly how you feel because you don't want me to worry about you, and I do the same with you. It's not healthy to bury our thoughts and feelings—not at a time like this. A Stephen Minister won't replace me. She'll be in addition to me. Besides, nobody is a stranger once you meet them."

Her silence confirmed that she was indeed protecting me. As we talked, Mom began to see the potential benefits of having a new listening friend.

"You need lots of different people to help you, Mom, especially as you care for John with Alzheimer's. You can't talk to him about your own feelings considering your own diagnosis, and you won't talk about him to our relatives or your friends. A Stephen Minister will understand, respect your desire, and protect your dignity as well as John's. They will not second guess your decisions, but they will be someone you can trust with your feelings. Anything you say will be held in confidence, and besides, if my experience counts for anything, I know that God will be the one to choose the perfect Stephen Minister for you."

Mom agreed to try it, and once introduced, she met with her Stephen Minister every week either in person or by phone until she had to say good-bye. After Mom died, her Stephen Minister Carol called me at home. She was calm but purposeful.

"Donna, I now know why God matched me with your mother. It is said Stephen Ministers receive more than they give, and I'm calling today to tell you that I've just been diagnosed with terminal lung cancer. Because of what I learned from your mother Anna, I am not afraid. She taught me how to get through this with dignity and peace. Thank you for sharing her with me. It's now my turn to receive care, and I wanted you to know that she will be my role model until I take my last breath."

Allowing yourself to receive care from others may be the greatest gift you will ever give them.

This simple story about these two extraordinary caregivers, both willing to accept the luxury of receiving care, is another testimony that God never stops using us until we take our final breath.

If you do not have a trusted friend who is a natural caregiver or a trained Stephen Minister available to you, I encourage you to reach out. You may need to take the first step. Talk to your doctor, visit a church to consult with the pastor, or seek out professionals who are crisis and growth counselors. Use the phone book if you must, but get help. Some people prefer to be part of a discussion group, and in most communities they already exist and will welcome you. Remember, you are not alone. God is with you and he will help you find "God with skin on" as you walk along the road of Good Grief.

He who dwells in the shelter of the Most High will rest in the shadow of the Almighty. I will say of the Lord, "He is my refuge and my fortress, my God, in whom I trust."
(Psalm 91: 1-2)

God with Skin On

The Lord is close to the brokenhearted and saves those who are crushed in spirit. (Psalm 34:18)

Jesus actually was "God with skin on." His miracles proved it. When Lazarus died, his sisters Mary and Martha were able to physically run to Jesus and express their sorrow and disappointment that he had not come to them sooner. Having Jesus as a close friend was indeed comforting. He even wept with the two sisters before responding to their request. When Jesus eventually called Lazarus out of the tomb, he came out—but even Lazarus eventually died. After all, life as we know it is only temporary.

Today, we can no longer see or hear God, and even if we could, the noise of the world can drown out God's still small voice. It is hard to maneuver through the minefields of life during a personal crisis or when we are unable to process man's inhumanity to man. Strong emotions during times like these may trigger irrational thoughts, endanger a person's health, and even change personalities. The good news is that since God's Spirit lives in us, we can be "God with skin on" to hurting people.

It's not as difficult as it sounds. All we have to do is be at the right place, at the right time and let God work through us. For example, the teenaged son of a friend was diagnosed with a life threatening disease. Upon hearing the news the entire family suddenly found themselves in a frightening world where they were forced to learn a new vocabulary in order to communicate with the doctors. My friend Carol and her husband worked on their son's treatment schedule, made lists of the possible life-threatening side effects of chemotherapy, and developed back-up plans if needed. It never occurred to them to talk about the impact this new lifestyle was having on them personally or how it was affecting their marriage.

As I was leaving the grocery store one day, Carol walked in with a faraway look in her eyes. Going shopping was the only time she allowed herself to be alone with her thoughts, but I soon discovered that she really needed someone to talk to. After a quick update on her son's situation, I asked how she was holding up. She revealed that she had begun arguing with her husband but didn't understand why. He had done nothing to deserve her anger. Carol sensed she was becoming increasingly protective, like a lioness with her cub, so much so that she even resented her husband's participation in caring for their son. As we talked, she suddenly realized that her anger was really with God, not her husband.

This prompted new questions about herself. Did this reveal a lack of faith or trust in God, a sign of disrespect? Is this why she had been unable to pray since her son's diagnosis. Standing in the grocery store that day, her real questions began to emerge. "Why, God? I thought I would be the one to get cancer. Why my son and not me? When are you going to heal him? How long are we going to have to endure this stress and uncertainty?"

Don't bury your negative emotions; talk to a trusted friend who is a good listener.

Was our meeting a divine appointment as Carol suggested? That day, she needed "God with skin on" to remind her that it's okay to be angry with God. It was an unlikely location, but at that time and place, my friend was able to dig up some of her buried feelings and ask some tough questions of God. It's nice to know his shoulders are big enough to handle whatever we can throw at him.

Timing is everything. Responding to the nudge of the Holy Spirit is faith's call to action. When you have the opportunity to be "God with skin on" take advantage of the situation. At various times in our lives, giving and receiving care may be just the conduit we need to reconnect the lines of communication with God. You will treasure the experience and the rewards are great.

How can we develop our ability to be "God with skin on?" Since the cornerstone of Christianity is the belief that Christ died to restore our relationship with God, I'm strongly persuaded that we become better caregivers as the relationship with our Heavenly Father grows. Haven't you noticed that people begin to look and act like their friends when they spend a lot of time together? If you want a glimpse of God, just focus on the good we see in ourselves and others. After all, we are made in his image.

The more time we spend in conversation with God, the sooner we become more loving and exhibit more joy, peace, patience, kindness, goodness, faithfulness, gentleness and self-control. The Bible calls these traits the fruit of the Spirit. Notice "fruit" is singular which means all of these traits will grow as our relationship with God matures. These are the characteristics to develop if we desire to be "God with skin on" to someone surprised by life.

These are the same characteristics that caused people to be drawn to Jesus, and they will draw others to us. Just like fruit on the vine, the fruit of the Spirit is not immediately evident. It first appears as a mere bud in the spring, and throughout the life of the plant it must be watered and fertilized. Likewise, in the springtime of our belief, we also need to be fed and protected from worldly pests so the fruit of the Spirit growing in us can come to full maturity.

Toxic people and our own destructive choices can slow our growth, and every loss in life can be compared with the pruning of a plant. While it hurts to be pruned, we can trust that God will use this situation to produce more love, kindness, peace, and joy in our lives. Through the seasons of our life, the fruit of God's Spirit will bud, blossom, and then ripen. Matthew 7:16 says, *By their fruit you will recognize them*. Unlike a vine or a tree, our spiritual growth is not subject to seasonal changes. If we choose to believe, the Master Gardener will till the soil of our hearts, preparing us for opportunities to be "God with skin on."

A Spirit-filled life both receives and gives which, in turn, builds community and creates harmony.

In addition to bearing the *fruit* of the Spirit so others are drawn to us, God gives us different *gifts* of the Spirit to share. From the very beginning God said, "It is not good for man to be alone." It is our diversity of gifts that helps us to stay connected—gifts of teaching, wisdom, discernment, preaching, music, administration, and more.

We live in a world where so many people are thirsty for love and a sense of belonging. If only we could truly see ourselves as the one Body of Christ, we would accept and develop the gifts God has given us instead of envying one another. Having different gifts should help us live in greater harmony and draw us closer to one another. Paul used a metaphor in letters to the churches of his time to explain how we should be working together.

Paul's message to the Ephesians was this: "From him [the Holy Spirit] the whole body, joined and held together by every supporting ligament, grows and builds itself up in love, as each part does its work." (Ephesians 4:16) Continuing in his letter to the church in Corinth, he wrote: "Now the body is not made up of one part but of many…If one part suffers, every part suffers with it; if one part is honored, every part rejoices with it." (1 Corinthians 12:12-20)

Grasping this concept is very liberating. We are called to be free—free to serve one another in love. (Galatians 5:13) We are free to help when the Spirit moves us, and because we have different gifts there is no pressure to be all things to all people. There's only one Savior and it isn't me or you. That's good news.

My friend Beverly has a special gift, but she didn't always recognize it as such. You could always count on Bev to spot a visitor in church. Bold and confident, she would welcome strangers not only with a smile but also with an invitation to a supper or a special event. Unfortunately, Bev was perpetually frustrated with other people because they did not follow her example. She would ask, "If I can do it, why can't they?"

Be an encourager and help others identify their strengths and gifts, and ask that they do the same for you.

When she realized that she had been given a gift of hospitality that perfectly matched her personality, it wasn't long before she stopped making comparisons. Instead, she became more loving and kind as she recognized gifts in other people. Bev has been "God with skin on" for so many shy people who needed her other gift of encouragement to feel a sense of belonging and help them recognize the value they have in their own right. She now shares the story of her growth, explaining that we cannot hold someone accountable for gifts they don't have.

Judging others whose viewpoints or experiences are different from ours is not what God wants us to do, and it is not conducive to being "God with skin on." Remembering Bev's experience reminds me that I need to be less judgmental, and be more forgiving when people disappoint me. Unfortunately, in the weeks following my mother's death, I forgot what I learned from Bev.

I felt hurt, disappointed, isolated from my relatives. My longing for the way things used to be was like a stone lying heavy on my heart. I suffered in silence because I didn't want to tell anybody how I felt. It took "God with skin on" to help me out of a dark place in my life. My very patient husband and one close friend sensed something was wrong and gently reminded me to focus on the relationships I had in my life. They helped me talk things out until I realized that dwelling on the close relationships I had lost through death, distance or changing circumstances was not healthy. Intellectually, I knew that everyone has their own problems, but grief has a way of blinding us so we are unable to see things as they truly are.

Many others suffer their losses in silence. So, if you want to be "God with skin on" act on your impulse to reach out to a person going through a difficult time. It may be a holy nudge. And if you are the one who thinks no one understands what you are going through, listen for the still small voice inside of you saying, "I'm here. Am I not sufficient? Just rest and let me heal you. Trust that this too shall pass." This reminds me of another "God with skin on" story.

Recovering from the second surgery was even worse than the first for my mother. It was much more invasive, and the pain was excruciating. The surgeon made an incision from the bottom of her breast bone to the top of her pubic bone so he could removed a new growth, all but a small section her colon, plus the fatty tissue around her vital organs—any place where cancer cells would likely hide. Once again, Mom called on God for the strength to endure the pain she had to bear.

One day during the second week of hospitalization, she hit a particularly low period. Her blood count had dropped significantly so she was given multiple blood transfusions—and then her lung collapsed. She was depressed, anxious, confused, and frustrated with her recovery. It was a very dark day for both of us. She needed "God with skin on" and because I was so emotionally involved, I could not answer this call. This time it was the hospital chaplain who came in minutes.

Mom did not want me to leave her alone, so I sat on a sofa across the room and listened as she spewed out her fears and questions she wanted to ask of God.

"You sound just like David," said the chaplain.

Having named the primary author of her beloved Psalms, Mom asked him to explain. Without hesitation, he opened the Bible and began to read David's words which were almost identical to what she had just said! Tapping into the life of one of my mother's favorite spiritual ancestors affirmed her feelings and gave her hope. Even though the account of David's trials and triumphs were written many centuries before, it motivated her to participate fully in the treatment for her lungs. Every movement hurt, but she knew—like David—she would get through it.

Six years later, it would be my turn to face my fears when I was diagnosed with breast cancer. Friends and neighbors sent notes and promised to pray for me, but I was still in turmoil. Balance and perspective was restored when the Holy Spirit moved a special person to call me. It was my friend Nigel who wanted to talk and pray for a complete healing as soon as he heard of my news.

Father Nigel Mumford, an Anglican priest and Director of Christ the King Spiritual Life Center in Greenwich, New York, has the gift of healing. It is remarkable how God had transformed the hands of this former Royal Marine that were trained to kill into hands that now bring a healing touch to hurting people. In our conversation, Nigel asked me to visualize what to do with all the promised prayers coming my way.

He said, "Imagine that the prayers for you are being collected in a funnel, a very large funnel that is full to overflowing. This is your funnel and you are to hold it in your hands and direct the nozzle of that funnel to the exact spot where you need healing—the site of the tumor, your fears, even toward the medical professionals taking care of you."

The doctors had not yet started radiation, and I was anticipating breast burns and blisters but also the possible damage radiation could do to my heart and lungs. As Nigel spoke, the image of the funnel clicked into place and I exclaimed, "This is God's radiation—prayers that target just the area that needs healing!"

That very positive, optimistic image stayed with me throughout my treatment, and every prayer in the funnel complemented what the doctors were doing to rid my body of disease. My mantra during radiation was "Shadrach, Meshach and Abednego," and just like those three boys who were thrown into the fiery furnace (Daniel 3:19-30), I did not burn or blister and my heart and lungs were protected. I am grateful that Nigel followed the prompting of the Holy Spirit to remind me of the power of prayer. He was just the "God with skin on" I needed.

Many of my Living Libraries had a way of reinforcing a belief in God, but they also knew the value of having an angelic presence during difficult times. Make yourself available for angel duty, and keep your eyes and ears open for the lessons you can learn as you visit the sick and comfort those who mourn.

For he will command his angels concerning you to guard you
in all your ways; they will lift you up in their hands,
so that you will not strike your foot against a stone.
(Pslam 91:11-12)

Facing Down Death

Weeping may remain for a night, but rejoicing comes in the morning. (Psalm 30:5)

We never know when it will be our turn to confront a life threatening event or illness. When it happened to me, it was as if I was suddenly dropped into a surreal dream. Everything seemed to move in slow motion, but not for long. I had decisions to make, and quickly. Being confronted with treatment options, most of which carry significant side effects with no guarantees, is daunting. Oddly enough, I didn't fear the words "you have breast cancer" or the thought that women die of this disease. It was the agony of decision at various stages along the way that caused the most pain for me.

Do I want a mastectomy or a lumpectomy? An axillary dissection? Should I submit to the recommended chemotherapy? If so, do I want to have all two or three drugs administered at each infusion, one being aptly nicknamed "red devil" after its color and side effects? Or should I go straight to radiation? Can I pray this disease out of my body? Should I allow them to destroy the good that remains after removing the tumor and 15 lymph nodes? My brain was beginning to feel paralyzed.

As I researched my options and prayerfully struggled with my choices, I thought about the paralytic in the Bible who was told by Jesus to "take up your mat and walk." The treatment plan was "my mat" and making decisions was a way for me to participate in my healing. But I knew that whatever the treatment, I needed to enter into it as my friend Gina did. She would look up at the IV and victoriously say to every drop of chemo that entered her veins, "Yes! Another cancer cell dies today!" Believing in what you are doing and viewing it as a partnership between you, God, and the doctor is very important. As they say, "Attitude is everything."

In spite of all my training and lessons learned from the dying, in spite of the physical and spiritual support I received, one question continued to lurk in the dark recesses of my mind: "How will I face down death?" This is a very human response to a life threatening situation. If we have no other role model, we need look no further than Jesus for the answer.

Just after he told his disciples he would soon die, Jesus went back to Jericho and healed blind Bartimæus. In other words, he kept on living and doing the work he was called to do! Should we not do the same when we are faced with the prospect of our own death? Even as he hung on the cross, Jesus continued to teach, guide and direct. To Mary and John he said, "Son, behold thy mother; Mother behold Thy son." He told them to take care of each other, a command we are all to heed.

The way to face down death is to keep on living and doing the work God has called you to do.

When it comes to facing down death, the disciples provide a good example. The Bible tells us that they feared dying at sea with Jesus asleep in the boat during a violent storm. Frankly, I wonder if he wasn't just resting his eyes, waiting to see how long it would take for the disciples to call on him. After Jesus calmed the wind and the waves, he turned to them and said, "Oh ye of little faith." The lesson for us is to remember that Jesus is in the boat of life with us as well, and he has promised to neither slumber nor sleep.

How we handle ourselves when we learn that we have to face death will vary. Some people search the world for miracle cures when traditional medicine can offer no hope for a cure. A colleague and professed atheist wrote to inform us of his terminal prognosis. His plan was to travel during the time he had left to "figure out the meaning of life," adding that he thought it has "something to do with service." It struck me that God continues to speak to our spirit and gives us innumerable opportunities to confront our skepticism and doubt to the very end.

My mother, like many others, drew even closer to her family. John, Larry and I were with her when she heard the dreaded words "it's inoperable; there is nothing more we can do." This is how she faced down death.

Mom took a deep breath and concentrated as the doctor explained in detail why there were no other medical options. The news penetrated every fiber of our being. Nobody moved, and we were afraid to look at one another. She was the first to speak. "How much time do I have?"

"Nobody knows that, but my guess is six months to a year."

"Well, Doctor, thank you for not pulling any punches with me. I wanted the facts, and I appreciate your candor and your honesty. But with all due respect, M.D. does not stand for Medical Deity! Only God knows how many days I have left, and I plan to continuing living and put myself completely in His hands. I'm glad my last days are not going to be spent in a hospital grasping at straws when I know that dying is part of life."

M.D. does not stand for Medical Deity.

She was somber but bravely accepted her fate without tears. Mom scanned our faces and acknowledged what we were feeling, too. "This is not an easy decision for me or my family—it's a very emotional time. But it is my life, and I want you to please understand that while I have no control over the fact that I am going to die, I refuse to live with death in my face or hanging over my head."

Looking for the approval from the authority figure in the room, she asked the doctor to tell her what he thought of her decision, adding "…as if I were your own mother." The young specialist conveyed his empathy by leaning forward to gaze into Mom's eyes and, speaking in a voice just above a whisper, he replied, "I believe you made a very wise and good decision, Anna." We left the building in silence.

As we approached the car in the parking lot, Mom stopped to ask if we were okay; then she smiled and changed the subject saying, "I'm hungry; let's go to lunch so I can take my vitamins." Nobody was really hungry, but after placing our food order at one of her favorite restaurants, Mom ordered a glass of wine for us. When it arrived, she smiled and lifted her lemon water to make a toast. She said with a big smile, "To life!" Another mental photograph was indelibly etched on my mind.

Later in the day Mom rested a bit, but after dinner Mom asked me to arrange an impromptu card party with the neighborhood ladies. Everyone loved playing canasta at Anna's house since they were sure to enjoy a home baked dessert. When the first game ended, her guests were going to get more than something sweet to eat. They were going to get a first-class lesson in how to face down death.

Mom signaled for me to make the coffee and turned to her friends. "Ladies, I have something to tell you. This is serious, so please listen and let me finish. I went to see a cancer specialist at the Moffet Center yesterday, and I was told that I have another tumor and, this time, it's inoperable."

All you could hear was a group gasp. They were speechless, and Mom paused to let her words sink in before she continued. "I know hearing news like this usually makes people feel very uncomfortable. Because of that, they usually tend to avoid the person with the disease. It's awkward. But you are my friends. Please don't do that to me! I'm telling you now while I still feel well—and since I am not going to have chemotherapy, I may feel this way for a long time. The worst thing you can do is to isolate me. I'm still the same person I was yesterday, and I don't want to be treated any differently.

"If you want to know what you can do, just treat me as you normally would and include me in our regular activities. I always wanted to live to be a hundred, but I guess that's not going to happen. But while I'm still here, I want to be able to talk and laugh with you and make the most of every day God is going to give me."

The silence was deafening and when she saw the tears in their eyes she added, "As I told my family earlier today, there will be plenty of time for tears, but not now. I'm not ready to go because we have more memories to make before then—so let's eat." Coffee was then served.

Mom alternated from being caregiver to care receiver for more than two years before she died, and continued to bake and cook for her neighbors who lived alone, especially when they were ill. She even organized and hosted her last Christmas party with 35 guests while under the care of hospice to thank the neighbors and her special friends for their love and support.

It is helpful to talk about death and dying so we can prepare one another for the challenge.

Mom was determined not only to coexist with cancer, but also maintain the quality of her life for as long as she was able. She had no intention of wasting one drop of energy. She still had work to do. My mother taught us all that while faith does not shield us from grief or sadness we can use our end times to share stories, enjoy the simple pleasures of life, and with God's help, make more memories. Her long goodbye, compared to an unexpected death, gave us the time we needed to prepare to let her go.

Considering my past fears, it was gratifying to have my mother look up at me from her bed two days before she died and say, "There always has to be at least one strong person in each family when someone dies, and I never thought it would be you." And neither did I. What a testimony to God's grace and empowering love.

Jesus said death is a bitter cup. He was right. I'm grateful that he can identify with us whether we are the person leaving or the one being left behind. I find great comfort and hope in what Jesus said to the believing thief hanging on the cross next to him, "Today, you will be with me in Paradise." With that knowledge and faith, we will be able to face down death with no regrets.

I can do everything through Him who gives me strength.
(Philippians 4:13)

Hospice is for the Living

*Even though I walk through the valley of the shadow of death,
I will fear no evil, for you are with me;
your rod and your staff, they comfort me.
(Psalm 23:4)*

Does this title scare you? Surprise you? Most people cringe at the word and associate "hospice" with the final act of death. In fact, the dying process can last many months or longer and go through various stages. A failure to understand the full role of hospice makes people reluctant to ask for much needed help.

When I began training as a Stephen Minister, it was not with the conscious intention of preparing to help my own mother face death. However, when the specialist surgeon told Mom she only had six months to a year to live, that was my call to action. Interestingly enough, her oncologist and primary care doctor both said, "Your mother's not ready for hospice." But because of what I had observed through my caregiving role, it was time to politely assert myself.

Be assertive when coordinating end-of-life care for your loved ones.

"I understand she's not going to die next week, but I know that hospice provides services that may help all of us right now. I'd appreciate it if you would write an order for hospice so they can visit her and decide for themselves whether or not they will accept her as a patient."

He did. They said, "Yes, the time is now." *Hospice is for the Living* was the title of the brochure Mom received describing the services they offered. In his book, *Last Rights*, Stephen Kiernan uses the subtitle, "Rescuing End of Life Care From The Medical System." It is a must read for everyone. Kiernan, for years a medical journalist and researcher, documents the advantages of hospice over traditional facilities that support patients at the end of their life. Hospice care is superior and it provides welcome support for other family members as well.

I must tell you that, while all hospice organizations share a common mission, some people may not live in close proximity to hospice, and the services they are able to offer can vary widely due to funding and the number of volunteers they have. Check the phone book or ask your doctor how to contact Hospice in your area. There may be more than one, so interview all available organizations to decide which will meet your family's needs.

Hernando-Pasco Hospice provided Mom with exceptional care primarily due to the large number of volunteers and generous donations from grateful family members. The initial meeting with Hospice was one of the most difficult things my mother and I ever did together. We would much rather have stayed in denial. But the sweet companionship and practical support from this organization lifted our burden and our spirits. Let me give you an overview now. When you later read Part III, you will learn in more detail how hospice care was delivered during the last nine days of my mother's life.

Once Mom was accepted as a hospice patient, she gained a new friend in a volunteer named Helen, a cheerful visitor who laughed and talked about "the good old days" with Mom. They discovered many things in common, including the love of knitting. Together they shopped for patterns and used the yarn my mother had bought to make what turned out to be my last Christmas present from her, a mauve colored coat scarf.

Mom also developed a special relationship with Carol, her nurse, but long before Carol or any of the home aides had to care for her. The nurse made routine weekly visits for months to check Mom's vital signs and we family members were given an open invitation to call any time of day or night if we had any questions or concerns. Having a medical professional on call to set our minds at ease was comforting; and, if needed, a nurse would make an unscheduled house call in less than an hour.

You may have to supplement the services of hospice as we did, but our hospice network of support included a number of volunteers who happily ran errands, provided respite care when family members needed a break, or they would keep Mom company when I had to take her husband John to the doctor or visit assisted living facilities to arrange for his future care.

When hospice services are limited or unavailable, many people create their own support system by engaging extended family members, neighbors, caring church ministries, or private nurses—especially at night so the primary caregiver can rest.

Hospice provided all medications with Medicare covering the cost of all prescriptions and supplies needed to keep her comfortable and pain free. Mom stayed at home, but for people who live alone or whose family members are unable to deliver the physical care needed, some hospice centers have residential facilities, such as the one my grandmother used. Compassionate hospice doctors made house calls, and the hospice social worker assigned to Mom's case visited regularly as well. Home aides provided personal care towards the end and, later, grief counseling was offered to family members for a year after my mother's death.

The hospice chaplain more than supplemented the spiritual care Mom received from her own church. Because of his consistent, weekly visits over the months, Mom was able to talk at length and with complete confidentiality about her spiritual concerns. She shared her personal beliefs with this sensitive non-judgmental man, and when Mom died, he uncharacteristically asked to say a few words at her funeral to honor their relationship. Once again, he confirmed that caregivers receive more than they give by saying, "Your mother did more for me than I could ever do for her. As I watched her prepare to die over these past six months, my own faith was strengthened more than I thought possible."

No matter how large the network of support, one's inner fears about dying may go unspoken. The true value of a caregiver to someone at this stage in their life is identifying those fears and how they can be alleviated. Ideally, family members and close friends should acquaint themselves with the most common fears so they can help their loved ones die in peace.

I've learned the following insights not only from hospice workers but also directly from the special friends and families I visited during the last months of their life. I hope this information will help alleviate your own fears. There are seven basic fears of dying, but know this: *God has not given us the spirit of fear; but of power, and of love, and of a sound mind. (2 Timothy 1:7)*

The Seven Fears of Dying

Hospice professionals do not treat the dying process as a secret. Family members and patients, if they desire, will typically be told what to expect as death draws near. Before I saw my grandmother die, my imagination was filled with many misconceptions, most of which were based on what I had seen on television or at the movies. If you can relate to this, acquaint yourself with the reality of what will happen in your particular situation to ease your anxiety.

It was difficult for me to concentrate while caring for my mother, so rather than reading about it, I was grateful to the hospice social worker who, with great sensitivity, was able to describe the behavioral and physical changes that typically occur from month to month after a terminal diagnosis, up to the very moment of death. Knowing what to expect and what to do when the time comes helped me, and it will help you, prepare and focus on the job at hand—addressing the fears of a person facing death.

1. The Fear of the Process of Dying

- Will death be painful?
- How will I get through this?

Unless you choose to suffer, you will have little or no pain when hospice is involved. Hospice doctors and nurses are specialists in pain management, and their mission is to deliver palliative care, unlike doctors in other specialties whose primary goal is to cure their patients.

The wonderful thing about hospice is that they allow the patient to take the lead and participate, if they are able, in making the decision about the type and amount of pain medication to take. It is essential to communicate the level of pain you or your loved one is having. Hospice doctors and nurses are trained to take the time to listen to what the patient has to say, both verbally and nonverbally. They discuss the up and down side of the options they have at their disposal, but it's the patient or responsible party who makes the final call—with no recriminations.

2. The Fear of Loss of Control

- Must I give up independence?
- Can I cope with being dependent on others?

Just because a person has been given a terminal diagnosis, they need not behave any differently or relinquish their independence at this stage. I asked my mother, "Are you really any different now than you were before you heard the doctor's prognosis?" She said, "No, I just have more information about the disease, and know the doctors can't cure it." Nothing had really changed, except she now had the cold facts. After she faced her fear and was able to vent her feelings, she did not lose control of her time and her life.

We all should continue to live normal lives for as long as we are physically able. My mother was my best role model, but more prominent figures have exhibited that same attitude.

Hospice personnel usually encourage people to make their own decisions for as long as possible; in fact, that's one of their goals—to help their patients and families maintain their normal lifestyle.

In fact, my mother's hospice nurse believed Mom was able to follow her daily routine for as long as she did because she was committed to caring for her husband. She refused to behave like a woman who was dying.

Agreed, people will respond differently to the news of their diagnosis and everyone has a different tolerance for pain. There came a time when Mom had to reverse roles from caregiver to care receiver. The good news is that when she needed to depend on others, it was an easy transition. Being introduced to hospice strangers at the last minute can be an uncomfortable, even frightening, experience. We were much better able to care for Mom knowing we had hospice support all along our sacred walk.

3. The Fear of Loss of Loved Ones

- What is going to happen to them?
- How will they manage without me?

Only the loved ones of the person dying can help alleviate this fear. Hospice cannot. If you are the patient's "loved one," it will take courage and willingness to talk openly about this fear. Do everything you can to reassure them that you will be okay.

If young children or dependent adults are involved, your loved one needs to know the details of the plan to care for them. Peggy was a widow with two teenaged children, but she had no relatives willing to raise her girls. Another friend Kathy was divorced with two young sons who did not want to leave the country to live with their father when she died. Linda was a married young woman with a loving husband and beautiful little four-year-old daughter she would soon leave behind. And Mike worried about how his young sons would grow up without their father as a role model.

With the help of family, friends, and their church community, they were all able to address their fears in different ways, but with the same result. All found peace once they knew what would happen to their loved ones when they died, particularly since they were able to participate in developing plans to raise each child. Having oriented the new mother and father figures to their children's likes and dislikes, they shared hopes and dreams for each of their babies.

Don, on the other hand, did not fear death or worry about his children because they were grown with families of their own. He worried about convincing his wife that she was going to be able to take care of herself when he died. Their children were scattered around the country and neither Don nor his wife wanted to disrupt their lives. So, Don took pride in teaching her how to do "his" jobs around the house. For example, when the smoke detector battery needed changing, he made her do it under his supervision.

Working together not only created wonderful memories, they viewed it as a mutual gift to one another. Don received peace of mind as his wife grew more confident in her abilities, and by accepting his advice and encouragement, she was able to transition more easily through the grieving process and into a new phase of her life when Don passed away.

4. Fear of Others' Reactions

- The fear in the eyes of others
- Their nonverbal communication, body language.

When a person knows that you know they have a terminal illness, they feel very vulnerable, and it takes a tremendous amount of courage to face the fear of death. Seeing fear in our eyes or hearing it in our voices adds to their burden. It is normal to cry and express your sadness at the thought of being left behind, but after the shock has worn off, try to behave normally. When you are with them, remember it's not about you. Make sure you have others to help you work through your grief.

One of the most important responsibilities of a caregiver is self care. Stress, lack of sleep, improper diet or exercise can so easily wear you down. The strain will begin to manifest itself in the way you look and act when you are with your loved one who may perceive they have become a burden to you. In addition to taking care of themselves physically, caregivers should have their own support system—at least one person who can help them vent their emotions or address their own spiritual questions.

Being good to yourself will make it easier for you to understand what physical and emotional changes will take place in your loved one. Then, when it begins to happen, they will not see surprise or fear in your face. For example, dramatic weight changes or mood swings are not uncommon and some are caused by medication. Have the doctor, pharmacist, or hospice nurse tell you what to expect.

My friend Joe's emotions fluctuated wildly following multiple surgeries, chemotherapy and radiation that failed to cure him. Hospice taught his wife and family members how to respond and how to cope with Joe. He would cry one minute and curse everyone the next, for no apparent reason. Eventually, Hospice was able to find a new medication to stabilize him so he could die in peace with his family by his side.

Joe's church family and friends also provided moral and spiritual support when his family needed it most. One friend came to talk with Joe regularly, and another even took him away for a weekend retreat at a healing center, providing much needed respite care for his wife. While at the center, Joe was reminded of the faith he had when he was a child, and thankfully, he was able to reconnect with those basic beliefs that restored his hope and gave him comfort.

5. Fear of Isolation

- Decreased or shortened visits from health care professionals and friends.
- Will I die alone?

Not many people want to die alone and yet some people get caught between their pride and their fear of isolation. If their appearance has changed due to hair loss, fluid retention, radiation burns, or the like, they may be reluctant to have others see them.

The only outings some people permit themselves are trips to the hospital or clinic for therapy, but at some point treatments cease if there is no medical hope for a cure. If that happens, the patient no longer has the benefit of interaction even with the health care professionals with whom they have developed a relationship.

Particularly for a person who has no family, this is another type of loss. Many individuals have relatives who live too far away to be a consistent presence in their life. In these situations, hospice can be a tremendous comfort. In my experience, I've even known hospice to supplement the care of elderly patients who live in nursing homes or assisted living facilities. Since such establishments are often understaffed, end-of-life care for patients in these isolated environments dramatically improved. Their pain was better managed and the stimulus of an increase in visitations from the hospice nurse, personal care aides, and a volunteer visitor eased their fear of dying alone.

If you have a loved one nearing the end of their life, help alleviate the fear of isolation with regular visits from close friends and family members. If you do not, consider becoming a hospice volunteer or participating in a church ministry to support someone with a terminal diagnosis or their caregiver. At the very least, make a referral to hospice or a church with a caring ministry that visits the sick.

6. Fear of the Unknown

- What can I expect?
- Will there be life after death?

My mother had great faith, but her nervous anxiety was evident when she was overheard saying to a dear friend who telephoned her the week before she died. "Well, Catherine, I guess I'm getting ready for my last big adventure; I wonder what it's going to be like."

No doubt your loved one will think about these and other related questions even if they are unspoken. Addressing them has physical, emotional, and spiritual implications whether it's done with or without the help of trained professionals.

The doctors and nurses who care for terminally ill patients and their families can factually tell us what to expect and, hopefully, do so in a sensitive, caring manner. Hospice and other medical professionals can monitor the noticeable physical changes that take place from several months to the hour before death. Knowing these signs will help you respond calmly and appropriately as the body begins to shut down.

Regarding spiritual concerns, doctors and nurses, even those with hospice, are often instructed not to discuss "religion." This is a job left for the chaplain in health care organizations. People at the end often welcome hope or reassurance that life does not end at death.

If you are unsure of your beliefs, have a priest, rabbi, minister, pastor, or a chaplain visit your loved one to address questions about life and death. Use outside resources to present a gift of peace regardless of your personal doubts or skepticism.

7. Fear that Life Will Have Been Meaningless

- Review of life history
- Need to identify positive aspects in one's life

How terrible it would be to feel this way. The person who will be leaving shortly needs to hear that they won't be forgotten. Don't miss the chance to tell them you love them and remind them of all the good they brought to your world. Reassure them that their life had purpose and meaning. Do it either in person or through cards and letters. Encourage others to do the same.

Addressing this fear will be difficult if we have close emotional ties to the patient. However, I promise it will be very rewarding, and you will have no regrets when they leave.

Your loved one needs to hear that their life mattered to you and that you believe they contributed something wonderful to your life. Go through family photographs together, share memories, talk about successes, and what they learned from their mistakes or regrets. If there is a need for reconciliation, do what you can to facilitate it and encourage others to do the same.

In addition to easing the fears of a friend or loved one, there are many practical caring things you and others can do as you walk them part way home. The next chapter will give you some dos and don'ts along with suggestions gleaned uniquely from those living with a life threatening illness and their caregivers.

Carry each other's burdens, and in this way
you will fulfill the law of Christ.
(Galatians 6:2)

Walking Them Part Way Home

I do believe, help me overcome my unbelief!
(Mark 9:24)

No one can walk your loved one home the way you can. While there is nothing to pack for this journey, you can help them sort through what they are leaving behind. If you are a close friend or even an acquaintance, you may accompany them along the way.

Helping someone make this final life transition is an intimate and a profound privilege. The walk may be short or it can take many months, even a year or more. To help you prepare, this chapter contains advice from the men and women who helped sensitize me to their needs—emotional and practical. There is no single formula to follow because our personal and cultural backgrounds are different. The first question most commonly asked of someone who has a health crisis is, "What can I do to help?"

Remarkable people who were willing to give me an honest answer to that question asked me to share their perspective with others. What follows is a collection of comments and suggestions offered by these men and women as we passed various milestones on our sacred walks. They may spark ideas on what you can do while easing the stress and worry of your own friends and loved ones.

Don't Ask Me How to Help

"I appreciate your asking, but I'm in the middle of a crisis right now, can't think clearly, and having to tell you what I need makes me uncomfortable. Please, if you think of something obvious, just do it. From time to time, a meal for me and my family would be appreciated. Just call and make sure we are home when you want to deliver it. Also, while I hate the thought of giving up my independence, I may occasionally need a driver particularly when I'm on medica-

tion or in a poor physical or emotional state. If you'd like to spend time with me, perhaps you could call and offer to take me to my next appointment. I'd enjoy the company, and maybe we can stop for lunch or coffee."

Linda, my friend Dave's wife, worked full time and could not afford to shuttle him to and from radiation treatments every day for weeks. When Linda gave me Dave's treatment schedule, his many friends jumped at the chance to spend quality time with him. The poster on his refrigerator read: "Dave's Drivers." Are you getting the idea? Someone has to coordinate such an activity, and it might be you.

For two weeks following my cancer surgery, one of my neighbors organized some of the women in my neighborhood to provide healthy meals. She was kind enough to inquire about allergies or special dietary needs in advance. At first I felt guilty and wanted to resist, but then I remembered what my special friends taught me about the luxury of receiving care. Having food appear was wonderful, even when two meals came at once. A meal can be kept for a day or two in the refrigerator, and casseroles and soups can be frozen for later use. Some friends even joined us for dinner, and cleaned up afterwards!

My friend Barbara shared this story about the time her illness lasted over a year. Initially she refused offers of help, but debilitating side effects of an aggressive treatment program left her too weak to get out of bed to care for her husband and two sons. Unannounced, a friend arrived one day with cleaning supplies, walked in, and got to work on her bathrooms. As Barbara tells it, "I was mortified! Do you know what a bathroom looks like after three men use it for a week or more? Looking back, it was the best gift anyone gave me and my family throughout my illness."

Barbara vowed never to forget this humble act of service, and today she does the same for others. She may not always clean bathrooms, but Barbara always shows up when a person least expects it and quietly does what needs to be done. Think of all the other random acts of kindness you can perform, such as grocery shopping, running errands, walking the dog, mowing the lawn, or taking care of children. Cards and letters are always appreciated along with CD's, inspirational and humorous books, or movies on DVD. Why not make plans to watch the movie together?

Don't Make Me Talk About My Condition

"After talking endlessly to doctors and my family about my diagnosis, treatments, and prognosis, the last thing I want to do is talk about it with

everyone else. When you ask me questions, it feels as if you are probing for details about my physical and emotional state. I appreciate your concern, I really do, and know you mean well, but talking about the details unnerves me and undermines the positive attitude I'm trying to maintain. Let me initiate the topic when I'm ready to share. Thanks for understanding."

After my own experience during and after treatment, I now understand what they meant. Even the question, "How are you?" made me feel uncomfortable at times. Let me explain. "How are you?" is a very common American greeting, not really an inquiry into the personal details of your health. But if a person has a serious condition, "How are you?" takes on a whole new meaning.

For a person not wanting to be identified by the disease or one who refuses to live with death in their face, this kind of "How are you?" reminds them that even though they feel well, they might not be well. Your reflected fear for their health can unintentionally plant seeds of doubt that may cause unrest or a sleepless night. Greet a warrior battling a disease the same way you would normally greet another and accept the normal answer, "Fine, thank you. How are you?"

When my uncle was first diagnosed with colon cancer, he went for a walk and wanted to run home screaming because so many people stopped him on the street and in the grocery store to ask about his condition. All he wanted to do was breathe some fresh air, and buy a quart of milk! His treatment was successful, but when he had a recurrence, he resolved not to tell even his good friends about it. "I don't want to be treated differently than anybody else. I'm not dying. I'm living, and I can't stand looking at their mournful eyes!"

Today, when someone now asks me the sympathetic "How are you?" I answer with a question of my own: "How do I look? You know, it's not how you feel that matters; it's how you look and who you know!" Gentle humor can take care of an awkward situation.

If you are tuned into the other person and follow their lead, you will know when they want to talk about their condition or their feelings. By contrast, some people may need to talk about their situation over and over again. If this is the case, remember that you may be the only effective listener they know. Be patient, pray for them and thank God you are not walking in their shoes at the moment.

Listen to Me

The deeper the sorrow, the less tongue it has.
(The Talmud)

"All my life, I've been saying, 'Listen to me,' first as a child to my parents, and then as a parent to my children. And if I've said it once to my spouse, I've said it a thousand times, 'You aren't listening to me.' Now, more than any other time in my life, I truly need someone to be fully present and hear me. Everybody wants to know what they can do, and all I really need is someone to listen to me. I don't want advice, but I could use a sounding board to think through the pros and cons of my options—someone who won't fall apart when I talk about my fears and concerns."

Being a good listener is an active not a passive activity. Listening involves practicing patience and having self-control. In the Book of Job, his friends sat with him for seven days and seven nights in silence before they spoke. That reminds me of my friend June.

She described how her neighbor would slip into her kitchen, make a pot of coffee, and sit with her in silence after her father died suddenly. June was too numb to even acknowledge her, so after a while, the neighbor would leave quietly with only a gentle touch of her hand. In time, the real June began to emerge and was grateful to see the friend whose familiar presence she sensed, the one who made no demands on her—not even to speak. A true friendship was born out of silence, giving June the confidence and trust she needed to continue the grieving process—this time, with words.

When emotions run deep, people may need encouragement to talk about them, so an important component to being an effective listener actually involves asking open questions. "Who, what, where, when, and how" questions help a person explore their feelings. "Why" questions tend to make a person defend their feelings or actions.

One friend in crisis described the good listening skills of a relative like this: "She was able to listen with her eyes." Listening involves being conscious of body language. Our ability to ignore distractions, our posture, eye contact, even a smile or nod of the head can tell a person we are tuned into what they are saying.

There is one other caution if you are going to go the distance with a person on a grief journey. As we listen, our thoughts can turn to our own past and losses in life. Be careful not to relive your story with them. It's helpful to explain why you are able to empathize with their current situation, but when a person is in the midst of their own crisis they do not want to hear about yours. If your wounds from the past are reopened, find a trusted friend of your own to talk about any unfinished business. Effective listeners are able to appropriately affirm feelings and reflect what they are hearing.

Affirming feelings. When emotions are strong or unfamiliar to them, it's important to tell a person that what they are feeling is normal. But the one thing you should never do is tell a person that you know how they feel. The late Leo Buscaglia, author and lecturer on life and love, used to say, "Don't you dare tell me how I feel! My experience of my experience is my experience of my experience; and your experience of your experience is your experience of your experience. You do not know how I feel."

Our past and our backgrounds account for the various ways people express themselves, possibly in a manner completely foreign to us. At times it may feel as if you are walking through the middle of a minefield. Don't take any reaction, even an explosive one, personally. In fact, a sudden burst of tears or a display of anger may even surprise the person venting.

When it comes to grief, there is no right or wrong way to express it. Grief just is. Expressing the myriad of feelings that accompany grief is the first step in the healing process. Affirming someone's emotions in a non-judgmental manner creates a safe and trusting atmosphere.

Reflecting what you hear. There are times when the thoughts of a person under stress can be a little scrambled. Listening carefully enables you to ask important reflective or clarifying questions so a person can actually "hear" what they are saying. Effective listeners are careful not to slip into "fix" mode or say anything that might negate the negative feelings being shared.

Debbie was suffering from low self esteem, depression and hopelessness when she taught me to pay attention to the subtle ways her feelings were being denied by others. In an attempt to build her up people would interrupt her flow and say something like, "Oh, you shouldn't feel that way." Another comment she loathed was, "How can you say that about yourself. You are so beautiful, talented, etc."

While her friends intended to make her feel better, their efforts were on the heels of Debbie's sharing deep personal feelings about herself. Rather than helping, her friends' remarks made her angry and she felt judged and reprimanded. When we go through change points in our lives, we can be extremely sensitive.

The effective listener's job is to encourage the person to explore their feelings. "Tell me more," is a better response. Asking a person to think about what might be the underlying causes of their feelings is much more helpful. You might also be able to reflect what you hear or see in their body language to help identify something they have yet to acknowledge. For example, "You sound angry," gives a name to the feeling they may have been reluctant to acknowledge, especially if directed toward God or others they love. A word of caution—don't become so emotionally involved that you lose objectivity. Some people may have long and complex family histories, and they just want to be heard.

A personal example of effective listening is the story about my first visit to a crisis and growth counselor during my divorce. It was she who explained that divorce is like a death in many ways.

God is the only hospice for the death of a dream.

In my first hour with the counselor, I rambled on about my fears and questions about my future. I was afraid of being alone and considered unlovable. I was angry for having wasted so many years and the loss of the children I would never have. I did not want to be a divorcee! Would my career survive if I followed through with an untimely transfer? Could I take care of myself? Where would I live? What will my family say? What did I do wrong? Will I ever have control of my life or my emotions again?

With only minutes remaining, my counselor reflected, "If I heard you correctly, you have only three questions to answer. One, do you want to move? Two, are you going to sell your house? And three, do you want a divorce?"

She not only heard me, she was able to help me identify the questions I could answer. After reassuring me that I wasn't losing my mind, she guided me through a rational decision making process so I could inch my way forward. This counselor never fixed anything, nor did she tell me what to do; but she did affirm my feelings and reflect what she heard me say about my future goals and plans.

Appropriately responding to the request, "Listen to me," will enable a person to feel a sense of relief, calm, and satisfaction as they regain balance and perspective primarily due to your listening heart.

Help Alleviate My Fears

"I'm afraid and worried about so many things—the dying process, how my family will get along without me, and who is going to take care of unfinished business. I have so many regrets. If only I knew then what I know now, I would have lived my life differently. How can I make up for the time I wasted or come to terms with all of this and more? Is it too late?"

In the chapter "Hospice is for the Living," the most common fears of dying are reviewed. Not everyone is concerned about everything on the list, and some people are truly at peace. But if there are fears, most people are reluctant to talk about the specifics even though it is a healthy thing to do. Showing empathy and asking a gentle question may help you assess what you can do to help or what outside resources might benefit someone you care about. For example, "If we were to change places, I think I might be worried or afraid. What's on your mind right now?"

Some people may be quick to respond, but others will need encouragement and regular opportunities to eventually feel safe enough to discuss their feelings openly. They may have always been a very private person, or a consummate caregiver who never needed much care before now. Once a person has addressed their fears and practical details, they are likely to feel empowered, even energized, and better able to prepare themselves and their loved ones for their inevitable passing and its aftermath.

Never make decisions when you are in an emotional state.

Help Me Maintain My Dignity and Control

"Please don't treat me like an invalid before my time. As long as I can still do things for myself, I want to do them. The only difference between who I was before this crisis and who I am now is eight hours sleep. In your desire to care for me, you seem to be taking over. At times, it feels as if I have lost control of my life, even my dignity, and I'm not yet ready to die. I want to be self-sufficient, and I want you to enjoy your life and work, too. If you don't, then I'll feel guilty. Don't hover over me unnecessarily. The day will come when I really need you, but until then, please allow me to live my life the way I choose for as long as I am able."

It's natural to want to do everything we can do for a loved one who is in crisis, especially when they have to face the reality of death. Many people with a terminal illness have many good months, even years, to live. For example, Pearl was eighty-one years old when I met her, still volunteering for the American Cancer Society. At the age of fifty-four, the doctors told her she had one year to live. Her advice after twenty-seven good years was, "Never give up!" She was truly *living* proof that M.D. does not stand for Medical Deity.

People like Pearl and my mother both viewed accepting help as giving up, and if they are intent on living and working, our being solicitous is counterproductive. One such person of notoriety is the late author and columnist Art Buchwald whose doctor told him he would only live for a few weeks. After settling into a hospice facility, he resumed writing his newspaper column, talked openly with characteristic humor about his situation, and finished writing a book much to the surprise of his doctors.

Here are a few other suggestions to keep in mind if you want to help a person maintain their dignity and control of their life. They were gleaned directly from conversations with my special friends as they grew closer to the end of their lives.

Let them speak for themselves. If a question is directed to your loved one, let them answer for themselves, if able. Too often a family member jumps in before they have a chance to answer and it's frustrating for the person. One of my care receivers told me they felt like a ventriloquist, able to change and throw their voice across the room. In some cases, the only thing a person has control over is their voice, so let them use it.

An important aside I learned is this: if a person is unable to speak, do not talk about the patient's condition in front of them. Grandma's hospice nurses taught us to talk to the patient even if they are in a coma, but they cautioned us not to talk about their condition or say anything that may cause anxiety or distress when you are in their room.

They modeled this by greeting Grandma by name every time they came into her room. After identifying themselves, they told her what they were going to do, and before treating her, they explained why they were going to do it to give her the opportunity to ask questions. Even during her last six days in a coma, they followed this same procedure for every pain injection and when they had to move her. The reason is that our sense of hearing is the last to go. People who have come out of a coma often repeat what was said even though they were unable to respond.

Focus on the person not the environment. If you have a weak stomach, visiting the sick may be a challenge for you. When someone is bedridden but mentally alert, they may notice how uneasy you are.

Your nonverbal reaction to their environment or to the changes in their physical appearance will make them feel self-conscious. Look beyond the bedside commode, the medical apparatus or sick room supplies, and focus on the face of the person you are visiting. Try not to be distracted by the sights and smells of a sick room.

Accept gestures of gratitude. Often people nearing the end of their life choose to give things away. Whatever the gift, accept it graciously even though it may be of no value or particular use to you. Margarita was 90 years old when she gave me the negligee she wore on her wedding day. She had kept this special garment all those years, and at the end of her life, she sent it to the cleaners and presented it to me to express her appreciation for our friendship. Remember, the need of the giver to give is tantamount.

My mother used her china closet to display her porcelain plate collection, crystal and other pretty little figurines. In the last month of her life, when anyone admired one of her treasures, she would take it off the shelf, and give it to them as a gift. During Mom's last Christmas, her favorite holiday, her nieces and nephews received prized glass Christmas ornaments. "Aunt Annie" was famous for her Christmas parties, and this was her way of ensuring they would think of her during a festive time of year.

Learn from them. We will all see the finish line in sight one day, and just as athletes study the other team in sports or our competitors in business, we have much to learn about how to do this "dying thing." It will be our last big adventure, so we might as well do it well.

One way to respect another person's dignity is to give them opportunities to make a difference in your life. Don't be afraid to ask questions. Seek their advice while you still can and accept their final gifts of wisdom. Encourage them to tell you their stories so you can learn from their regrets while you still have time to avoid similar mistakes.

Reassure Me that My Life Mattered

"I feel like such a burden to everyone these days. I'm no good to anyone or for anything any more, and I wonder if my life will have any lasting value."

Depression and doubt are always lurking in the background when a person accepts the fact that they will lose the battle to stay alive. It is common for them to express feelings of uselessness and a lack of self worth, particularly if they have always been an "in-charge" kind of person or the consummate caregiver themselves.

As you walk them part way home, let them know their life continues to have value to you. This is one way to help lift their depression and doubt about the legacy they will leave behind. Take every opportunity to express appreciation and admiration for their past accomplishments and what their relationship has meant to you. Tell them that the very fact that they are allowing themselves to receive care has value. What a lopsided world this would be if everybody wanted to give and nobody allowed themselves to receive.

In his wisdom, Solomon wrote in Ecclesiastes, Chapter 3: *There is a time for everything, and a season for every activity under heaven: a time to be born and a time to die.* It's a lovely chapter that puts life and death in perspective.

Share Your Faith with Me

"What do you believe? Do you think there really is a God? Is it true that there is life after death, or is this all there is? What do you think eternal life will be like? Will God receive me?"

Whether an atheist, agnostic, or a person of faith, not everyone is comfortable initiating conversations about what they believe. If you are walking someone part way home, keep your antennae up and listen for the subtle openings you may be given. Losing your health is one thing, but coming to terms with losing your life is a monumental task and you may have the opportunity to bolster the courage of someone you love. One day Marco's humor revealed a desire to talk by saying, "Nobody knows for sure what's going to happen when we die, which is why I chose to believe in God. He's my insurance policy. If I'm right, I'm home free! If I'm wrong, I won't know it anyway." There was some truth in this tongue-in-cheek remark, but there is more to it than that.

Even people with great faith need to be reminded of God's forgiveness and promises, especially of eternal life.

In Hebrews 11 it says, *"Now faith is being sure of what we hope for and certain of what we do not see."* People like Marco may also benefit by talking about what they really believe or would like to believe. Hearing this scripture read to them along with the many promises of God contained in the Bible may be just what they need to hear. If you do not respond to the opportunities to talk about faith in God you may regret it for years to come.

Grace is one of my more recently discovered living libraries. We occasionally talk about the lessons she has learned during her lifetime. On one such occasion, she recalled the death of her husband some 40 years earlier. She said, "You know, I do have one regret. One day toward the end of his life, my husband seemed lost in his thoughts, so I asked, 'What are you thinking.' He quietly said 'the unknown.' Just two words. I still regret not asking him to tell me more. I just said 'Oh' and walked away. I should have shared my faith with him; it could have strengthened his when he needed it most. I will never know if he was afraid or if he had doubts, but I may have relieved some unexpressed anxiety and given him hope—even a sense of anticipation. This was one lesson I learned too late." Be alert to opportunities to share your faith. It's one more way to make a difference in someone's life.

Create a Peaceful Atmosphere for Me

"I hate being sick and isolated from my family and familiar surroundings. I dislike all the noise, the clutter, the smells and reminders of death and dying. If at all possible, I want to stay home because I dislike all the distractions of a hospital or nursing home and the inconvenience it causes my family just to be with me. I want to be surrounded by my favorite people and things."

If your loved one is in a health care facility, do what you can to make their room look familiar. Keep the area around them free from clutter and harsh lights. Surround them with their favorite things—pictures, mementos, flowers, and artwork. Wear their favorite colors. If possible, let them breathe fresh air and see the sunshine. You may consider replacing the bedding with colorful covers from home.

It is easier to hide all medical supplies, personal hygiene items and pill bottles in nightstand drawers, closets and cabinets, boxes under the bed or behind floor length tablecloths if they are at home. Arrange bedside chairs so that visitors can be seen and heard without difficulty. Don't isolate your loved one from the rest of the family. During the day, have them rest in the living or family room and even lay on the couch or recliner as long as they want. The change of scenery will do them good.

Once the physical environment is improved, there is more that can be done to create a peaceful atmosphere. Drawing on selected items in your caring tool kit will be helpful. My favorites include poetry, music, devotionals, healing prayers, and inspirational books—anything that can lift the spirit and make a person smile. If your loved one has vision problems, you can read to them so their mind is filled with positive messages, particularly when their interest in current events begins to wane.

One of the best gifts is music. Physiologists tell us that music has an almost immediate effect on our entire nervous system. Unlike any other sound that fills the air, music helps alter our physiology since it enters the medulla, the part of the brain connected to our spinal cord. Soothing, classical music, calming instrumentals, or familiar songs, praise songs or hymns wash over the psyche, bringing peace to the mind and spirit.

It is common for a person to lose interest in current events, so talk about their favorite memories; look at family photo albums together and listen to their stories again, or for the first time. Mom got increasingly disturbed with the evening news as her illness progressed. To those who didn't understand, she explained, "Why should I fill my head with thoughts of violence and man's inhumanity to man just before I go to sleep?" Is it any wonder one of her favorite verses, particularly at this time in her life, was from Paul's letter to the church in Philippi? It concludes this chapter.

Give Me Permission to Go

"I'm no longer afraid to die, but I don't want to leave the people I love just yet, even though I'm tired and ready to go. When the time comes, I don't want to feel guilty about leaving so I'd like them to give me permission to leave. Does that sound strange? After working so hard to care for me, I don't want to disappoint them. I wish I knew what they are thinking. Will they be okay after I'm gone? Will they remember me?"

After a person's fears associated with the dying process have been addressed, they are then free to prepare for the journey home. Some of us may have to leave a little earlier than expected, but home we all must go. Hospice nurses tell us that our desire to control events is one reason people struggle to hold on to life, some more than others. Mom waited to be told, once more, that there would be no discord in our family and reassurance that her husband John was in a safe, secure facility that would take care of him before she left us.

Grandma waited until her son arrived before she died. As soon as Uncle Mario walked into the room after work to join his sisters and me, she heard his voice. After he said his goodbye and we gave her permission to go, it was as if her breath was connected to a faucet that was slowing being turned off—a trickle, then a drip, then silence. Removing any emotional obstacle will help open the door to a peaceful passing.

Hospice nurses tell us that other people wait for family and friends to leave because they don't want anyone to see them die, so there is no need to feel guilty for not being there. Knowing how fragile life is and how little we control the timing of our passing, we should take advantage of every opportunity to express our love and respect for those closest to us. If we do and we make the most of the time we have together, however long it is, we will be consoled by our memories even in the case of a sudden death.

There is no doubt that Mom and I made the most of our time together. Our sacred walk strengthened and prepared both of us for her inevitable journey. Even if we weren't together, we would speak by phone each day, usually in the morning, and share a daily devotion as well as discuss plans for the week or an upcoming visit. On one occasion, she casually said, "I hope God is going to receive me."

I said, "Of course, he is. You know that, don't you?"

"Yes, I hope so," she replied with a hint of nervous laughter.

After our call, Mom's expression of doubt continued to bother me. *Why did she make that statement? How can I reassure her so she would have confidence and peace?* I turned to the Bible for inspiration, and after a while wrote this letter which I found pressed in one of her Bibles after her death.

Dear Mom,

I just finished talking to you this Saturday morning. When we hung up, I started thinking about something you said, "I hope God is going to receive me." Your time has not yet come, but I'd like to share some truths with you on that subject. I think that intellectually you know that God is willing and able to receive you. And when he feels the time is right, he will prepare a banquet in your mansion—just as he promised—beyond the likes of which you have never seen!

If you are not emotionally secure in that knowledge, remember that the Bible says he will receive you, and its stories are true! God gave us His Word so that we may feel secure and be comforted. Don't forget that Jesus came to earth to show us through his miracles and tell us with his own mouth that he died for us "while we were yet sinners." Anything you may think of in your life—past, present, or future—that would separate us from God is forgotten! It's as if God sees us through a purifying filter that makes our lives pleasing and wholly acceptable to Him, and that filter is Christ. Being received into the kingdom of God is a gift—freely given out of love when we believe. From where I sit, you have gone beyond a mere statement of belief.

You know that "faith without works is dead." Your faith is alive—can't you feel it? People around you can see it so clearly. With the help of the Holy Spirit living in you, your faith has become something tangible to all who know you. You have had the courage to do the work God has given you to do. Even though you may not have always succeeded to your satisfaction, your desire to do right has been inspiring and pleasing to God. And another thing…

We are the sum total of all our experiences. It is because of our failures and our human condition that we grow closer to God year by year. That's how he planned it. The gift of being received into heaven cannot be earned. We only strive to obey God's commands to grow closer to him. The crowns we earn on earth by "doing good" will be thrown at his feet when we are received.

Our failures, our sins, are opportunities to learn and grow. One of the things I admire about you is you were never afraid to fail. You plunged right into life and always looked forward to your next attempt, your next challenge. And the work God gave you changed from year to year—depending on the lessons you learned as Daughter, Wife, Mother, Career Woman, Aunt, Friend, Neighbor, and Sister in our blood family and in the family of God. I'm not the only one who loves you "warts and all". As you said; God does! What matters is how close you are to Him today because of your experiences in those different roles.

Think of how mature and intimate we (you and I) have become over the years because of all that has happened to us and our ability to share our highs and lows. Just imagine how close God feels toward you. After all, He's the one who created us and set up this whole system of growth and redemption.

You taught me and Larry to learn from our mistakes and move forward. "The past is dead." That's a quote from you! God heard you teach us, and saw you struggle with decisions. Granted some of the time you did the right thing kicking and screaming, but you did it! God got you through some angry, dark days. But He also gave you sunshine and wonderful experiences you and I will never trade for all the wealth in the world. Perhaps it was because of the hard times that you have such a zest for life and a curiosity about it all.

You also know that Jesus said, "What you do to the least of these you do to me." God has used you all your life to "do" for Him. Whether it was spending your first paycheck at the age of 13 to buy clothes for your sisters, or ministering to the lonely people living at Chatham; comforting Mary Ann in the face of family opposition after Bennie died; taking in Mary as a boarder and being her role model; sending your children to parochial schools to learn about God instead of squandering your hard earned cash only on worldly pleasures; honoring your parents and lovingly helping Grandma transition from this life to the next; being mother <u>and</u> father to me and Larry all your life and praying unceasingly for our safety and happiness (even during the years when you were mad at God); and, the most *personally challenging, honoring your vows of marriage in spite of separation or physical and emotional abuse.*

These few examples of faith in action don't begin to tell the story about your obedience to Christ's greatest command to "love one another." Love is not just a word to you. You act it out every day of your life, and that love—God's love that He personally placed in your heart—has had a tremendous impact on the lives of so many. Your life matters; you make a difference!

Your heart and home have always been open to everyone. Growing up, I remember we often had people at our dining room table Larry and I didn't even know, but you did not want them to be alone on a Sunday. Even now, you still organize gatherings to create a loving atmosphere where no one is excluded and all feel special—and you do this knowing that most of them will not reciprocate. Each time I ask you why you continue to put yourself out, not expecting anything in return, you say "because it gives me pleasure." You see, that's proof that God is working in you. The gift of hospitality, cheer, happiness and love you give others is because of the generous soul you have been given by God—and he will want it back.

Another reason I believe God will receive you is that you communicate. God wants us to be in dialog with him and you are. You praise him, you admit you made mistakes, you seek reconciliation, you ask for forgiveness, and you thank him for all the blessings of your life. And that's just the way God wants us to be—not perfect, but always aware and growing.

Then there is our family. I believe God Himself was speaking to you through Bill and Barbara when they said that the love you feel now, when you are in crisis, "is only your love being reflected back on you." It's hard to believe, but it is true that God loves you even more than I do, and he weeps with you as you suffer physical and emotional pain. He has more compassion than you, me or any human can have for the sacrifices we make in His name.

God wants you so much to have peace at this stage in your life. That's why He has given you his gift of Faith. Faith that you will be received by Him. Faith that will give you peace that passes all understanding. Out of all the gifts He has given us, He saves the best till last—eternal life. Here are some verses from the Bible to think about as you recuperate from surgery:

Psalm 23:4, *"Even though I walk through the valley of the shadow of death, I will fear no evil, for you are with me; your rod and your staff they comfort me."*

Psalm 16:9-10, *"Therefore my heart is glad and my tongue rejoices; my body will rest secure, because you will not abandon me to the grave, nor will you let your Holy One see decay."*

Proverbs 12:28, *"In the way of righteousness there is life; along that path is immortality."*

Luke 9:24-25, *"For whoever wants to save his life will lose it, but whoever loses his life for me will save it. What good is it for a man to gain the whole world, and yet lose or forfeit his very self?"*

Hebrews 2:14-15, *"Since the children have flesh and blood, he too shared in their humanity so that by his death he might destroy him who holds the power of death—that is, the devil—and free those who all their lives were held in slavery by their fear of death."*

Ecclesiastes 7:2, 4, *"It is better to go to a house of mourning than to go to a house of feasting, for death is the destiny of every man; the living should take this to heart. The heart of the wise is the house of mourning, but the heart of fools is in the house of pleasure."*

Philippians 1:20-21, *"For I know that through your prayers and the help given by the Spirit of Jesus Christ, what has happened to me will turn out for my deliverance. I eagerly expect and hope that I will in no way be ashamed, but will have sufficient courage so that now as always Christ will be exalted in my body, whether by life or by death."*

Isaiah 43:1-2, *"But now, this is what the Lord says, He who created you, Anna, He who formed you, Anna: Fear not, for I have redeemed you! I have called you by name; YOU ARE MINE! When you pass through the waters, I will be with you; and when you pass through the rivers, they will not sweep over you. When you walk through the fire, you will not be burned; the flames will not set you ablaze. For I am the Lord, your God, the Holy One of Israel, YOUR SAVIOR."*

Mom, regarding any doubt about being received into heaven or fear of death, you are in good company. Even the apostles, especially James, did not understand what Jesus was talking about until they actually witnessed his death AND resurrection. James was the first of the 12 disciples to willingly die because he knew Jesus had conquered death, the doorway to eternal life. Christ said, "Blessed are they who have not seen and yet believe." You are my blessed mother, and don't forget that.

Remember, too, that it is not God who gives us a spirit of fear, doubt, anxiety. The devil is trying to rob you of your peace—don't let him do it. You are particularly under attack because he thinks you are in a weakened condition. But it is only your body that is weak. Your spirit is strong because it is the Spirit of God that dwells in you. Ask, in the name of Jesus, for the spirits of fear, doubt and anxiety to get out! 1 John 4:4, "You, dear Anna, are from God and have overcome them, because the one who is in you is greater than the one who is in the world."

So, my dear mother, as you requested, I pray for healing, acceptance, and peace for the mortal life you have—and it is not over yet!

Remember, only God knows the number of our days, and He asks that we live each one to the fullest, pressing on to do His work.

I believe God wants you to fully recover from this last surgery, to inspire us with your spirit of survival, your love and continued zest for life.

Cling to your optimistic nature and offer it to God so he can make you "an instrument of his peace" as it says in the prayer we brought home from Italy.

I can't wait to see you in July with our pictures from Ireland. I look forward to our special walk around the neighborhood and our next visit to the beach, this time including Roger!

Love, Donna

Walking someone part way home, even for a short while, is a profound experience. If your friend or loved one is open to sharing their thoughts, listen to them. They will teach you how to be a better caregiver, and you will have the privilege of learning how to keep life in perspective even when difficult circumstances threaten to overwhelm. Walking in their shoes is inevitable and their lingering voices of experience and wisdom will inspire and remind us to walk in love with a sense of purpose and self control.

And finally, brothers, whatever is true, whatever is noble, whatever is right, whatever is pure, whatever is lovely, whatever is admirable—if anything is excellent or praiseworthy—think about such things…and the God of peace will be with you.
(Philippians 4:8-9)

Lingering Voices from Heaven

Do not let any unwholesome talk come out of your mouths, but only what is helpful for building others up according to their needs…Get rid of all bitterness, rage and anger, brawling and slander, along with every form of malice. Be kind and compassionate to one another, forgiving each other, just as in Christ God forgave you.
(Ephesians 4:29-32)

If you want to know how to maintain a positive attitude and live life to the full, just ask someone who is facing the end of theirs. The lingering voices of many of my mentors and special friends continue to enhance my life and give me perspective. I can still hear them say, "If only I knew then what I know now…so let me tell you what's really important."

If wisdom is learning from our mistakes, even greater wisdom is learning from the mistakes of others.

Have you ever wondered what words of wisdom you will pass on to others after you have experienced a life changing event? In the passage above, Paul's lingering voice to the Ephesians is an excellent summary of much of the advice given to me by those nearing the end of their lives. Unfortunately, it is often in conflict with our very human nature and, therefore, impossible to follow without God's help. Our minds need be transformed and trained to tap into our divine nature so the quality of our relationships can improve and we can learn to live and work in harmony with one another. Too many of my friends reached the end of their life with regrets and they didn't want me or their loved ones to make the same mistakes.

What follows is a synopsis of conversations with my mentors and special friends that have made an impression upon me. Four topics are most commonly discussed; sharing these collective insights and stories gives us food for thought when we encounter difficulty with relationships, poor choices, painful situations, or life in general.

The Importance of Forgiveness and Reconciliation

Throughout life there is nothing that creates more unrest, tension, inner conflict, and anxiety than an unforgiving heart. Forgiveness releases the control our past has on our present. Forgiveness is soothing balm to our spirits. Forgiveness is an integral part of one of God's great commandments and its importance is underlined by being mentioned at least 139 times in the Bible. How can we love our neighbors let alone our enemies, if we are unwilling to forgive? The famous quotation by the English poet Alexander Pope says it all: *To err is human. To forgive is divine.*

If we believe that Christ gave his very life for us and for all humanity in order that we may be reconciled with God, who are we to hold a grudge? The author and distinguished professor of theology Henry Nouwen spoke of the importance of reconciliation and its benefits, particularly before we have to face death. In *Bread for the Journey: A Daybook of Wisdom and Faith,* he writes:

> How can we be prepared to die? By not having any unfinished relational business. The question is have I forgiven those who have hurt me and asked forgiveness from those I have hurt? When I feel at peace with all the people who are part of my life, my death might cause great grief, but it will not cause guilt or anger. It will be easier for our family and friends to remember us with joy and peace if we have said a grateful good-bye than if we die with bitter and disillusioned hearts. The greatest gift we can offer our families and friends is the gift of gratitude. Gratitude sets them free to continue living without bitterness or self-recriminations.

Mental health professionals tell us that the number one inhibitor to finding peace is our inability to forgive. The longer and tighter we hold on to anger, resentment, pride or our need to be right, the more difficult it is to reconcile. More than anyone else, Jesus had legitimate reasons for not forgiving those who hurt him, even killed him. He knows the hurt is even greater when someone in our own family is the source of our distress. His own people conspired against him, abandoned him, treated him unjustly, and tortured him. Even to those who crucified him, he said, "Father, forgive them for they do not know what they are doing." (Luke 23:34)

We, too, will be able to forgive with God's help. When we do, we no longer have to be a slave to our feelings. Rather than being a victim of an unforgiving heart, we can be a victor over the death of our relationships! Let me tell you a story about a couple of winners who were able to reconcile just before one of them crossed the finish line.

Two days before he died, Cameron asked someone to get a message to his sister Ellen. He had just been released from the hospital yet again. They had been estranged for years because of Cameron's alcoholism, and his health was failing due to the collateral damage this disease caused. Ellen wrote her big brother a letter of love, forgiveness, and encouragement to finally beat his addiction to alcohol. He was so moved when he read his sister's letter that he called for an old family friend, a retired pastor he knew since childhood. Through this beloved surrogate, strengthened by the knowledge of Ellen's unconditional love, Cameron was able to reconcile with God as well as his sister—and made a decision to turn his life around. Sadly, this would be his final turn for the worse. Cameron was hospitalized again the next day, and died.

On the day of his funeral, Ellen received the response to her letter when the pastor delivered Cameron's apology for "making sport" of her and his family all these years and he wanted her to know he loved her, too. They were reconciled at last.

Don't let your legacy to anyone be an unforgiving heart. Think of how many times you have prayed, "…And forgive us our trespasses [or debts], *as we forgive* those who trespass against us." Be careful what you pray for, you just might get it.

Forgiveness and reconciliation are closely related, but are not the same. You may forgive or be forgiven, but it requires both parties to restore the relationship. A bumper sticker I saw recently said: *Prayer doesn't change things: it changes people.* Reconciliation happens when you work at rebuilding trust, and it can be done unilaterally by acknowledging the role you played in whatever caused the rift in the relationship—and by making every effort to change your behavior. Whether or not the other party makes the same commitment is irrelevant. You will benefit from the exercise regardless. Pray the Prayer of Abandonment and feel a sense of relief when you finally let go of the situation.

If both parties work at it, lines of communication are restored and reconciliation is possible. Alternatively, harboring negative feelings can result in a toxic situation. We cannot survive for long in a toxic environment without becoming sick in body, mind, and spirit. The diligence we take in getting rid of hazardous waste, polluted waters, and the unclean air we breathe is out of proportion to time we should spend cleaning up our relationships with family and friends.

Many homes are equipped with a carbon monoxide detector to warn us of the toxic gas we cannot see that can cause physical death. A lack of forgiveness and an unwillingness to reconcile are our internal detectors warning us of hidden dangers that poison our spirit and our soul. If left unchecked, we are drawn closer to an emotional or spiritual death from a heart that is turning to stone.

It's a bittersweet moment when someone waits until they are on their deathbed to restore a broken relationship. The sweetness comes from the beautiful release of a burden carried for so long. The bitterness results from the fact that you cannot recapture the past. Most people who reconcile after long periods of time are usually heard saying, "If only we had done this sooner." "We should have…would have…and could have…"

Don't waste time fostering a festering anger. Make the choice to forgive and reconcile now. The six most challenging words in the English language are, "I admit I made a mistake." Use them. Forgive if only in your heart. Reconcile when possible. Then, leaving the past behind, enjoy the moment and the inner peace that will surely come. I've watched many people grow stronger physically, emotionally and spiritually when they made the choice to work through disappointing relationships, hardships, and grief rather than turning away. When forgiveness, reconciliation and love reign, the fear of death disappears.

If you were not able to reconcile with a loved one before they died, inner healing is still possible. Your loved one is no longer angry with you, and from where they sit, they would want you to be happy. Write a letter to them and say what you would have wanted to say in person, or use a surrogate to talk to them. Be open and honest with your feelings. Accept your part of the problem with your past relationship, ask for forgiveness, and tell them that you have forgiven them, unconditionally. Do not wait any longer to reconcile and be at peace in the here and now.

One final note on this subject: we must remember to forgive ourselves. God has. Psalm 103:12 says, "As far as the east is from the west, so far has he removed our transgressions from us." Do you know how far the east is from the west? Scripture says when we repent, God remembers our sin no more. So, there is no reason to keep beating ourselves up over the past if we have a penitent heart. If we are harder on ourselves than God, we will be stuck in the past and unable to enjoy life to the full. With the advice we have been given, we can do better.

Mistakes and Poor Choices

Mistakes happen. We don't always make good decisions in life. The overall lesson is: take the time to learn from them! If you see nothing positive coming out of a mistake or a bad decision, be patient. God will use it for good and reveal the benefit to you at a later time. *And we know that in all things God works for the good of those who love him, who have been called according to his purpose.* (Romans 8:28)

When we do something we regret, acknowledge it and accept responsibility for your actions. There is no need to blame others. We all fall short and accidents happen perhaps as a result of mistaken or poor judgment. Don't feel sorry for yourself; just work through the consequences and move forward having learned a hard lesson.

Transferring what you learned from one situation to another will help you avoid making the same mistake twice. Mistakes help us to grow and become better for having failed in some way. In the long run, we will have very few regrets if we approach mistakes and bad decisions with these thoughts in mind.

Coping with Growing Pains

Growing pains are part of life, be they physical, emotional or spiritual. Young people sometimes experience joint pain during growth spurts and old people have joint pains when their muscles and bones begin to show signs of wear. In our youth, we experience the emotional pain of peer pressure, failure to make the team, or when shifting loyalties cause us to lose a friend or our first love. These situations help prepare us for the emotional pain we will experience as adults.

When we mature, however, a broken relationship of any kind is not only painful, but it can also have a significant ripple effect on many others within our various social circles. For some, this is second only to the spiritual pain suffered when their faith in God has been shaken by the hand of man. Everyone has a different spiritual journey and life story to tell, but the people who call on God to heal them or to provide the spiritual anesthetic needed to ease the variety of growing pains in life seem to have peaceful endings.

Lingering voices from heaven reminded me of this advice and helped me cope with fear and pain when I was diagnosed with breast cancer. I regretted my choice to take estrogen for 15 years because it was the most likely cause of my predicament. Forgiving the doctors who encouraged me to stay on that controversial drug took time. The day before I was to have surgery, I was reminded of one of the lessons my mother shared with me years before. Just prior to my last pre-op test, I was told that it would be painful. I wasn't prepared for that.

The doctor had to use a larger than normal needle in order to accommodate the special dye that had to be injected into my chest to help identify the sentinel lymph node which would be the target for biopsy. The fluid contained tiny bits of metal which had to be forced through my dense chest tissue. The dye would remain in my body so during the next day's operation, the surgeon would be able to trace the path any additional cancer cells might travel to reach my lymphatic system.

After hearing this, my childhood fear of doctors and needles began to reappear. You see, I jumped and broke the syringe when I had my first penicillin shot! My heart raced, and then I heard Mom's lingering voice say, "Shhh, just breathe into the pain. Don't run from it because that's where the Lord meets you—in the pain."

I closed my eyes, took a few deep breaths and visualized my grabbing onto God's hand. As I relaxed and focused on the truth of the lesson I learned from Mom, I saw an image of Christ. His profile was unmistakable with the crown of thorns on his head and his back stripped bare of clothing waiting to be scourged. Just then, the whip hit him and bits of flesh and drops of blood spattered in all directions.

Focusing on that image, I silently prayed, "Dear Lord, forgive me for being such a wimp. Here I am lying in a clean hospital with medical staff trying to protect and preserve my life. You endured all that for me, so there is no reason to be afraid of a little needle for that matter."

A voice distracted me, saying, "Are you alright?" It was the doctor.

"Yes, but please tell me when you are going to do something because I don't want to be startled."

"I'm half way through," he replied.

Even though I was pleasantly surprised, the fear returned. "Well, the needle's in, but now the metal particles are sure to hurt." Once again, I followed Mom's advice and breathed into the pain. A few minutes later, I asked if it would be much longer. This time the technician responded.

"We've been done. I'm just adding some pressure to the site of the injection. It's all over." There was no pain. Both the doctor and technician were amazed, and I was grateful that I had Mom's lingering voice from heaven to remind me of a lesson learned.

Some physical pain is caused by stress and holding onto feelings like anger and fear. There is a connection between mind and body, so the sooner we accept the reality of what's happening to us, the sooner we will be able to make the best of a bad situation.

After two bouts with cancer, one survivor described her life-threatening illness and dependency on others this way: "On one level, I would have preferred not to have gone through the experience, but because of it, I have grown into a better person. I'm more aware of the important things in life, and can actually thank God for this disease. Because of it, I have a greater awareness of his presence, and more loving, caring friends than at any other time in my life." Out of physical and emotional pain, a woman of faith, inspiration and compassion emerged.

If we adopt this type of positive, realistic attitude when faced with a crisis, we will not ask the question, "Why me?" Instead, the question will be, "Why not me?" Some journeys through the valley may be long, but with a little help from our friends, we will make it.

Enjoy Life, But Be Prepared

If the saying, "Older people don't change; they just get more so" is true, I was privileged to know some very positive people in their latter years. As they reflected on their lives, most of them said, "All in all, life is good. It's not without its challenges, but life can be very good." They attributed their attitude to a belief in God which enhanced their life. Influencing their behavior, their faith was a source of hope and strength, and motivated them to enjoy life to the full. Because of their faith and belief in an afterlife, their death was not necessarily a cataclysmic event for them.

Most of these extraordinary people were grateful to have a chance to be philosophical about their circumstances knowing full well that their life could have ended suddenly by accident, heart attack, a mysterious infection contracted after a routine hospital procedure, snake bite, or being a victim of a violent crime or terrorism. Their point in discussing these things was to teach me the necessary balance between enjoying life and taking the time to be prepared. Being prepared frees us to get on with the business of living without dwelling on death.

If I had to summarize their advice on how to enjoy life to the full it would be to never stop learning, not procrastinate, pray, build healthy relationships, forgive and forget. Because life's too short, develop your gifts, follow your passion, continue to work and contribute to the needs of others, and most of all, remember to laugh. Man is most comical when he takes himself too seriously.

As end of life draws closer, the more our thoughts turn inward and any question or concerns expressed are usually deeply personal and more spiritual in nature. We truly are preparing ourselves for the unknown. I overheard the last conversation Mom had with Sister Therese, her long-distance friend.

"Sister Therese, it looks like I'm getting ready to go—and I have so many questions to ask God when I get to heaven," said Mom.

Laughing, Sister Therese replied, "Oh, Anna, you won't have any questions when you get there. You won't need to ask—you will know."

Mom confessed that she was afraid, so Sister Therese reminded her that, while a spirit of fear is not from God, it is part of our human nature. Knowing that can help us come to terms with fear and our faith can help us overcome it. We must never let the devil or anyone else thwart us from living out our purpose in life or rob us of our joy—from the days of our youth to the end of our life. The lingering voices from heaven continue to remind me to live each day as if it were my last—and if it is not, to fall on my knees and give thanks.

When we are ready, willing, and able to help someone enjoy life up to the end and be with them as they prepare to leave this life, we can learn so much about life as well as the dying process. Providing any form of emotional, spiritual, or practical support will result in receiving so much more than you give. Like mine, some of your friends may even give you a rare sense of what dying feels like. For those who had faith, it did not appear to be so bad.

Give, and it will be given to you.
A good measure, pressed down, shaken together
and running over, will be poured into your lap.
For with the measure you use, it will be measured to you.
(Luke 6:38)

What Does Dying Feel Like?

Now we see but a poor reflection as in a mirror;
then we shall see face to face.
Now I know in part; then I shall know fully,
even as I am fully known.
(1 Corinthians 13:12)

During my mother's career in apartment management, a woman named Pearl came to live in her building. Pearl was a very wealthy, self-assured sophisticate, but extremely lonely. She befriended my mother, stopping by her office every day just to talk. If Pearl had any faith at all, she never mentioned it, except to say that she did not believe in an afterlife. Later, when Pearl was hospitalized with a terminal illness, Mom visited her—even on the day of her death.

As she approached her room, Mom heard Pearl screaming at the top of her lungs, "I don't want to die! I don't want to die!" Upon entering, she found her thrashing on the bed, yelling obscenities at the attending nurse and aides who were trying to calm her down. Suddenly, Pearl died of a heart attack. I remember my mother telling me the story and saying, "Poor Pearl. I pray I never die like that, kicking and screaming."

Years later, I met Florence who was raised in a Christian home by missionary parents. As a young girl she memorized many parts of the Bible and enjoyed reading its prose and poetry. But when she fell ill, her behavior was very similar to Pearl's. She had been a political journalist and editor all her life, traveled the world and even lived abroad for a time. Florence happily mingled with what society would call the great and the good. Too busy to think about the future, she found herself alone and without means in her old age, having lived only for the day.

Like many of us, Florence fell prey to some dastardly deeds of others and had her share of broken relationships. As a child she was taught to hide her emotions, so she grew quite skilled not only at hiding, but also at harboring, feelings of resentment and bitterness stemming from her past. When I met her, she was overwhelmed by the consequences of the bad choices she had made in life, but pride prevented her from assuming responsibility for her actions. Her negativity manifested itself by becoming completely self absorbed, blaming family, friends, caregivers, the government, and even the church for how her life would end. Nothing anybody did gave her lasting comfort.

At the age of 91 years, with only her body failing her, she steadfastly refused to forgive. She resented attempts to help her reconcile with her past. Florence had no peace. Her behavior and attitude in her latter years were completely inconsistent with her years of service to the church and what she had been taught about how to live. She knew about God but when she rebelled against her parents and left home, she didn't take the time to get to know him. Her faith appeared to be the faith of her father's and not her own. She died in anger and with regrets.

The moral of the life and death of these two very different women is this: In our final days, our masks will be removed, and any pretense of piety and self-righteousness will be revealed. Death can feel like an enemy; the dying process can be tortuous if we choose not to forgive, not to reconcile with ourselves and others, and if we refuse to accept the gift of faith and hope in eternal life. Other endings tell a different story.

Mom

It was about a month before she left. On one of my cherished visits while I was doing dishes, I thought Mom was reading in the living room. Then she called to me and said very casually, "Donna, you know I think the time is getting closer."

I grabbed the dish towel to dry my hands and walked into the living room. "Why do you say that, Mom?" She clearly was experiencing something that was completely foreign to her and she wanted to talk about it.

She lifted her hands from her lap and rubbed her thumbs across her fingers, as if trying to feel the invisible. "It's hard to explain. I feel like I'm separating. There are times when I think I'm only half here—like I'm floating." Her demeanor was calm; she was not upset, just curious. She spoke factually about what this phase in the process of dying was like to her.

After listening intently, I tried to match her calmness with a dispassionate but loving analysis of what she had revealed to me. "You're probably right, Mom. Neither one of us has ever died before. Are you in any pain?"

"No," she said. "It's just very different and peaceful, like I'm detached from what's going on around me."

I replied, "I don't know what to say, Mom, except it sounds as if the weaker your body gets, your spirit will continue to grow stronger until one day it will simply break loose—and you'll be free." I waited for her comment but she just sat there peaceful and pensive, so I added, "Isn't it wonderful you aren't in any pain!"

"Hmmm," she said with a nod of her head. "It's hard to put into words; but I just wanted you to know that I think I'm getting ready."

"Well, thank God you're not leaving today! Besides, we have things to do!" She agreed with a chuckle knowing that she was being prepared and happy she was able to prepare me.

Sister Therese

Sister Therese died a few years after Mom, but she also prepared herself and me for her death by sharing in her own way. She was determined to never stop doing the work God gave her until her final breath. Her letters, my memories of our visits to the hermitage, and our telephone conversations helped me piece together a picture of her last days.

Not long before she passed away, Sister Therese called to tell me about an incident that happened to her. It made such an impression on me that I was moved to capture the details immediately after our conversation. It will give you a glimpse into the depths of her faith as well as the joy that came from believing she was in the exact place God wanted her to be and doing exactly what he wanted her to do—serving and praying for others. Despite chronic pain, she was content and daily pressed on with her chores even though her health was quickly failing.

One Friday night, Sister Therese collapses onto the floor of her hermit's cottage, riddled with arthritis and suffering from a severe case of fibromyalgia. Her joints are swollen, and her knees curled up under her. *The pain, oh, the pain!* Now fully awake after responding to nature's call following some sleep, she notes that it is 2:30 in the morning. "Father, what happened?"

She tries to move, but nothing happens. She tries harder and harder—up, down, side to side, engaging her back, hands, arms and elbows because her legs just do not work. Minutes, then hours pass since what was supposed to be a quick trip to the bathroom. The struggle to get to her feet continued, and the resulting rug burns on her back and upper limbs turned into bruises on her thin skin. "My God, my God, why have you forsaken me?"

Gradually, the gold and pink colors of sunrise reflect off the mountains, spreading light across the morning sky. "Lord, help me get up. Maybe I can roll over to the chair. Oh, no! I have to go to the bathroom again. I didn't know we made water even when you don't drink any." Too exhausted with the night's struggle she rolls up her pajamas and absorbs the liquid. Later a haplessly tossed towel provides a welcome receptacle for more bodily fluid. An afghan is pulled from the bed to protect the modesty of this frail little woman.

Throughout the day, the suffering and struggle continue as attempts to use the chair and then the bed for leverage fail. Morning turns to noon and throughout the afternoon hours the sun slowly heats the desert hermitage, but nothing can compare to the heat generated by the fire of prayer.

"Abba, help me patiently await the renewing of my strength and my ascension. While here, let me use the time to connect more intimately with you and intercede for those I know and love, and for friends who are too sick in body, mind or spirit to pray for themselves. Help me continue to do the work you have given me to do."

The hours of the day tick by and the desert sun takes its time moving from east to west across the mesa. "I must keep trying before darkness falls." The bruises enlarge and the skin, already thin, begins to tear and throb. Soon the sky is colored as if by a master painter with brush strokes of blue, pink and purple, first pale then deepening in dark hues that then turn gray then black. The second night begins.

As she lies where she had first fallen, the stillness and silence she cherished for so many years begin to disarm her. Her pain makes her cry out to God again, "Abba, have you forgotten me? Give me strength to lift myself off the floor. Don't let anyone find me like this because they will send me back to the mother house for care. I want to die here in my desert home and be with you always. In your mercy, hear my prayer."

The silence is finally broken by the hooting of her friend the owl who normally sits near the chapel. He keeps her company through the night and finally sings her to sleep with his soft whooing and cooing. Comfort indeed to this lovely lady so in tune with all of God's creatures.

The second sunrise comes and goes, and as the sun streams in the window, it catches the eye of the sleeping hermit. Her time has not yet come.

Upon awakening, she notices the owl is gone and a new opportunity to get up awaits her. Determined and strengthened by the gift of sleep, she grabs hold of the lever and bottom of the chair and with every ounce of strength she was given overnight, she manages to stand on shaky and very sore legs. Grabbing her cane, she makes her way into the bathroom and showers with songs of thanksgiving and praise on her lips. Refreshed by the soap and water, clean from head to toe, she checks the clock as she dresses. It's 8:30 a.m., about 30 hours since the fall. It's Sunday—Palm Sunday.

"I must go to church on this, the beginning of Holy Week. But how? I'm so exhausted. Where's the paper? Look, a Mass at one o'clock this afternoon." She slowly finishes dressing and manages to hobble around to get some nourishment. She walks to the prayer porch and meditates, makes a trip to the chapel to read her morning scripture and devotions. Carefully, she climbs into the driver's seat of the car and begins her cautious journey to church. It's a Spanish Mass! As she gets caught up in the joyous celebration of a packed assembly, she whispers to herself, "God saved the best for me in this last Mass of the day."

Positioning herself on the end of a pew, people climb over her but one woman, noticing her cane, sits beside this gentle, humble woman of God and helps her up and down during the service. A protective angel! The procession is glorious and it has been a long time since she has heard such beautiful singing and music coming from the choir and a variety of musical instruments. Her critical ear is still sharp after decades of directing an all-girl chorus and playing the organ. She delights in the talent and passion of the entire congregation.

She later said, "If it had not been for my spending 30 hours on the floor I would have missed it! Thank you, Jesus, for such a beautiful gift. My suffering was such a blessing because it set me up for Holy Week where I would meditate on the Passion of Christ. All things DO work together for good for those who love God and are called according to His purpose."

Epilogue: A Few Months Later

July 15, 2004: Sister Therese died today, three days shy of her 73rd birthday. A priest found her body which had been lying in the sun just outside the chapel facing the hills.

That morning, she literally gave her heart to the Lord as she sat on the prayer bench, no doubt thanking Abba for another night of fellowship with Him and her gift of intercessory prayer. Her bed was not yet made nor the air conditioner turned on after a cool desert night, but her car was by the chapel. The priest who arrived to say Mass at four o'clock finally spotted the blue hem of her garment and found her body.

No doubt her last vision was of the rising sun spreading early morning shades of color across the sky and the mountaintops before painting the desert floor. No doubt her friends the bunny and the owl were close by, comfortable with her presence and waiting for the sound of her gentle greeting. As she sat on the bench to just "be" with God and let the pain from her early morning movements ease, she was given her heart's desire to die in the desert alone with her Lord. God must have said, "Enough, beloved Child, it's time to come home. Well done, good and faithful servant."

Dave

Every single time I spoke to Dave, particularly during the last nine months of his life, I was reminded of the scene in the Bible where Jesus turns to those trying to dismiss the little children playing at his feet and says, "Let the little children come to me." (Luke 18:16) He then warns: "Anyone who will not receive the kingdom of God like a little child will never enter it." (Luke 18:17) Of this I am sure, Dave is there! When it came to his faith, Dave, above any man I have ever known, accepted this gift with childlike simplicity and enthusiasm.

A few weeks before he died, our pastor and I went to his home for an intimate Eucharist and to pray with Dave. When his head was anointed with oil and the pastor blessed him, in that solemn moment, he said with characteristic glee, "WOW! That was great! That was really great!" And he let out one of his big, loud laughs that couldn't help but make you want to join in.

"A joyful heart is good medicine and a broken spirit dries up bones."
(Proverbs 17:22)

We asked Dave how he was able to maintain his positive attitude as he endured the side effect of some of his treatments and the knowledge that he was dying. He gave the credit to his many friends and his wife Linda who rose to the occasion. Dave was so proud and grateful that they were united in their faith and optimism as to where he was going.

When anybody asked Dave how he felt, he usually answered, "I never have bad days." He looked beyond the problem of the moment and anticipated the good to follow. David described dying like this, "I feel like I'm being scrubbed, cleaned and polished, getting ready for something big—another wonderful experience God has planned for me."

His wife Linda gave me permission to share one of his final exchanges. A day and a half before he left us, Dave was in a very weak state. As he lay in his hospital bed, someone asked, "How are you?"

Naturally there was a delayed response, but Dave managed a smile and said, "It's like a little bit of heaven." Was God giving him a glimpse of what he is enjoying to the full at this very moment so he could let go?

Kathy

It was the last full day of Kathy's life. She knew she was dying, but said she felt as if she was preparing for a party. From her hospital bed, she called our friend Gail. "Quick, get over here and bring me my usual from Starbucks." She barred anyone but her confidantes from entering her room, so she could talk and say her good-byes. Kathy was wired. One minute she felt full of nervous energy, talking about how glad she was to see you and the plans she had made for her two teenaged sons; and in the next, she reluctantly grabbed her oxygen mask to breathe.

"Do you know what I really would like?" Kathy asked.

"You name it and you've got it," I said.

"A beautician. Do you think we can find someone who would come to the hospital to do my hair before the boys arrive tomorrow?" They had been visiting their father preparing for the eventual move when Kathy passed away. As I persisted in dialing one salon after another, she sat smiling and propped up in bed, surrounded by her papers. She rifled through the latest poem she wrote, her to-do lists, and thank you notes, along with the CD's she listened to when she was alone.

The hour was getting late, and it was time for the nurse to help manage the pain. While Kathy accepted the fact that we needed to say good-bye, she knew no matter what happened over the next 24 hours, we would eventually see each other again. Besides she said she knew she was surrounded by angels that would watch over her. In the middle of the night, the need to rid herself of pain outweighed her desire to see her boys. The hairdresser hadn't come anyhow, and she didn't want her sons to see her in this condition. They knew she loved them, and all her planning for their future was complete.

The time had come, and the growing pain was responsible for the growing anxiety. At one thirty in the morning, Kathy was beyond her ability to bear it any longer. She called her oncology nurses who had tried so desperately to keep her comfortable, and asked them for another dose of pain medicine and something to calm her nerves. They complied and Kathy fell asleep. Her boys will always remember their mother full of life—alive! And she is.

When I recall these end-of-life stories, I am filled to overflowing with gratitude. Each story has confirmed for me the truth of the saying, "As you live, so shall you die." The kindness and mercy we show others while we live will be returned to us when we die. We may stumble and fall or backslide from time to time, but God knows our hearts. Responding to faith's call to action may be easier if we embrace the sentiment in the Prayer of Thomas Merton adapted from *Thoughts in Solitude*:

> God, we have no idea where we are going. We do not see the road ahead of us. We cannot know for certain where it will end. Nor do we really know ourselves, and the fact that we think we are following your will does not mean that we are actually doing so. But we believe that the desire to please you does in fact please you. And we hope we have that desire in all that we are doing. We hope that we will never do anything apart from that desire. And we know that if we do this, you will lead us by the right road, though we may know nothing about it. Therefore, we will trust you always though we may seem to be lost and in the shadow of death. We will not fear, for you are ever with us, and you will never leave us to face our perils alone. Amen.

May the final gifts of those who have gone before add to our knowledge, make us wise, bring us peace, and help us make the most out of our lives and relationships so we can live and die with no regrets.

I have told you these things, so that in me you may have peace.
In this world you will have trouble.
But take heart! I have overcome the world.
(John 16:33)

Part III

Experiencing Death: A Sacred Time

The Last Days—From Trial to Triumph

What is more, I consider everything a loss compared to the surpassing greatness of knowing Christ Jesus my Lord. (Philippians 3:8)

People who have yet to experience the death of someone close to them have often asked me what it was like to care for my own mother as her life neared its end, even as she took her last breath. Their curiosity reflected in our conversations revealed their concern about their own ability to rise to the occasion when the time comes, asking questions such as:

"Will I be able to be there for someone I care for at the end of their life."

"How did you do it, practically and emotionally?"

"What does it feel like to be with someone you love as they prepare to die?"

"What do you see or hear at the moment of death?"

"Do people look different after death?"

"How did you feel?"

The most honest and complete way to answer these intimate questions is to return to the strictly personal story that began this book—the story of my mother's last days. Together we have already explored the fears people have about dying or the dying process, the benefits of accepting the reality of our mortality, and considered the pros and cons of tending to pragmatic details before a terminal illness befalls us. Reviewing the personal vignettes and advice from my mentors and special friends will help us walk someone part way home. We also have, in the Prayer of Abandonment, a spiritual tool to use when life throws us any of its unexpected surprises. Unlike anything else, clinging to faith when our world has been turned upside down gives us hope and an ability to inspire hope in others as they prepare to transition from life to life.

Before completing Mom's story, there is one more lesson I learned about "good grief." It answers the question, "When will I stop crying?" The bad news is that you will never stop crying. We often make the mistake of wanting to get through the grieving process quickly so the pain goes away. The good news is that the time between tears gets longer, and the amount of time you spend crying gets shorter. However, whenever you or someone else scratches this emotional wound, don't be surprised when your eyes fill with tears. This is part of having "good grief."

You will never stop crying, but the time between tears gets longer and the amount of time you spend crying gets shorter.

Good grief is being in it—opening ourselves up to it and learning from it. Even if we try to run from grief, the memories of our loved ones and our experiences with death will remain in our minds, hearts, and souls forever. Every Memorial Day I cry, and I was only two when Daddy died. The fresh pain of young mothers and children who have lost their husbands and fathers to wars in the 21st century scratches that spot deep inside of me. We are the sum total of all of our experiences and each one is part of what makes us who we are today.

Good grief makes us more compassionate, sensitive, caring, and calls us to action. Good grief prepares you to help others walk part way home and to comfort those left behind. I am not asking you to follow my example, but I am asking you to do what I've done. Remember, share your stories, and do not be afraid.

Our family circumstances at the time of my mother's prognosis and ultimate death were complicated, as they often are. Up to this time, she had been caring for her husband John, who had Alzheimer's disease. Even though she was dying from ovarian cancer, Mom declared, "As long as I am able to put the pills in his mouth, I will do it." She took her marriage vows seriously.

After living with a family member with psychological and emotional abnormalities, I'm convinced mental illness is contagious. Caring for someone like John can make you feel as if you are losing your own mind. Mom lived for two and a half more years after her diagnosis, a miracle in itself. But on April 9, she knew it was time to relinquish her role as John's sole caregiver. For the first time since her recovery from surgery, she had pain and she needed help.

Reading the account of how our family dealt with the situation and ran the full gamut of raw emotions will illustrate why we were able to laugh in the midst of our tears. Sharing in Mom's last big adventure by walking her part way home was the ultimate privilege, a joy, and a life-enhancing experience. This is how "good grief" came together for us.

Monday, April 9

Start by doing what is necessary; then do what's possible; and suddenly you are doing the impossible. (Saint Francis of Assisi)

After a frantic start to the day, the harrowing rush to the airport, and the frustration experienced with the limo service in Tampa when I landed, I finally made it to my mother's home. She had summoned me the day before. Little did I know that, when the day was over, I would look back on my travels as the most relaxing part of my day.

Mom opened the door, greeted me with a smile which looked like she had pulled it up from her toes, grabbed my neck to kiss me, held on tightly and whispered in my ear, "Thank God you are here. It's been terrible!"

"Where is he?" I asked.

"In the bedroom," she answered.

Just then John appeared, with a stiff half smile on his face, looking pretty disheveled. He had on a tee shirt, baggy bleach-stained trousers, socks and no shoes. Mom had told me on my last trip that he refused to wear his good clothes. He insisted that he liked his pants this way—dragging on the ground below the heel of his shoes, fraying. Alzheimer's makes you very stubborn. The slacks were new the day John thought the Clorox bleach was weed killer. Mom spotted him through the window, but before she could stop him, he had spilled the bleach on himself. He continued to wear the pants around the house to spite her. Since he had no control over her dying, he exercised his control over how he expressed his anger at the worsening situation.

I reached for John to gently greet him and asked how he felt. He said, "Not good," and immediately he went to lie down on the couch. Mom followed me to my room to unpack, but I plopped my unopened suitcase on the bed and quietly asked her what had been happening.

She said, "It has been awful. He keeps asking to be taken to the hospital again saying his pain prescription is not working. He paces around the house, screaming in my face, 'Ann, help me. Give me more pills!' I called the doctor's office and had him talk directly to Liz, his nurse, who explained to him that going to the ER would not help. They would only give him the same prescription.

"What he really wants from the ER is another shot to knock him out. He said he wants to die. He walks around holding his head and his stomach, saying he is having anxiety or panic attacks and he can't tell me if the pain is physical—'the thing' in his stomach—or mental. I don't know what to do!"

I asked her how she was feeling, and she said her pain was getting worse, but had not told the nurse because she knew a stronger dose of pain medicine from hospice would prevent her from taking care of him.

Knowing that her nurse was about to make one of her regular visits, I said nothing. Within five minutes, there was a knock at the door. It was Carol from hospice. Thank God! John reappeared, and after Carol asked how he was feeling, she suggested he watch TV while she could talk privately about female things. I promised him that as soon as we took care of Mom, he and I would spend some time together to see what I could do to help him next. He slowly moved back to the couch.

Fortunately they had just eaten something. Mom was always so good about taking care of both of them. Eating healthy foods was part of her personal program of building her body and immune system to stay well for as long as she could. The Easter holiday was coming and her children would all be with her. She anticipated a happy time, particularly since she secretly never thought she would make it to Easter.

While I sat on the bed calming her, Carol checked her vital signs and listened to Mom describe her worsening condition, but in a most positive light. I gently guided the conversation around to pain, and Mom admitted her need and her fear of the next level of drug. After Carol explained to Mom why she should consider taking something stronger than Tylenol at this point, she informed us of the various options that helped other patients. They discussed the pros and cons and continued talking until Mom asked, "What do you think? Should I try it?"

Carol gently, without pressure, said she thought it was worth a try and I seconded it adding the reassurance that since I was here, she didn't have to worry about taking care of John or the house for the next week. I would do the driving and even take him to the doctor's office for her. After making a call to the hospice doctor, Carol told Mom she would be receiving new medicine soon. She counted Mom's existing pills to make sure she had enough to ease her anxiety and help her sleep.

As Carol left, she reassured Mom as always that she would check on her in two days. "See you Wednesday."

Mom's eyes lit up and said, "At the Blue Dolphin. I'm taking you to lunch!"

"Oh no, you don't have to do that. We're not allowed to do that."

"You have to eat lunch, don't you? Meet us at the restaurant; I'm counting on it." She added pleadingly, "Aw, Carol, I really want to do something different with you this week."

"Okay, we'll see how my schedule looks. I'll call you. And, of course, you can call any time of the day or night if you need me."

Mom loved Carol. She was so kind. Mom called her a "softy" who loved her children and grandchildren and took in stray people as well. Carol was keeping the children of a friend for a while because they had no place to live. No details were shared with me, but I thought, "Everybody has a story."

After Carol left, Mom and I had a few precious moments to really hug and kiss, and talk about how wonderful it was going to be this coming weekend with Larry, Connie and even Roger joining us on Easter Sunday night. Now that she was calm and more cheerful, I suggested she stay in bed to rest while I talked to John in the family room.

"My pills aren't working and I want to go to the hospital, but she won't take me and she won't let me go with anyone else."

Suddenly Mom appeared. She had been listening and could not stand for me to hear only his side of the story. She wanted to explain to him one more time, in front of me, why she stopped him from calling the neighbors to take him to the ER.

"It isn't right for you to keep imposing on other people, John. If they take you to the hospital, do you expect them to wait for you? The last time Larry and Roger spent four hours with you in the emergency room. You can't do that any more, John. The neighbors have their own problems; how can they spend that much time with you? You already have the medicine they prescribed for you the last time you went. All you want is a shot to knock you out. If you insist on going, call 911. I can't do it any more. I'm sick too, John. Don't you understand?" She broke down and cried.

I intervened to restore calm to the situation. "Okay, John," I said. "Now that I'm here and Mom has been seen by her nurse, let me call and talk to your nurse or doctor at the VA and see what they recommend." He thought that was a good idea and went back to the couch. I called Liz, the nurse, from the bedroom and told her the situation. I had worked for months with the Veteran's Administration to enroll John in their program. He was entitled to medical benefits after serving in Japan at the end of World War II. I knew the nurse well from our many appointments.

Liz suggested I take him to the emergency room at the VA hospital in Tampa, and advised, "Do whatever you have to do to get him admitted to the Psychiatric Ward for an evaluation after they discover there is nothing physically wrong with him." I asked her to talk directly to John so he would agree to go with me.

She told him the truth. They could do nothing more for him at the clinic, and the local hospital did not have the kind of specialists he needed. However, if he wanted to try the emergency room at the VA hospital in Tampa, they might be able to have a specialist help him. After all, they had access to doctors at various teaching hospitals in the area. He continually asked for reassurances from her and finally agreed to go.

Liz shared our concern about who would care for John when Mom died. She advised that if he voluntarily admitted himself for an evaluation, the VA would help us find an assisted living facility to care for him. My efforts to identify a suitable long term care facility had failed up to this point.

After we hung up, I asked John to think it through and make sure that this was something he really wanted to do. It had to be his choice. He said, "Yes. It is necessary."

"Okay, I'll take you because this is your decision, and I want you to have help." He decided to pack an overnight bag in case they kept him. While Mom helped him, I went to my bedroom and called hospice to explain the situation and requested someone come to stay with Mom while I was gone. She was still able to get around the house on her own, but I noticed she was very shaky with all this stress and had begun having attacks of vertigo.

Under the circumstances, hospice decided to send Josephine, a nurse, to be with her until midnight. They promised she would arrive by 3:30 p.m., so taking them at their word, John and I left at 2:45 leaving Mom with her books by her side and one of her favorite CD's playing soothing music to calm her spirit.

On the drive to the hospital, I suppressed my anxiety about leaving my mother with a stranger in her vulnerable state. Earlier that morning, when I walked Nurse Carol to the car, she told me that things were going to get worse from now on, and I needed to get John out of the house. To myself I said, "This is for you, Mom."

On the drive, John refused to talk, so I was alone with my thoughts and reflected on the day John was officially diagnosed with Alzheimer's.

It was last November when everything fell apart. After surviving two surgeries, it was hard to believe, considering how well Mom looked and felt, the doctor could say she only had six to twelve months to live. It was a shock for everyone, but too much for a husband with mental illness. It wouldn't be long before John himself had to be hospitalized. After hearing that he would soon be losing the only person in his life who ever loved him unconditionally, John started to unravel.

It was my birthday, and Mom and I had planned a mother-daughter day out, but John was in a terrible state and we could not leave him. He lay in a fetal position all day and would not speak. Mom thought he may have suffered another mild silent stroke. We had to keep repeating our words and use touch to get his attention. The only thing he did on his own was come to the table for meals when Mom called him, but he just sat there. He had to be encouraged to eat and did so with his hands, or used a fork to push food off his plate onto the floor or his lap. The day before we had taken him to the beach, thinking a change of scenery would help. He lay curled up on the shore he once loved to visit. At least he was getting some fresh air and sunshine.

Mom confided that she had to help maneuver him to the bathroom because if left alone he had begun to urinate on the floor or toilet seat. Even when she was with him, he refused to use the toilet paper she handed him when he had a bowel movement. Instead he would grab a hand towel to wipe himself. Mom had to clean and disinfect the bathroom and wash his clothes four or five times a day. John refused to wear adult diapers.

I decided to write a letter to John's doctor that summarized his behavior and suggest he be tested for Alzheimer's. It took me nearly an hour to finally speak to his nurse Sheri. She listened to the entire saga, and after another hour passed, Sheri called back and instructed me to take him to the hospital immediately. "We will pre-admit him, and someone will be waiting for you. Bring the letter with you so the doctor can read it first hand."

The next trick was to get John in the car voluntarily rather than call 911. As I was describing the plan to Mom, John entered the living room. "Good, John, you're here. Please sit down with us. We've been worried about you, so I called your doctor to tell them how sick you have been. He just called to ask us to bring you to the hospital for an evaluation."

John looked as if he was shocked back into this life, and said, "When?"

"Right now," I said. "They are waiting for you. Let's pack some things and go so you can get the help you need." John did not move, but Mom began packing his pajamas and robe, his tapes, a Bible and toiletries. He mutely looked on. It was some time after lunch.

When we got in the car, John, who chose to sit in the back seat where he could stretch out, began to speak. Fortunately, Mom rode up front with me where I could hold her hand. He began a diatribe all the way to the hospital. His tortured mind was working overtime. Paranoia had set in.

"That's it, Anna. Throw me away! Just transfer the problem to somebody else. They can't keep me, you know. They'd better not lock me up! I'm going of my own free will, but you think you are going to get rid of me. But you won't." He told her what a terrible person she was and brought up hurtful distortions—anything negative about her past that he remembered, lashing out with confidences shared about the years of her youth.

With tears in her eyes, she looked at me, wounded and incredulous. I squeezed her hand and whispered, "He's sick, Mom. Don't listen to his lies. He doesn't know what he is saying."

As he ranted and raved, Mom tried to explain, "I am not trying to get rid of you, John. I'm trying to help you. You are sick, and I have just been told the cancer is back. All I can do for you now is take you to the hospital, but I am not abandoning you. I am not going to leave you there, but you need to go so someone can help you." He was beyond listening. He was full of anger and fear, totally self absorbed. It was useless to apply logic.

When we arrived, we only had to wait two minutes before a couple of nurses came to the front desk and took us upstairs to his room, pre-registered and everything! Thank you, Sheri! John was asked to change and get comfortable in bed. Mom helped him as I arranged to have the television activated in his room. My mother refused to leave him, and continued to reassure him that when we did, we would be back. The nurse tried to help by telling him that they were going to run a series of tests to find the cause of his pain. Eventually we were able to leave with the promise of returning the next day after we all got some rest.

From the hospital, we went directly to their church to talk to Pastor Jim about the latest events—both Mom's terminal diagnosis and John's hospitalization. We prayed and he promised to go see him. We went home to recover from the day's events.

The next morning when Mom called the hospital, we assumed John was having tests because he didn't answer his phone. When we called the nurses' station we learned that he was pacing the halls all morning, so we asked them to tell him that we had called and would see him later. Mom was terrified that he might feel abandoned.

We couldn't go to the hospital in the morning, because the hospice personnel were coming by to introduce themselves to Mom—first the social worker, Karyn, then the nurse, Carol. Even though I had completed the preliminary paperwork the previous week, they had to speak to Mom personally for her medical history, list of allergies, vitamins, and other medication. She had only been taking a mild sleeping pill that gave her about two to three hours of sleep.

They needed copies of her Living Will, and she had to sign the Do Not Resuscitate order, and tell them about her funeral arrangements. It all seemed like an out-of-body experience. Both Karyn and Carol knew how draining and emotionally traumatic this was for Mom and me, so they were very gentle and got through with the administrative details as quickly as they could. Now it was their turn to talk; Mom wanted to know about the services they offered to help her maintain the quality of her life as well as what they would do to ensure she would have a pain-free death.

After they left, Mom had no appetite, but she forced herself to eat a light lunch, just enough food to take with her vitamins. Mom refused to waste another minute thinking about herself. All she wanted to do was get to the hospital. She was a nervous wreck, full of fear and anxiety over how John was going to react.

When we arrived, John was pacing the hallway. Mom greeted him with characteristic love and warmth. After asking how he was doing, we listened to him tell us about his tests and which doctors he had seen. I left them alone to have a private conversation, expecting him to ask Mom about how she was so she could tell him about the people she met through hospice. That never happened.

While she spent time with John, I met with the hospital social worker to advise her of Mom's situation and talk about John's aftercare. I didn't want him to come home because Mom was less and less able to care for him. The news was not good. She said he would be released into Mom's care that evening or no later than the next day. She gave me little hope and mentioned one or two support agencies I could call to explore getting professional care for him after Mom died. I learned that John's diagnosis was dementia and, as I had suspected, Alzheimer's disease.

After spending over an hour with the social worker, I went back to his room. One look at Mom's face told me something was very wrong. She sat calmly listening to John, but when he saw me, he stopped, so I waved and walked away, thinking they needed more private time together. When it began to grow dark, I finally broke in and said, "John, you better tell Mom she has to leave now. She's not well, and she hasn't even eaten anything all day."

He said, "Okay." Before we left, Mom told me, in front of John, that he thought we had forgotten about him. We both continued to reassure him that we would be back tomorrow, because he would be coming home the next day, but not until all the test results were in and the doctor had a plan for his follow-on care. He kept repeating, "I'm not going back to prison. They can't keep me here."

As we walked away from his room, Mom started to cry, and nearly collapsed into my arms. "He read his chart! He read his chart! He thinks I'm trying to lock him up, that I'm going to abandon him. How could he have seen his chart?" Just then a male nurse came to our aid and helped me get Mom to the car.

The nurses had left his chart on the table outside the door of his room rather than returning it to the nurse's station. As John walked by, he took it into his room and read the entire thing. It had the consultation notes from his doctor, the neurologist, his test results—and the letter I had written to the doctor describing his behavior along with my suggestion to test him for Alzheimer's disease. In his condition, he only retained part of what he read, and thankfully, thought one of the medical staff had written it. Alone, without the support of his wife, the neurologist had actually informed John of his diagnosis, dementia and Alzheimer's. But he didn't remember being told, so reading about it before we had arrived shocked him.

John was incapable of asking Mom anything about her own condition, so all the while I thought they were having a "normal" (how could I be so stupid) husband-wife talk, Mom was being subjected to his ranting and raving. He accused her of concocting lies about him and conspiring with me to lock him up.

Naturally, I reported this to the nurse supervisor before we left the floor, but the damage was done. All I wanted to do was get Mom home and fed. Our original plan was to go out for a nice meal after leaving the hospital, but she was so upset, she couldn't eat. We went home. Neither one of us had an appetite. How can you when you begin the day with hospice and end it the way we did? I only ate some of the split pea soup Mom had made for John. It was his favorite. She forced herself to have a small bowl with her vitamins, saying she needed to regain her strength to care for John when he came home.

Mom was dying of a broken heart that evening, not cancer. All joy had left her. There was no smile, only lifeless despair and utter emotional and physical exhaustion, at least that's how it seemed to me. I felt as if I were in some sort of twilight zone, nearly crazed myself with the prospect of bringing this crazy man home to live with her when I returned to New York.

Looking at her frail and sapped body lying on the couch that evening, I was unable to control my emotions or my mouth. "He should be in an assisted living facility, Mom." But when she said she actually wanted him to come home, I lost it. Anger, resentment and disgust with the medical system, with Mom's prognosis, and with her stubborn attitude made me say dogmatically and with all the authority I could muster, "But I don't want him to come home; and you can't take care of him any more!"

"Yes, I can." she quietly said. "The doctor told me I have six months to a year before I die, and I'm still able to drive and take care of myself—and him."

Protesting, I responded, "But I want to take care of you. I want you to have peace. I want to fill your days with laughter, friends, and give you your heart's desire."

Mom could always see things as they truly were. "What you want is for me to live a fairy tale and I want to live life—a normal life which includes pressing on through bad times. That's how we can appreciate the good, by surviving the bad and not turning our back on responsibility. Yes, I want to have quality of life—my life! And John is part of my life. He is the work God has given me to do. You cannot deny me this."

I persisted and screamed," But I don't want him here. I hate him!"

My beautiful mother looked up at me as she lay on the sofa, and in a weakened but pleadingly firm voice said with such clarity of thought, "Please, honey. Please. Don't make me choose. Don't make me choose between you and the work God has given me to do. As long as I have breath within me, I will take care of him. I will be the one to put the pills in his mouth. I took a vow for better or worse, for richer for poorer, and in sickness and in health. He is so sick. If I had a sick dog, I wouldn't abandon him and throw him in the street. How can I do that to another human being? If you love me, you have to be with me on this."

I began to wilt, and Mom continued, "This is the man who helped take care of my mother, the one who helped me carry Grandma to the bathroom when she stayed with us. How can I abandon him when he is so sick, vulnerable? What would that do to his self esteem?"

I recalled the stories about John's immigrant father who slept on the roof with the homing pigeons he raised, and how neither he nor John's mother set boundaries for him as a wayward teenager, starved for attention and expressions of love; of how he was rejected by the rest of his family because of his behavioral problems.

Mom continued, "Donna, don't you understand? John was never taught how to love or how to forgive. He doesn't even care that God forgives him, because he can't forgive himself. He's a tortured sad soul and doesn't deserve to be rejected just because he's mentally ill."

Her tender heart was not able to penetrate my heart of stone. My resolve to protect my mother remained firm. I stood over her and yelled, "But I hate him, and I hate what he's done to our family. He's ruined every holiday, every special moment, and every trip we've taken. He is an ungrateful user and abuser, and I don't want him at my mother's death bed! I can't live through another scene like the one he made when Grandma died! I refuse to have a demented, ungrateful, sick-o in your face. I want you to have peace; I want to be there with Larry. I wish he would just disappear!"

My poor mother. What did I just do to her? It was all about me. She began to cry, and then, to my shame, she apologized to me through her tears. "I'm so sorry; it's all my fault. I brought this man into our house. I'm so sorry," she sobbed. "It was my pride. I didn't want to be divorced again. By the time I found out how sick he was, it was too late.

"What would my family say? I thought I could change him. I thought if I could get him help, he could be cured. I mortgaged the house several times to help. I thought if we moved to Florida as he was getting older, things would be different. I heaped this sorrow on my family. I'm so sorry. But now it's too late. I can't abandon him now. Please help me. If you love me, please be with me. I need you."

With those words I finally entered into my mother's pain, not mine. I fell into a heap across her prone body, and with the venom still stinging in my throat and tears freely flowing from my eyes, I begged her forgiveness. Why did it have to come to this for me to understand? Promising to never try to take control of her life again, even at this stage, I vowed to honor her choices and her life's work forever. "Mom, please forgive me; can you ever forgive me for my selfishness, insensitivity and anger at this helpless man?"

"There is no need to forgive, darling. You were just expressing your feelings. They are just as valid as mine and I need to acknowledge them." As always, I marveled at her grace. "There are no secrets between the two of us. We love each other warts and all. You are my precious girl and we will just move forward from here. Now let me get some rest."

Sitting beside me in the car, John sighed, but he still refused to talk to me. I was ashamed that I resented the years my mother spent caring for this very sick man. Each time I visited them, I wanted to stay longer, but she insisted I return to my own life. Mom persuaded me that she was still able to get along with the network of local support she had, saying, "And if you stay and hover over me, it will only remind me that things aren't normal. I don't want the guilt I would have if I kept you away from Roger." As John sat slumped in the passenger seat next to me, I began the memory replay of a time she walked me to the car as I left for the airport.

Each time I visited Mom and John, I left feeling helpless and frustrated because Mom and I had so little time to be alone and talk. After one particularly grueling stay, I began to cry as she walked me to the car. "I'm sorry, Mom. I wanted to have some quality time with you, to take you for a walk in the sun; but instead I went from one doctor to another with John. I spent the entire time collecting medical records from each of his doctors, talking to administrators, and doing all the paperwork needed for the VA and Medicaid applications."

She interrupted my pity party with a hug, then took me by the shoulders and looked straight into my eyes. "But, sweetheart, don't you understand. What you did for me was better than taking me for a walk in the sun. You gave me peace. And remember, it's easy to love the lovable. Jesus said, 'What you do to the least of these, you do to me.'"

With that, I remembered one of the seven fears of death. What is going to happen to my loved ones? So I mustered up a smile and said, "You're right, Mom; I'll remember. I promise."

As I drove off with my arm waving out the window, Mom stood by the curb with her ever-present smile and waved back, reminding me of a baby saying "bye-bye." I prayed for both of them all the way to the airport, turned in the rental car, walked into the lobby of the terminal and roamed around the shops, not knowing what to do with myself until boarding the plane. I was filled with so much pent-up emotion that I wanted to scream—to curl up in a ball and sob. But I couldn't. "I have to find something to do, someway to distract myself!" I spotted the bookshop.

It was late, and nobody was around except a lone sales clerk. She smiled. I tried. Our eyes met once more, and she did something extraordinary. She came around from the cash register, walked right up to me and said, "You look like you could use a hug. What's the matter?"

I burst into tears and blurted out, "My mother is dying." She put her arms around me and asked how she could help. "Find a book that will distract me—something I can read on the plane to maintain my control and dignity." The book I bought still sits, unread, in my bookcase. There was never any concentrating on my return flights. All I could think of was leaving Mom alone to care for this poor, sick demented man while she, herself, was dying. Mom had enough faith for both of us, and her sharing it gave me the courage to leave and trust they would be all right.

And now, here I was driving John, this poor soul, to yet another hospital. Only this time John will not come home. Mom's life as his caregiver had just ended. With Mom's stronger medication, someone else will have to put pills in his mouth and it wasn't going to be me. I could not, would not, divide my time between the two of them ever again. She was the priority, and that was that! I prayed, "God, I abandon John into your hands. Be with me and help me find the care he needs so my mother can die in peace."

Nurse Carol was right this morning when she said, "Things will get worse from here." She had no idea how much worse. My eyes stung with tears as I pictured Mom sitting with a stranger at this very moment. Silently I vowed to return and spend uninterrupted quality time with my mother—to make her laugh again.

This was the right thing to do for John. His condition was beyond the scope of care that could be provided by lay people. Larry and I would remain his advocates and ensure he had the professional help he needed for the rest of his life. Driving as if on automatic pilot, I saw the hospital looming two blocks away. Soon we would be in the Emergency Room.

It didn't take very long for various tests to begin, in spite of the fact that there was nothing physically wrong with John. It was hospital procedure, and none of the various doctors and nurses I spoke to truly listened to me. The battery of tests required that I push him in the wheelchair from one location to another for hours. Then the word came. Because they could find nothing wrong with him, he was going to be sent back home with me.

When I was finally able to speak to a doctor, I reviewed our situation and told him about the similar batteries of tests he had recently—once with the HMO and again when he entered the VA system. He had been checked out thoroughly by doctors, a urologist, and an oncologist. I referred him to the medical records I brought with us, including the report from his psychiatrist indicating obsessive-compulsive behavior and depressive psychoses—even last November's diagnosis of dementia and Alzheimer's.

Something else is wrong and I pleaded with the ER doctor to order a psychiatric consultation and have him admitted for closer evaluation because he just could not go home. "He is very ill, and his wife—his only caregiver—is dying." They ignored me. When I said I had to leave him to return to my mother's death bed, I was threatened with a law suit for abandoning a senior citizen. So I was forced to stay and wait for him to be discharged.

Throughout the day I kept calling Mom so she would not have a moment of anxiety. Our chats were cheerful, reassuring her that John was getting lots of attention. They helped, but so did Josephine, the 24-hour nurse.

Mom delighted in her, "She's wonderful. Guess what? She's Italian from New York, has had cancer, too, and a healing. She fixed me the dinner you prepared the last time you were here—you know, the turkey loaf you put in the freezer. And she made mashed potatoes, string beans and a salad. I'm teaching her how to play cards, Kings in the Corner. We're getting along just great. Can't wait for you to meet her."

By this time, nearing 9 p.m., the ER was empty and I was pacing. A man in a white coat and green scrubs passed me on his way out. Noticing my distress, he stopped and asked if I was all right. I asked, "Are you a doctor?" When he said he was, I cried, "Please, please help me."

Through my tears, exhaustion, and hunger, I told him our story, and pleaded with him to do what he could to have John admitted. "He needs a psychiatrist to evaluate the situation. Based on his medical history and the current home environment, you can't make me take him home. The worse my mother gets, the worse he gets. One of your staff in the ER threatened a law suit when I said I wanted to leave him to go to my mother's side. Is there anything you can do?"

He said, "Wait here." Ten minutes later, he came out, followed by a nurse who confirmed that they were calling a psychiatrist. The angel in the white coat wished me luck as he disappeared through the automatic doors, no doubt leaving for home himself.

Soon the psychiatrist asked to see me. I had to repeat everything I told the ER doctor about John's prostate cancer and incontinence from the radium implants, his liver surgery, chronic pain, mini strokes, dementia and Alzheimer's diagnosis, his behavior patterns and Mom's recent turn of events. He asked me to wait while he talked to John privately.

In a while, the doctor called me back into his office to inform me that John had agreed to admit himself to the Psychiatric Ward for evaluation of anxiety and pain, and to find the right combination of drugs to help him. But wait—John appeared in the doorway and said, "I changed my mind." Just then, a nurse joined our meeting after completing the necessary paperwork to admit him.

The doctor gave John assurances that he would be helped, but added since he was voluntarily admitting himself, he could leave if he wanted to. I encouraged John to listen to the doctor and reminded him that it was his idea to come here to seek help. The VA was affiliated with University Hospital and Tampa General Hospital, and they promised to have a team of pain specialists find the right medication for him. The doctor concurred and promised to treat him for not only his pain, but the panic attacks he had been experiencing. "It's worth a try, don't you think? We've waited all day for this. What do you say, John?"

He nodded, but pointed a finger in the doctor's face and said, "Okay, I will trust you, but I don't want to be locked up."

With that, we were escorted to the Psychiatric Ward where he had a private room. There were no locks on the doors. He had a television to watch, and there was a snack room. He was free to roam the halls. The attendant told him the main door to the ward was locked to protect the really sick people from wandering outside and getting hurt.

I asked the nurse if they had the list of his medications from the ER we brought. They did not, so I stayed until the hospital pharmacy delivered it, and he had his sleeping pill. John was permitted to keep only his pajamas, his Bible and a shirt.

After helping him get ready for bed, I said goodnight and said I shared the hope he had of finding needed care. "Now that you are in good hands, I have to leave you, John, to take care of Mom." The parking lot was empty.

I arrived home at 10:30 p.m. Mom was glad to see me and eager to serve me dinner. Between her and Josephine, they prepared my plate and wanted to know everything, particularly why it took so long. "Everything is fine. But you know how hospital emergency rooms are. There was a lot of waiting around, a battery of tests to rule out any physical problem, and finally a psychiatrist was called who spoke with John. Together they agreed he should stay and be evaluated by a team of specialists for his physical and mental pain."

Managing her expectations while assuring her he was in good hands, I said, "It may be a while before he can come home, because they want to keep him and watch how he reacts to various drugs. They really want to get to the bottom of his problems, and are confident they can help. He's very sick, Mom, but he's in a really good place. How does that sound?"

She relaxed and breathed a sign of relief. "Wonderful!" she said. "I hope and pray they really can help him." Josephine reinforced my message, saying to my mother that it was her turn to rest easily.

As I ate my first meal of the day, they told me about the fun they had getting to know each other. I finally asked, "Mom, since I've been gone all day, have you tried the new medication for your pain yet?"

Her sheepish answer was, "No."

Josephine explained, "She wanted to wait until you came home in case she had any side effects, and she wanted to be clear headed when you reported on John."

I asked, "Are you in pain right now, Mom?"

"Yes," she said, "but it's time to take the old medicine and my sleeping pills."

"Well, Mom, if you're going to try the new prescription, it might be best to take it now while Josephine, a trained nurse, is here? What if you do have a bad reaction? Carol is not supposed to come again until Wednesday."

She asked for Josephine's opinion. "I think Donna's right, Anna. Why not try it? It's the smallest dose. I'll stay for a while. I'm supposed to be here until midnight anyhow, so why not take it, go to bed, and see what happens?" Mom took her first Oxycontin that night.

Tuesday, April 10

This was my day with Mom. It took longer for her to wake up. She used to be an early riser. Mornings were her favorite time of day. She would walk into the kitchen, see the sun streaming in through the windows and cheerfully and enthusiastically say, "Thank you, God, for another day." The drug had helped, but she was slower in movement and speech than she had been. She was a little unsteady, so I fixed her breakfast. As she ate and then took her tea and vitamins, we discussed the help John was getting. He did not have a phone in his room, so she relaxed and, as usual, planned her day.

The most important thing on her mind was shopping for Easter Cards. She really wanted to write notes to people who had been so good to her—some family members, Sister Therese, her pastor, and friends from out of town who had sent her many cards and letters during her illness. I wanted to take her to lunch at the beach. We did both.

Mom didn't want to take the Oxycontin again because it made her a little "thick tongued." She always did have a high tolerance for pain, but I reminded her that the nurse suggested she take it as prescribed to stay in front of the pain. She agreed and rested before she dressed for our ladies' day out. .

First stop—the card shop. Using the walker hospice provided was a new experience for Mom, and maneuvering it in the crowded store was tricky. "Damned walker! I hate it." After carefully selecting each card with a specific person in mind, we bought the stack she had accumulated saying, we'll come back if we need more. We never did.

A special day out had to include Hudson Beach. She and John would go there regularly to be among the children and families during the day, or to watch the sunset. More recently, they had installed a small boardwalk along the edge of the Gulf of Mexico, only a city-block long. It enabled her to walk more securely than she could on the sand, despite her neuropathy. She loved being able to watch the seagulls soar and pelicans dive for fish. The beach always calmed both Mom and John. He did not like to move around much, so he usually sat with an ice cream cone at the local beach shack and watched people while Mom got a little boardwalk exercise.

Today, she decided we should eat at the full service restaurant across the street and pretend we were on a mini vacation. As I helped her out of the car, she asked, "Do you think if I held onto your arm, I could make it to the restaurant without using the walker?" She did not want people to stare or be reminded of her condition.

"Absolutely," I said cheerfully, and then helped steady her.

"No, not that way, this way! This feels better." She adjusted my grip so she could hold on to me, rather than my holding her arm. We slowly made it to the front door. "Okay!" She said with a sense of accomplishment, adding with enthusiasm, "Look, we can eat outside."

The restaurant had an outdoor patio with an awning to shade us from the Florida sun. I spotted a table at the very back and center of this airy space. After carefully weaving our way through the lunch crowd, Mom settled into the chair facing the room, but I was the lucky one because I could see her against a backdrop of lush Florida vegetation and palm trees swaying in the breeze. That vision will be forever framed in my mind's eye, complete with the contrasting bright blue sky and a few white fluffy clouds over her head. Disappointedly I said, "Aw, Mom, I forgot the camera. You look so beautiful with the sun on your back. I wish someone could take our picture."

She grinned and leaned across the table saying, "We don't need a camera; we're making memories that will never fade." I agreed and fought back the tears.

We ordered grilled grouper sandwiches and iced tea. After a sip, she said, "I don't know why I ordered iced tea; I don't like it. Think I'll stick with water." As we ate, I watched her every move, delighting in her freedom, her peaceful day—the first one without John in a long, long time. She talked to the people at the next table, commenting on their beautiful children. She could see the sunbathers on the beach and in the water just across the street and was pleased the waitress was very nice. That's what usually brought her back to a restaurant, nice wait staff; she would refuse to return to a place that did not treat her or, more importantly, John with respect.

She said happily, "This is my kind of day!" Every day was perfect to Mom if it was sunny, not too hot, with low humidity. When our lunch arrived, I wondered if it was the company or were not these the best grouper sandwiches we ever had? "Delicious," she said. To prolong our stay, I talked her into splitting a slice of key lime pie for dessert, but she only had a couple of small bites, ever conscious of not eating too much sugar. Cancer loves sugar and even at this stage she had no intention of giving in to it.

On the way home, we stopped at the supermarket. By then, Mom was fading, so she stayed in the car while I went in and grabbed a few things. I would do the big Easter shopping later in the week. When we got home, she decided to nap saying, "I'll write the cards later." Then the phone rang. It was Helen confirming her visit tomorrow. Mom yelled across the room, "Tell her to meet me at the Blue Dolphin at 12:30 p.m. for lunch—my treat!" My mind wandered to a day the previous November when we first met Helen.

It was the week Mom courageously invited hospice into her life. Encouraging her to take full advantage of their services was part of my goal to build a network of support for her and John. Since she insisted that I return home to New York, I wanted her to make another friend who would visit regularly.

"You need people to talk to, Mom. It will help you cope with John."

"But I have someone. I talk to you, and I have a Stephen Minister."

"Yes, but that's different. Making a new hospice friend has other benefits. She will run errands or shop for you when you need help, in addition to being another person to keep you company during the week. Besides, I know you don't want me to worry about your being lonely. Hospice said they would handpick someone to meet your exact specifications."

She was softening, so I continued. "Wouldn't it be nice to have some intelligent conversation? John isn't much of a companion for you since he only responds when you say 'it's time to eat' or talk about the cat. That's not enough. Remember, hospice is for the living—to improve the quality of your life. Won't you try it?"

I listened as she talked to Charma, the volunteer coordinator. "Listen, Charma. I appreciate the help, but you must remember I'm not a kid and I really don't want to talk to a kid. I'm still well enough to continue to do everything myself, so all I would like is someone I can relate to, perhaps play cards with, or someone who might walk with me in the neighborhood, and most of all someone who can keep a confidence."

Charma said, "I think I understand; let me see who I can come up with." Mom eventually received a call telling her Helen would be visiting. "I think you'll like her."

The day before Helen was due, the hospice chaplain, Chuck, stopped by to introduce himself. He wanted to get to know Mom and her family, but the session had turned into an interrogation by John about Chaplain Chuck's theology and a monologue of John's problems and pain, as well as his views on religion. Mom was getting anxious, frustrated, and a little embarrassed. She finally mustered the courage to speak.

She began, "I have a question, Pastor. Are you here to see me or John? I have no interest in being a bystander in a religious debate between you and my husband. I hear this stuff all day long. I was under the impression that you were here to see me. I have a lot of questions I'd like to explore with you. Are we going to have any time at all to talk alone? Please explain your role and the purpose of your visits."

How proud I was of my mother's assertiveness. She knew what was at stake. She was the patient, and she wanted to get ready for the journey she would travel alone. The chaplain began to set her mind at ease and delicately talked about how he would try to meet her needs without completely neglecting John. He said he would talk to them separately in subsequent visits, first spending time with Mom, and then checking in with John. There was an unexpected knock at the door.

I quickly opened it and stepped outside and looked down on a little lady with a beaming face and smiling eyes. "Hello, I'm Helen from hospice. I'm a day early, but I was in the area and decided to make sure I had the right house before I visit tomorrow."

Just then Chaplain Chuck opened the door to leave. After introducing Helen to Mom, I walked the chaplain to his car. Standing in the driveway, I vented some of my own frustration with our complex home environment, John's physical and mental condition, and Mom's determination to take care of him. I exposed my anger, and he assured me he and the rest of the team would be monitoring the situation and would call me if they thought it was time for John to go to an assisted living facility.

When I went back into the house, Mom looked so happy. "Here she is. Helen, this is my daughter Donna."

"Yes, Mom, we met briefly when Pastor Chuck was leaving."

"You won't believe it. Helen's from Pittsburgh. She reads and volunteers at the library I go to. And she knits! In fact, she used to own the shop where I bought the yarn for the sweaters I made!"

"Great. Did you tell her we have not been able to find a pattern for the scarf you want to make for me?"

"Not yet. Helen, I have some beautiful yarn I bought to make myself a

sweater, but it's too hot now, and besides, what do I need a new sweater for—under the circumstances? I would like to make Donna a beautiful coat scarf. She can use it in New York. We had looked for patterns the other day, but were unable to find any. Do you have any books?"

Helen said, "Yes, I do. I have lots of books. I'll bring some the next time I come."

They decided to save any further conversation for a real visit, and Helen left.

When the door closed, Mom started to really laugh for the first time in a while, slapping her thigh. "I told Charma I didn't want a kid. But, I didn't think she would be sending me an old lady." She laughed again at that statement saying, "I guess I'm an old lady, too, but she's older than I am! Did you see her wrinkles? She looks so frail. Did you notice the poor dear has osteoporosis?"

"Yes, but what did you think of her, Mom."

"I think she's wonderful! I admire her so much. She's still driving and volunteering and doing things for other people. We had so much in common. I just think it's funny that, if you go just by looks, it appears that I should be the one taking care of her!"

"Well, just wait to see how the relationship develops. Remember, Charma said she would send someone else if you are not completely comfortable with her as a new friend."

"Don't worry, honey. I'm okay. I really liked her. It's funny how you don't ever look at yourself the same way you do other people. We'll get along just fine. I'm looking forward to seeing the patterns so I can make you that scarf for Christmas."

Helen and Mom saw each other every week for the next five months and had become good friends. Both of them enjoyed sharing memories of their lives, and it was lovely to know how much laughter filled the air when they were together. As Easter approached, Mom knew she didn't have much time to show her appreciation, so planning a ladies' luncheon for the next day was very important to her.

That evening, after my first full day alone with Mom, we watched a television movie together. She sat on the end of the sofa in the family room, and I stretched out with my head in her lap so she could mindlessly play with my hair, something she did all my life. If she would stop, I'd nudge her—my way of telling her to continue. Every now and then she would smack me in the head because she was getting tired. Sometimes, she would tug on my hair and ask, "Are you awake? Don't go to sleep! Are you watching?"

During the movie, we had to contend with Baby, her jealous cat. He was the one who normally participated in an evening ritual of head scratching. Baby would climb onto Mom's lap and purr while she petted him. Once he had had enough, he'd jump down, contented. But tonight was my night.

After the movie, we played cards and then delved into the books we were reading. I made her nightly cup of Flor-essence tea and watched the clock to make sure she took her medication on time: two sleeping pills, one anti-anxiety pill, and a pain pill. Tonight it was early, only 11 p.m. She usually stayed awake until midnight, but she thought perhaps she would start getting ready for bed earlier. She knew I was tired, still catching up after the ordeal of the day before.

I tucked her into bed and made sure the night light was on because she usually got up in the middle of the night. Recently, she told me how shocked she was to catch a glimpse of herself in the mirror as she hurried to the toilet, pulling up her nightgown on the way. She said she jumped and exclaimed, "Oh, my God, it's my mother! Grandma was right when she told us, 'You, too, will be where I am some day.'" We both laughed at the circle of life. After all, man is most comical when he takes himself too seriously.

Just before I kissed her goodnight I said, "Mom, remember how you used to pray with me when you tucked me into bed: 'Now I lay me down to sleep, I…."

She interrupted me with a pat on my arm and a shake of her head, "That's not how I pray today. Do you want to hear how I pray today?"

"Yes, I do."

Closing her eyes, she softly began, "Heavenly Father, my Joy, my Shield, my Comfort, my Salvation, my Rock, my Savior, Almighty God, Everlasting Father, Prince of Peace, Jehovah, Abba, my Strength, my Protector, my Redeemer, my Healer, Jesus, Holy Spirit, my Lord. Bless the Lord, O my soul, and all that is within me, bless His Holy Name. Bless the Lord, O my soul, who heals all my diseases, who redeems my life from the pit, who forgets all my iniquities, bless His Holy Name. Bless the Lord, O my soul."

She may have finished Psalm 103 in its entirety. I don't know because I was transported to another world eavesdropping on my mother and her God in intimate conversation. After a pause, she opened her eyes and turned to me. "That's how I pray every night and then I sleep."

I kissed her, left her room, locked the doors, turned off the lights, and retired to my bedroom to wallow in deep sorrow at the thought of losing her. My sorrow was also mingled with gratitude for the ultimate healing she would soon have. I slept with anticipation of her tiptoeing into my room the next morning, so we could snuggle and have our special pillow talk. That never happened again.

Wednesday, April 11

Mom usually was up before me, but not this morning. I heard no noise so I decided to check on her. When I reached her bed, I was startled to find her brows were furrowed, wincing in silent pain. She could barely talk, but she was able to whisper, "The pain. The pain."

"Where, Mom, where's the pain?"

Through clenched teeth she said, "My head, my spine, my legs, neck, shoulders—everywhere. All over. It's terrible."

"Okay, Mom, I'll call hospice to get help. It's going to be all right."

It wasn't 12 hours yet so I wanted to make sure I could give her the pain pill straight away. Of course the answer was "yes." This was Wednesday, and the nurse would be here at lunchtime. It was very difficult sitting her up to take the pill, the pain was so bad, but she also had to go to the bathroom. I positioned the walker and held onto her as she slowly and painfully made her way. It was so hard to watch her suffer, but I took consolation in the fact that the pill took effect in minutes. After resting a little longer in bed, she was able to get up and come to the table for breakfast.

Around 10 a.m. Mom had a visit from her Stephen Minister, also named Carol. She had been the other faithful person who visited Mom. Mom enjoyed taking walks with Carol, holding onto her arm and sharing stories of their lives as well. Unfortunately, Carol herself had to be hospitalized for a while. But Carol called each week and sent lovely cards and inspirational messages that lifted Mom's spirits. One my mother particularly liked describes the limitations of the disease:

Cancer is limited
It cannot cripple love,
It cannot corrode faith,
It cannot eat away peace,
It cannot destroy confidence,
It cannot kill friendship,
It cannot shut out memories,
It cannot silence courage,
It cannot invade the soul,
It cannot reduce eternal life,
It cannot quench the Spirit,
It cannot lessen the power of the resurrection.

I took a walk while Carol spent time with Mom. Carol found me outside as she left the house. When I told her she didn't have to worry about calling regularly since I had no intention of leaving, she said, "Yes, I know. Your mother and I said our good-byes today." With tears in both of our eyes, Carol drove away. Oh, the grief she must have felt when she had to say goodbye to Mom and realize this very special friendship had to come to closure.

Back in the house, Mom was wearing her best face and refused to dwell on the situation. Instead, she wanted me to address envelopes while she wrote notes in the Easter cards she bought the day before. She chuckled every time she asked me to help her with spelling, saying it was never her strong suit. On a more serious note, she commented that she was having difficulty with her memory and noticed her handwriting was getting worse.

"Do you think it's in my brain?" she asked.

"I don't know, Mom. Not even the doctors know exactly where it is. What difference does it make? You know it's a progressive disease, but the main thing is you are not in pain."

She agreed and turned back to her cards saying, "These poor people. Do you realize some of them will get their card after I'm dead! Too bad, I'm writing to them anyhow."

She wrote to friends, cousins in Italy, Australia and even sent birthday cards to her brother Sonny and her niece Anastasia who shared a birthday in June! I promised they would get them. She did not read the notes to me, so I don't know exactly what was on her mind. Later, one of my friends gave me the card Mom mailed to her:

Dearest Deirdre,

Thank you from my heart for all your little notes; the comfort they give me cannot be expressed. We really don't know each other except what Roger and Donna relate to us, but somehow you have a special place in my heart. It's as if you know without my telling you what's going on in my life.

It's a big pill to swallow, and swallow I must. No other way out. But God is sooooo good. He uses all the balm Jesus gives me to make it easier to swallow. I'm so blessed by my children and spouses. They are incredible in the joy, comfort and balm they give us.

I pray for your peace of mind in your own life and pray God's blessing on all of you. We will both continue to pray, my dear Deirdre.

Anna

Mom had no illusions. She knew exactly what was happening to her and got the most out of each day, without tears, without complaints, without anger. She exuded peace. It was as if her heart was guarded in every way.

She began another card and suddenly asked, "What's today's date?"

"April 11."

She stopped short and took a quick breath of air. As soon as our eyes met, I knew.

"It's our anniversary. Your dad and I would have been married 61 years today." Enough said.

Just then, the phone rang. It was Nurse Carol so we reminded her that we were meeting at the Blue Dolphin for lunch. Since Mom had suffered the episode with pain earlier, she decided to come to the house first to check on her condition. As usual, she was wonderful with Mom. Reluctantly, Mom agreed to a stronger dose of Oxycontin in the evening so she could wake up without pain. But first, Carol explained, "You don't have to take this, Mrs. Colibas. I know you don't like it because it slows your speech and makes you feel groggy. But, it's a trade off. You have to deal with the side effects or live with the pain." It's your choice.

Recalling that morning, Mom chose the pill. Carol also gave us Oxyfast in a dropper for emergencies. Its effect was instantaneous when a few drops were placed under the tongue.

When Mom went back to her bedroom to get ready to go, Carol took me aside and spoke quickly but very quietly so Mom couldn't hear. "You do realize that I am only going to lunch because I believe this is one of the things on your mother's list. She needs to do this before she can let go. It is very important to her, and we need to help her work down that list to have peace. I think she is getting closer. However, she wants to make it through Easter and see Roger. I could be wrong, but I want you to be prepared."

I told her I understood perfectly and said, "Whatever she wants, she gets. She rules, and my brother and his wife feel the same way. As Mom has said, there will be plenty of time for grieving—but now, we are going to 'do' lunch!" I felt the chill of things to come, but shook it off as Mom reappeared with a smile of anticipation for the Easter lunch she had arranged.

It took two of us to help Mom to the car without her walker, and Carol followed us to the Blue Dolphin where Helen was waiting. We had a wonderful time with Mom insisting, "Now I want you to order whatever you want, and don't worry about the cost. This is on me!" The conversation was light and friendly—a perfect ladies' luncheon with

Mom actively participating. But half way through the meal she became rather quiet. Her energy was being sapped by the dreaded disease, but thankfully, she had no pain.

After we paid the bill, we slowly walked to the parking lot and said good-bye to Carol. Helen followed us home. The plan was for her to stay with Mom while I did the Easter food shopping according to the grocery list Mom prepared. On the way home, Mom could barely keep her eyes open and said uncharacteristically, "Do you think Helen would mind if I took a nap when we got home, or would she be insulted?"

"Mom, of course she wouldn't mind. That's what she's here for, to keep you company, and it would give me peace of mind knowing she was with you while I go to the store. I don't want you to be alone even for a second. Take a little power nap, and then you can visit."

"I've never done that with Helen. We always have a great time. She is such a wonderful person and I enjoy her company so much, but I can't help it. I'm so sleepy."

"It's the medication," I told her. "Besides, you have always been the one to take care of Helen, baking cookies and meals for her to take home. She always said that you take better care of her than she does of you. She'll be delighted to sit and read a book while you rest a while. It will give her a great sense of purpose. Besides, you promised her she could help you when the time comes."

"Good. Then I'll do just that. But you had better get the right ham, the low-salt one. I want to make sure we have a really good Easter dinner. And I want chocolates, and we still have to bake the lamb cake."

As soon as we helped her into bed, she fell into a deep, peaceful sleep. Helen truly was needed, but not as much for Mom as for me. I allowed myself the luxury of tears, as we noted how fast her body was failing. Carol said it on Monday and now Helen confirmed the situation, "It's going to get worse, my dear. You must be strong."

It seemed like only minutes before Mom appeared in the doorway of the living room, and asked incredulously, "Are you both still here? Did you get all the shopping done?"

"Not yet. I'm going now. You know how it is when you talk to Helen; time just flies by. I'll go now."

She was upset with me. "You can't expect Helen to stay. Do you know how long she's been with us?" Mom was always worried about being a burden to someone else.

"Don't worry about me," said Helen with her big grin and twinkling eyes. "I have no place to go. We can have our own visit now while Donna does the shopping. Come here and sit with me."

I did the fastest shopping anyone has ever done at the closest store, not where Mom told me to go. Unfortunately, they did not carry the brand of ham that Mom specifically wanted me to buy. When I returned, the first thing Mom asked was, "Did you get the ham?" She was irritated. "You were supposed to get the ham yesterday," she said with an admonishing tone. I reassured her there was plenty of time to get a ham for Easter Sunday, adding, "After all, it is only Wednesday."

She didn't want to hear that. She was such an organized person and believed in making lists and planning ahead. Menus always hung on the refrigerator along with shopping and to-do lists so she wouldn't forget anything. Beside each item you would see check marks indicating "done" or dashes that meant "still to do or buy." The menu was on the fridge, but the list was in her head and she wanted to mentally check one more thing off as "done." She was determined to be in charge of Easter dinner and make sure we followed all the traditions she taught us.

After Helen left, I began thinking how we would spend the evening without dwelling on John or her failing condition, but then the phone rang.

It was John's counselor from the VA who called to inform us they were getting ready to send him back home. I moved to the other room where Mom couldn't hear me and said, "Over my dead body." Apparently the woman calling, assuming the role of John's advocate, did not believe the severity of Mom's situation. She was testing the waters to see if his coming home was an option while they were still working with him. They knew nothing about John's past except from him, so I began to tell her about his problems. My voice carried and Mom got the gist of my conversation and asked to speak to the woman herself.

"Would you like to get a medical and psychological history from his only caregiver for the past 33 years?" I handed the phone to Mom.

Mom knew of his deep-seated problems which began in childhood and ultimately developed into obsessions and various antisocial behaviors. This time Mom asked me to leave the room. She did not want to reveal her secret life with John to me. But I listened anyway.

She recapped her condition and the many doctors with whom she had spoken over the years on behalf of John. She said that she wanted to confide in her only if she could be certain that the information she was about to give would be passed onto his doctor. "You are his last hope—

and mine, since I can no longer care for him. He needs professional care for the rest of his life now, and I can't go to my grave with the information about him if revealing details would help the doctors care for him."

I listened from the other room until I heard Mom begin to cry. When I took the phone from her grasp, her hand went limp. Walking away from my mother, I asked the social worker if she now understood how imperative it was for them to continue treating John and help us find an assisted living facility for him. She seemed finally to comprehend the reality of the situation, and said she would call back with a time for us to meet with John's doctor.

Now that Mom knew I overheard the conversation, she unburdened her soul to me in even greater detail, giving examples of her humiliation and shame brought on by John's behavior over the years. As she spoke through her tears, I felt my body melting in sympathy, hot with anger and rage, then icy cold as the chills went up and down my spine. My feelings overwhelmed and frightened me.

Mom asked that I never reveal the details to anyone except Roger and Larry. She was confident that they had hearts of compassion and would be capable of forgiving this very sick man, as she hoped I would. While I shook inside, she was the one who needed to be calmed. I gave her an anti-anxiety pill hospice had provided and both of us sat quietly listening to soothing music.

When Mom had dozed off, I went into my bedroom to scream into my pillow for the burden she carried on her shoulders for 33 years. It all made sense now. Her insomnia. Her over-protection of him. Her assuming all the household responsibilities, handling the finances, and not pressuring him to work outside the home. It all made sense.

Over the years when we would ask her how she could continue to live with him, she would say, "And what am I supposed to do? Leave him? Who would take care of him? He would become a street person. Nobody will take care of him. I'm the one who promised to care for him until we are parted by death." In order to be true to her vows, Mom had to learn how to forgive. She could not live with the guilt if she abandoned him. I was reminded of someone else who said, "Father, forgive them for they know not what they do." It was I who felt guilt and shame.

Mom had a divine gift of being able to truly forgive and forget. Throughout the rest of the day, she characteristically acted as if nothing had ever happened. We never spoke of it again. I had to put what I had just learned away in another compartment of my mind. Mom was still alive and there was more living to do. To help me as much as her, I suggested we call her friend Renee and ask her to come over for a visit.

Her eyes lit up. "Good idea. Maybe she'd like to play some cards."

I agreed but added, "Even if we don't play cards, you can have a good visit just with her instead of having all the other ladies over. It will be more relaxing." Renee was happy to come especially as I whispered to her on the bedroom phone that Mom was beginning to fail.

After dinner, Renee arrived, and before too long June and Pat came for an unannounced visit. Mom's house was always open to everyone. The look on the faces of her friends when they saw her said it all. They knew there had been a drastic change since John was hospitalized on Monday. Pain medication slows you down, and word quickly spread throughout her network of friends by the next day.

Thursday, April 12

Mom awoke in pain again, but this time I was ready. Just a drop or two of Oxyfast did the trick within seconds. With the aid of the walker and the security of my hold on her from behind, she was able to get to the bathroom then back to bed. She fell asleep again but when she awoke she was pain-free and hungry. However, the drugs had a cumulative effect. Lifting her to a standing position was awkward and stressful for both of us because she had always been so fast, bounding out of bed, ready to attack the day. Even now, she refused to stay down and made it to the kitchen table to eat properly. I thought what a difference a day makes and remembered how she got me out of bed on school days.

As soon as I heard the alarm, I would pull the covers over my head. That did little to muffle Mom's voice, "Everybody up! Up and at 'em!" She would clap her hands. "Donnnnnnn, Larrrrrrrrr, do you hear me? Are you awake?" How I hated that then, but now I longed to hear that strong, purposeful voice calling to me! Even two days ago, she had said, "So, what shall we do first today?" This was typical of the way she attacked each new day. This one was different.

Instead I heard apologies. "I'm so sorry, honey, to have to lean on you; don't hurt yourself."

"Don't be silly, Mom. I'm not hurting myself." *Stay in the moment, Donna! There will be plenty of time to cry later.* "We'll just take it slowly. Once you get some food in you, you'll feel better." Soft boiled eggs. She loved them served with bits of soft bread mixed in with the eggs. Very nourishing and exactly what she fed to us when we were little, especially when we were sick.

She wanted to feed herself, but because of the drugs, I had to help guide the spoon in her hand to her mouth. After she ate, she sat on the couch with her feet up, and settled in to try and read a book. Just then the phone rang. It was Carol from hospice checking on her. After telling her of the difficulty getting Mom in and out of bed, she suggested they send over a hospital bed. But I didn't tell Mom. I used my bedroom phone to call her neighbor Sue and asked if she could help me when the delivery came.

When it arrived, Mom was furious. She screamed, "No, no! You are not going to turn my house into a hospital. I do not want a bed in my living room!" The adrenalin rush must have been fierce because before we could blink, she bolted upright on her own and burst into tears. Sue and I walked her into the bedroom, and told the delivery man to wait.

"Mom, Mom. Nothing's going to change. We are not going to put a bed in the living room or dining room. We are just going to switch your double bed for a single bed, one that will be easier for you to get in and out of. Please stay calm. If it doesn't work, we'll get rid of it."

Turning to Sue, "Sue, you keep her steady on the walker while I get a chair." I brought a dining room armchair into the bedroom and placed it in the little hallway next to her walk-in closet that led to her bathroom. There she could sit and look through to a large window at the front of the house with her back to where we would be working. We moved quickly.

Amazingly, Sue and I stripped the bed and moved the mattress, box spring, frame and headboard into the garage, and used her bedspread as a dust cover. While we were doing that the man sent from hospice was setting up her new bed. We vacuumed around him, and the instant he finished, Sue and I made the bed with Mom's own linens. After we repositioned the night stands and chairs, we helped Mom turn around to a very familiar setting. It took us less than 15 minutes. "See, Mom, nothing has changed except the size of your bed. You are going to be so much more comfortable, and it will be so much more convenient for you when you want to get in bed."

Sue remained with her as she calmed down while I completed the required paperwork. When I walked back into the bedroom, Mom had asked Sue, herself a trained aide, to help her wash and change into a clean night dress and bed jacket. She then rested in her new bed.

Later that afternoon, she was up and back in the living room. Right after she got settled, the doorbell rang. More neighbors—Grace, Pat, June and Pauline came to visit. You would never have known anything had happened that day. It was a lovely visit. I made coffee and served some cookies Mom had made the week before. Everyone was placed immediately at ease by Mom's cheerful attitude. They talked about clubhouse events, and plans for Easter. The ladies didn't stay long, and after they left, Mom needed to rest again. It had been an exhausting morning.

Once in bed, she asked for her favorite Italian CD, and I entertained her by pretending I was dancing with someone like the night we arrived in Alcamo, Sicily. Her cousins took us to a nightclub with friends. Mom said, "I used to love to dance when I was young. I still do you know, but now I dance in my mind." My throat tightened and I forced a smile saying that I remember how she loved to jitterbug. After a few minutes, I could see her eyes wanting to close, so I changed the music to something more soothing so she could nap.

Larry called from work as she slept. It would take two and a half hours to get to Mom, and he wanted to know if he should come before Saturday after he heard how fast she seemed to be failing. Knowing how busy he was, I told him to wait a while to make sure I wasn't overreacting. I wasn't.

I sat by her side as she slept, and then Mom opened her eyes. Smiling and stroking her hand, I asked her opinion about whether or not Larry and Connie should come. "Hey, Mom, Larry called earlier and wanted to know if you'd like to see him today instead of Saturday." She was slow to respond, so I asked again. "Today is Thursday, Mom, and Larry wants to know if you want him to come now instead of waiting for Easter weekend."

All she could do was nod her head, "Yes."

Refusing to give into my desire to cry, I gently said, "Okay, Mom, I'll call him at work from the other room so you can continue to rest. I'll be right back."

He answered. "Larry, Mom is asking for you." That's all I had to say.

"I'm on my way. I'll call Connie at work and we will be there as fast as we can."

"Don't panic. She's okay; but sleeping a lot this afternoon. Be careful. I love you."

Mom heard me enter her room and looked at me. "Okay, Mom. He's on his way." She just nodded approvingly. I sat next to her and, throughout the rest of the afternoon, read to her, stroked her hand or her hair, played a variety of her favorite music, and silently prayed with thanksgiving that she had no pain. She looked so peaceful and so beautiful.

Around 5:30 p.m., she opened her eyes, speaking only in a whisper, "Donna, I don't think I'm going to be here when Larry arrives."

My heart stopped. The air pressure in the room seemed to change and the oxygen thinned. I took a breath to respond and tried to match her calm. "What do you mean? Larry and Connie are on their way."

She repeated, "I don't think I'm going to be here when they get here."

"Would you like me to call their house to see if they left yet?" She slowly nodded and I pressed the programmed button on the cordless phone by her bed and walked out of the room. Connie answered. "Connie, is Larry there?"

"Yes, he's loading the car. We're leaving now."

"Get him to the phone - quick!"

He spoke, "Hi." And I heard Connie pick up on the other line.

"Mom wants to talk to you. But you need to stay calm. She asked me to call to see if you left the house yet, because she doesn't think she's going to be here when you get here. She wants to talk to you now." There was a pause. "Are you okay?"

"Yes," he said quietly.

As I walked back into the room, I said, "Stay calm; I'm giving the phone to Mom now."

It was hard for her to begin talking, but once she did there was no alarm in her voice. I listened on the extension as she spoke gently and factually. "Larry, I don't think I'm going to be here when you get here, and I wanted to tell you I love you."

"Yes you will. You're not going anywhere yet! We'll be there in a couple of hours. We're leaving right now."

"I can't promise, Larry. I think I'm going to leave before then. I just wanted you to know how much I love you both."

"We know, Mom. We love you, too." I could hear the strain in his voice and the tears in Connie's. "You'll be there. Just hold on. We're on our way."

"I can't promise; but I'll try. I don't know. I feel like I'm going now. I love you." She handed me the phone as she drifted off.

"Larry, Connie. It's me. Be careful. Listen to me. I need you. I need you. I need you. Please drive safely. Don't let me lose you, too."

"We will. We will. We're on our way. We love you."

"I love you, too." *Click. Click.*

The world stood still while Mom slept. I sat there watching her and studying the regularity of her breathing. As I examined the possibility of Mom dying while I was alone with her, I could feel the chemical changes taking place throughout my body. It felt like the barometric pressure in the room dropped and rose again. My skin tingled. What would I do if I was alone with her when she died?

I was grateful for all our preparation. There was nothing left to do but stay in the moment. Everything was done—the cemetery plot, the shipping, the casket, the obituaries for Florida and Pittsburgh. Hospice had the phone number to call to activate the process. The hospice nurse told me that when Mom actually does leave us, all we need to do is be with her and each other. We were to relax and call them—but only when we were ready. There was no need to rush. Because of our advanced planning and advice, there was a sense of security and empowerment in this uncontrollable situation. All that was left to do was to pray for Mom, and Larry and Connie's safe arrival.

She opened her eyes and I kissed her. "Joya mia," I whispered. It was the loving greeting Grandma had used throughout her life. It means, "You are my joy." Looking down at my beautiful mother, I was at peace. "You're okay, Mom. Just you and me together, but Larry and Connie are on their way and Roger will be here on Sunday. Don't forget you want to see him, too." She nodded her head and smiled.

"Do you want to listen to more music or Nigel?" She mouthed Nigel's name, so together we listened to the CD of our dear Nigel reciting healing prayers for us when our own words failed. All I could do was whisper, "Jesus" and silently pray the Prayer of Abandonment once more.

Father, I abandon my mother into your hands.
Do with her what you will.
Whatever you may do, I thank you.
I am ready for all. I accept all.
Let only Your will be done in her…
Into your hands I commend her soul;
I offer it to you with all the love of my heart…
Without reserve,
And with boundless confidence,
For you are our Father.
Amen.

Time seemed to stand still until I heard the horn and looked at the clock. It was nearly 8:30 p.m. "They're here, Mom." The door swung open and Larry and Connie were in her bedroom in a flash. Mom was thrilled to see them. Her eyes lit up and big smiles spread across everyone's face. Mom even lifted her arms to receive the plethora of hugs and kisses. What sweet relief to experience such joy and hear the laughter. I never knew we would be given so much grace and poise at a time like this. Nobody cried and there was no mention of Mom's phone call and fears. We were all just happy.

As Larry talked about the traffic and relief that they arrived safely, Mom started shoving the covers as if she were going to get out of bed! We looked at each other and not knowing what to do, we asked, "Where are you going?"

"Gotta get up. Time to eat!" Mom actually said this with a straight face, but we laughed in amazement. Shrugging our shoulders and without words, we agreed to honor her every wish.

There was no attempt to restrain her, no admonition that she would be better off resting in bed, no platitudes.

"Okay! Let's help you." As Larry and Connie took charge of Mom, I ran into the kitchen. For years, I had been Mom's sous chef, but tonight I would run the kitchen solo.

Connie and Larry prepared her for the journey to the table—first a trip to the bathroom, a quick wash and comb of the hair, then the robe. She was too weak to walk, even with the help of two people. A creative thought emerged. Let's put her in the dining room armchair!"

The chair that sat at the head of the table had been placed by the bed for visitors, and the next thing I saw was Mom being carried in it from the bedroom. It was like a scene from the film Cleopatra where Elizabeth Taylor looked down upon her slaves from her portable throne as she made her entrance through the adoring crowds. There she was, flanked by slaves Larry and Connie, looking like a queen—a reluctant queen—but a queen nonetheless.

Mom felt silly, and yelled, "You're going to hurt your back!" She apologized for being so much trouble, but we diffused her negativity with humor and kidded her about being our favorite monarch. It was not only wonderful to see her out of bed, but as we began to eat Mom was able to feed herself. If we tried to help steady her shaky hand, she responded with irritation, "I can do this myself!" We could hardly believe the rally.

Later, after we gave Mom her tea and pills, she went to bed and slept through the night and so did I. Connie and Larry slept on the sofa bed just outside her room and checked on her periodically.

Good Friday, April 13

Friday was nurse Carol's day, and when we told our Cleopatra story, she arranged for a wheelchair to be delivered. It was a gift from God because not only did it give Mom dignity and comfort, it also relieved her concern about Larry's back when he helped her move from room to room. In addition to the wheelchair, hospice provided a Home Health Aide to help us care for her physical needs.

Connie, being a nurse herself, was capable of being "in charge" of this aspect of her care. However, Mom was comfortable with hospice support and it allowed her to maintain her dignity with her children. The home aide also brought additional supplies we would need to care for Mom during the day and throughout the night.

First, Mom now had a bedside commode so she didn't have to take what felt like the extra mile to bathroom. Having the facilities so close was much easier for everyone. They also brought her an "egg crate," a bubbled piece of foam that fitted on top of her new mattress. Besides being more comfortable, it helped prevent bedsores if she were to lie too long in any one position.

Precautions were taken to ensure sterile hygiene was practiced by providing rubber gloves, orange sticks for cleaning nails, liners for the bed to help lift and keep linens clean, disposable panties, bacterial sprays, room deodorizers, and the like. You name it, we had it; but Mom never was aware of our storehouse of goodies. We kept things out of sight, under a skirted bedroom table for the television or the closet so she never had the feeling of being in a hospital. Nor was she embarrassed when visitors came to call. She always did hate clutter.

Working together to create this loving environment was a bonding experience for our family. We were united with a common goal—to give Mom peace, comfort, security and tender loving care. Family harmony was always very important to her, and later we would hear her whisper as she drifted in and out of her dreams, "No discord; no discord."

Because the hospice aide knew how important it was to give as much control to the patient as possible, she asked Mom if she wanted to be washed. To our surprise, she answered, "I want to take a shower." And so she did!

It took two people to get Mom into the bathroom and undress her. The aide guided the process of transferring Mom from the bed to the shower chair, using the wheel chair; and clever Connie put on her bathing suit so she could help wash Mom from the top of her head to the tip of her toes. As they tended to her personal needs, I changed the sheets and cleaned the bedroom.

All of a sudden, I heard Mom, give me a mocking call, "Donna, they're skirting me." My ears perked up, and after a pause, I heard my mother wistfully repeat, "They're skirting, skirting me. They're skirting me." Only I understood what she was saying and ran to the shower door.

"I hear you, Mom. I hear you. I know what you're saying. I remember. I remember. I love you, Mom." Flashbacks—Mom was having a flashback—and so did I.

Eighteen years earlier, Grandma lived the last 21 days of her life in a hospice facility in Pittsburgh. It took more than two people to care for her round-the-clock needs since she was paralyzed along one side of her body. The nurses were wonderful and listened attentively to Grandma's stories. They hung on her every word and met her every need. We had decorated her room with pictures and family mementoes to create a familiar environment. The room looked like home with a chest of drawers, night stand, and bedside lamps—no harsh fluorescent lighting.

Since it was hard to care for Grandma wearing her own night clothes, one of the hospice nurses bought a supply of ladies' nightgowns—floral prints, ruffles and bows—and made hospital gowns out of them. She split the gowns completely up the back and attached matching ribbons to the neck and back so the gown would not slip off the shoulders. A regular night gown, which they tried to simulate, would bunch up under the patients' back and legs, but this lay neatly on the side of the patient's body. If anyone had an "accident" changing the gown would be easy and comfortable for the patient.

One Friday afternoon when Mom and I visited Grandma after work, we asked her how her day had been. She became animated and said, "It was wonderful! Such a wonderful day."

"Really? What happened?" Mom asked.

"They skirted me! They skirted me! Wonderful! They skirted and skirted!"

"Skirted?" Mom and I looked at each other, both stumped at what she could mean.

"They put me in a chair and skirted me!"

The light bulb went on. "They must have given her a shower," I said.

"Yes!" Grandma said, "They skirted me and washed everything! Even-a my

hair." Then she started to laugh. Cackle, actually. That's how Grandma sounded when she thought something was really funny. "They even-a washed my butterfly!"

"Your butterfly?"

"Yes. That's what Mary calls this." She pointed 'down there' and cackled some more.

A Grandma memory, simple pleasures we take for granted, recalled from November 1983, but today is Good Friday the 13th in April 2001. Grandma always said, "You too will be where I am some day. Dying is part of life. I can handle passing from this life to the next and so will you." That concept doesn't really sink in until it happens to you. Now, for the second time in my life, I heard, "They're skirting me!" Mom was mimicking Grandma. She knew all too well what was happening.

Because of a shared memory, just a word or phrase was all that was needed to recall a memory frozen in time. But now, I didn't want to laugh. I wanted to scream, "No, no, not you, Mom. I'm not ready to let you go!" All I could say was, "I hear you, Mom. I understand. I love you."

There's no time to cry. I had to finish making the bed, get her clean nightgown ready. I slit it up the back, and prepared to do her hair. I knew that Grandma and she would be together before long, and some day it would be my turn. Why cry? Dying is part of life. And if Mom had to die, I was determined to do whatever I could to make sure the experience was the best it could be. To do that, I needed to stay in the moment.

After Connie and the aide finished dressing her, Larry wheeled Mom into the kitchen. There was an electrical outlet between the kitchen and the dining room where I could plug in the hair dryer and the curling iron. I did what I had been doing since I was 12 years old, and fixed my mother's hair. She always said it looked better than when she went to the beauty shop. Some styling gel massaged onto the head I knew so well, followed by a skillful use of brush and blow dryer and curling iron (rather than rollers, these days), then a comb through, a little teasing, final styling and hair spray. "There! All done. You look gorgeous. Look in the mirror." She loved it! But she was tired.

She wanted to sit on the couch with her feet up—her favorite position. The kitty could jump on her lap or she could play solitaire on a tray, or read. She also could doze if she liked. Today, she wanted to play cards with Larry—Kings in the Corner, a game she learned from one of her lady friends. Her eyesight and concentration were failing, but

Larry pretended not to notice. Soon visitors began to arrive, one after the other—Pauline, Pat, June, and Mom's sister, my Aunt Angie.

Mom was amazing considering her near-death experience of the other evening. Her conversation was cheerful and, as always, did not focus on herself. Instead she wanted to know everybody's Easter plans. Since she had plenty of company, Connie and I took advantage of the situation and slipped out of the house to finally get the ham at Publix—the exact one she wanted. When we got back, the visitors left and Larry helped her back to bed while I planned dinner and cooked the chicken marsala and rice we would eat later.

Larry, Connie and I took turns sitting with her, and whenever she opened her eyes, we held her hand and spoke softly to let Mom know she was not alone. Once again, we did not think she would ever get out of bed again. The day's activity seemed to sap her of any remnants of energy.

Larry and Connie needed to take a nap of their own. They were still recovering from the emotional scare they had the day before when Mom thought she was dying, so I held vigil. All of a sudden, Mom began to stir and became very agitated and confused as if waking from a nightmare, "Where is he, where's John?"

"He's in the hospital, Mom."

"No, he's not. He was just here. I saw him." She was frightened. "He said, 'You thought you were going to get rid of me, didn't you? Well, you're wrong. I'm here and I'm staying right here. You are never going to get rid of me!'"

"Shhh, it's okay, Mom. You were just dreaming. John is not here. He is safe in a hospital. He is never going to hurt you, or scare you, or bring shame on you or this family ever again. He is with the doctors—a whole team of doctors are working with him. He's in a locked unit in the hospital and they are helping him. Shhh, just relax. He is not coming home again, Mom. They're transferring him to the assisted living facility we told you about. You never have to worry about him again. It's finished, Mom."

She breathed out and said, "And so am I," recognizing the finality of it all. "So am I."

I wasn't prepared for that. She closed her eyes, and as she quieted down, I kissed her forehead and stroked her hair as I allowed myself the luxury of tears which were running down my cheeks before I knew it. I could tell no one of the anger I felt. With every fiber of my being I prayed. "Please, God. Heal her mind. I abandon her into your hands, but give her peace on her death bed." I could hardly breathe.

Only two days ago, Mom had told me about the source of her nightmares when she unburdened her soul about John's problem to his social worker and me. I had told Roger by phone, but there had been no chance to tell my brother yet; besides, what would be the point? I needed him to be the clearheaded one when we saw John again. It would only put him in an awkward position. There would be plenty of time later. Right now, I had to focus on Mom's desires. No discord. No pain. No tears. It would be too hard for her to bear.

Still…I sat wondering. Why had she not told me before? She knew we all knew something was wrong with him. Why couldn't she confide in me? Of course, she never wanted to burden us and she wanted us to be kind and gentle with John. She knew we would worry even more than we did about her, about both of them, and she wanted us to be able to live our own lives, not hers. At some level, she experienced life vicariously, through us, because her own dreams of a happy marriage were never realized.

No good thinking of that now. John was out of the house and I did not want to be distracted from caring for our mother. Mom always taught us to focus on the present and not to live in the past. What was it she said? "Don't cry now; I'm still here and we have more memories to make." Did we ever! Mom had a surprise in store for us.

Later that evening, Mom rallied—again. As we recapped what we had been doing while she slept, she began pushing off her covers again, saying, "Gotta get up. Time to eat." That was our cue to go into action.

Connie and Larry got her up, saw to her bathroom needs, and wheeled her into the kitchen for dinner. I warmed up the chicken marsala and rice and we had a lovely meal together. Mom ate as well as she could. Connie cut the chicken in tiny pieces and helped guide her weakened hand as she tried to feed herself. A little chicken; then some rice. "How about some apple sauce? How is it, Mom?"

"Mmm, good!" she said, as she pushed Connie's hand away. "I can do this myself. Mmm, good."

After we had our fill and the dishes were cleared, Mom, still sitting at the kitchen table said, "Well, what are we going to do now?"

"What do you want to do?" we asked with a little chuckle.

"You wanna play cards?" Now we did laugh! "How about a little canasta?" she said enthusiastically. How could we refuse?

I said, "Let's play partners," thinking that the game would go faster and we could help her win. "You and Larry against Connie and me." That was basically how we were sitting at dinner.

Sarcastically Larry said, "This is going to be fun. Mom, you know Connie always wins."

"No, I don't, Larry." Connie lied, especially when it came to playing cards. But then, almost anyone could beat Larry. Playing cards was never his forte.

We winked at each other, got the decks, and began to shuffle. I dealt the cards which meant that Mom was the first to play because she sat to my left. Mom picked up her cards and began to arrange them in her hand. "Oops," we said in unison as she dropped some of them onto her lap.

We all jumped to her aid and she grumbled, "Just a minute, just a minute; I'll get them." And warning us with that card-killer confidence in her posture, she added, "Don't worry Larry, we're going to whip them."

Connie and I laughed and both joked. "Win? You've got to be kidding, Mom. Look who's your partner." Larry laughed, too.

Connie and I winked at each other. Our unspoken plan was to let them win. Then the game started.

Mom was the first one to open and not only put down some good cards, but she had two red three's as well. Connie and I held onto our cards, waiting for a couple of rounds to go by before picking up the pile with one of our pairs. Larry made a couple of plays on the board in front of Mom, and she smiled her card-killer smile, "Good job, boy!"

Connie and I still held our hand and began collecting nothing but wild cards; however, we had nothing to go with them. Mom continued to rack up points and Larry decided to hold back some of his wild cards until later. I discarded to Mom thinking it was a card she could use, but she passed it up. After she picked from the pile, she started moving cards around in her hand and then, slowly and deliberately, she began laying them down.

There we were, Connie and me, sitting with a fist full of high cards, most of them jokers and deuces. Incredulous, we said, "You're not going out, are you?" In silence, she just kept laying down cards. "Mom, answer me! Are you going out?"

Unsuccessfully, she tried to stifle the coy smile on her face and said, "I don't know yet." We sat helplessly as we watched her lay down one card at a time. She revised her answer to, "Maybe," and then with a final flourish, she laid down all her remaining cards!

"Ahhh! You can't go out," Larry, cried. "You have to ask me first."

He was sitting on some high cards he wanted to get rid of himself; but none to compare with what Connie and I had in our hands.

"Sorry, son. But I told you we were going to win; and I wanted to stick 'em." She squealed with delight and looked at me with a great smile of satisfaction. It was brilliant! Still in shock, we counted the minus points in our hands and tallied the score. The next few rounds went pretty much the same way. Connie and I struggled to get back in the game because we are both very competitive. If we had "let" Mom win, she would have known it because she was surprisingly sharp that evening. Mom beat us fair and square! She was back, and as we read each other's mind, someone said, "Can you believe this?"

"Why are you all laughing?" Mom questioned.

Larry answered. "Mom, don't you see the humor in this? Here we are playing cards 24 hours after you called to tell us you didn't think you would be here when we arrived, just yesterday. And now you're sitting here whipping our butts at Canasta!"

She was mortified. Mom rested her bent elbows on the table, put her face in her hands, and nearly cried, "I'm such a fraud." Shaking her head with her face still covered, she repeated, "I'm such a fraud. Oh!" she gasped and looked up in a flash, "Please don't tell Roger. It'll be all over Connecticut that I'm a fraud. I'm so embarrassed."

"Don't feel bad, Mom. We're thrilled. You really did think you were dying; we know that."

"I really did!" She said, with such a pathetic, yet endearing, whine.

"We know; but we're so glad you didn't," I said, "And Roger isn't going to tell anybody. He's going to call any minute to share a prayer and the lyrics to a hymn they sang at church today at the Good Friday service. He just got back from his trip and can't wait to see you."

Chuckling, Connie chimed in. "And, Mom, remember you always said we should make memories. We're going to remember you like this—laughing, playing cards and having a good time. This is a gift we will enjoy forever. So don't feel bad."

"Okay, okay. But the next time I call and tell you I'm dying, don't come!" We roared with laughter, but she was serious. "I'm so sorry I scared you. It must have been awful." We never talked about it again.

Just then the phone rang, and it was Roger who had a long talk with Mom about the people, especially the children, in the Dominican Republic he met on his trip with Habitat for Humanity. She delighted in all of his travels and interests. They were kindred spirits. They ended their telephone visit with his reading the words our church choir sang from Mendelssohn's *Elijah.* It was dedicated to her that Good Friday afternoon:

> For God commanded angels to watch over you;
> That they shall protect you; in all your living keep you,
> For their hands will uphold and guide you,
> Lest you dash your foot against a stone, stumbling.
>
> For God commanded angels to watch over you;
> For their hands will uphold and guide you,
> For they shall protect you, in all your living keep you,
> Protect and keep you."

She was moved to think that she would be remembered by the singers she enjoyed so much when she visited. "Can you bring the music with you so I can read it again?" she asked. When she handed the phone back to me, something told me to ask him to bring the Prayer Book from church as well.

Mom showed signs of weariness from sitting in the wheelchair for such a long a time, but it was too early to go to bed. "Let's go in the living room so I can lie on the couch for a while; maybe I'll try to read," Mom said.

We talked about our Easter traditions and how she was still upset that I left so much of the shopping until the last minute. Inwardly, I felt a twinge of hurt because she did not recognize all that I had done for her that week. I admonished myself, "Such pride!" Mom was just being normal, not dwelling on the looming loss we were coming to terms with as her body failed her. She never dwelt on the negative. She would yell at us when we did something wrong, but then smother us with kisses in the next minute. Forgive and forget was something she mastered. I wanted to be like her.

Her last holiday, Easter—a celebration of the Resurrection—had to be special. "And don't forget the candy tomorrow," she said. "Get a large chocolate egg filled with fudge, nuts and fruit like the ones we used to buy in Pittsburgh." And then there was the Lamb Cake. I was to bake the cake, and she wanted to make Connie her chocolate cream pie—and she wanted to color Easter Eggs.

"Okay, Mom, I've got the list. Connie and I will do the last minute shopping and we'll be all set for Easter. I promise." She just looked at me with that "wait and see" look and we changed the subject. She tried to read, but could not. Again she wondered if it was the cancer or the drugs that affected her eyes.

After a while we convinced her that it was okay to go to bed a little earlier than usual because it was nearing the time to take her pain medicine. She said, "I feel so out of it when I take it. I want to be alert and able to talk better. It makes my tongue thick."

"We understand you just fine, but it's your choice, Mom. Just remember what Carol said. You can choose pain or grogginess."

"Okay I guess you're right; but let's wait a little bit longer," she said. We did and in fact we listened to the Garrison Keeler tape of *Bruno the Fishing Dog* on Lake Woebegone. It made us laugh and talk about our childhood and what wonderful memories we had about being at the cottage with Grandma and Grandpa as kids. She finally said, "Okay, I guess it's time to go to bed." We all settled down for bed, and the three of us took turns checking on Mom throughout the night.

Saturday, April 14

The morning routine was pretty much the same. A little Oxyfast when she awoke very early in pain, falling back to sleep, and then Connie and Larry getting her ready for the day. Just as Connie was about to begin to give her a sponge bath, the home health aide arrived. She took over and we were pleased to see how well she treated Mom. She cleaned her nails on her hands and feet, brushed her teeth, and artfully changed the sheets with Mom still in the bed. Before leaving, she checked and replenished all the supplies we needed. Mom was grateful for the home aide from hospice because she really didn't want her children to have to take care of her, even though we viewed it as a privilege. It helped her maintain her dignity with us.

When she was cleaned and ready for the day, Larry went in to sit with Mom while the aide gave Connie and me some pointers. "I noticed when I brushed her teeth this morning she still had rice in her mouth."

"Oh, my God!" Connie and I stifled a shriek. "That's from dinner last night. We knew she wasn't chewing very well, but we never dreamed…"

She consoled us. "It's okay, but from now on I think you had better stick with soft foods, nothing that could irritate her throat or cause her to choke if she doesn't swallow it, and try to get her to drink lots of fluids." We planned future meals accordingly.

This day she let us feed her. We could see the change in her body with the combination of the rapidly spreading cancer and the cumulative effects of the medication. Her mind, her attitude and her spirit, however, were terrific despite the slowing of her speech. She ate a small bowl of oatmeal, apple juice, and took her vitamin pills with water that she drank through a straw at this point. Yes, she still wanted to take her vitamin pills! Then it was back to bed to listen to music and recover from the exertion of the morning's routine.

I called Aunt Angie and Aunt Jennie, Mom's two sisters who lived nearby and suggested they come to visit as soon as they could. They would arrive after lunch.

Mom did not stay in bed for very long. She wanted to be where the action was. As noon approached, she said, "Do you know what I could go for—a hamburger!"

We laughed and, of course, said, "That's a great idea, Mom. I haven't had a hamburger on the grill for a long time."

"Me neither," she said. "I want a big, juicy hamburger."

Connie jumped in the car and went to the store while I set the table and Larry turned on the grill. Of course, Mom could not hold the hamburger, but we chopped it up and fed it to her with a fork. Connie was on her left with the apple sauce, and I, on the right, cut the meat into tiny pieces with tomato and mayo. Chew. Swallow. Drink. She felt as if she was having a taste of forbidden food and it was delicious. For the past two years, red meat was definitely not on her cancer diet! Mom laughed and said, "At this stage, what does it matter?"

In fact, Mom was feeling so good that afternoon, she noted how well the Oxycontin knocked out her toothache. She said, "I was going to go to the dentist, but I figured - what for?" She shrugged her shoulders then seemed to be alone with her thoughts for a moment, before she shared them. "I also need new cushions for these kitchen chairs and I was going to buy them before Easter, but what's the point. They'll do for now." She laughed. "Don't have to worry about that anymore!" She was in the process of letting go of the everyday details of life.

We swallowed the lump in our throats and joined in, "Yes, and isn't it wonderful that God has answered your prayers to be pain free, Mom. You don't even have a toothache! And the chairs look fine."

She said, "The real problem with the cushions is that I washed them last week before you got here, Donna, and the covers shrunk. I had to take the padding out to get the cushion back in before you got here."

What? Was she really doing housework, baking cookies, and taking care of John until just five days ago? Has it only been five days?

After lunch, Mom wanted to go back into the living room. It was Larry's turn once again to jump into action. He was Mom's gentle giant and my heart swelled with pride, love, and admiration as I watched my 6'4" baby brother lift his mother in and out of bed over the last two days, carry her to the bathroom, place her in the wheelchair, hold her hand, and read the Psalms to her. Mom quietly said to him, "You have such wonderful arms and such big hands. I feel safe when you hold me." Once again, he placed her comfortably on the couch, as Connie and I cleaned the kitchen.

Mom sat holding her book, but because she could no longer focus, it sat on her lap as we talked. Larry watched TV in the family room, while we three women reviewed the Easter menu, our to-do list and waited for the visit from her sisters.

As we talked, Mom looked at me and said, "What? I can't hear you. Is something wrong with my hearing, too?" Mom then mocked me by mumbling in hushed tones.

"Sorry," I said smiling. "I guess I'm just trying to be gentle."

"Gentle is good, but you're practically whispering. I never have any difficulty in hearing Connie!"

We all laughed, and Connie agreed saying loudly, "Yep. Nobody ever says they can't hear me!"

"Yeah, but you make some people jump when you talk." I said this loudly so Mom could hear me.

But Mom turned to look at Connie and asked, "Why is she yelling?"

We cracked up and just as I said, "Ya can't win," Aunt Angie arrived, so Connie and I went shopping. If anything happened, both Larry and Aunt Angie would be with Mom. We went to the Mall and made the rounds of specialty candy shops and bought a variety of homemade Easter eggs including her favorite fruit and nut, molded pieces of dark chocolate, solid chocolate eggs wrapped in colored foil, green grass, Easter egg dye, jelly beans, and tulips for her dining room and kitchen tables. She already had the Easter balloon which I had bought during my last visit. What a celebration of resurrected life this was going to be!

When we arrived home, we found that Aunt Angie had been joined by some of Mom's closest lady friends. They were having a great time, and left around 4 p.m. Aunt Angie went home but promised to return the next day, Easter Sunday, with Aunt Jennie who had been unable to come. She was having a bad day due to advancing Parkinson's disease.

All this stimulating activity sapped Mom's energy. In her bedroom, we had positioned three chairs, two on the right, and one on the left of her bed.

Her hospital tray table on wheels held her boom box and it was large enough to hold the supply of her favorite CD's and a box of tissues. She closed her eyes and enjoyed having us talk or read to her as she drifted off.

After about an hour, there was a knock at the door. It was like Grand Central Station. Neighbors Grace and Sue had come to say "good-bye" because of what they heard from her earlier visitors. Mom was as gracious as ever. "Ohhh. It's Grace and Sue. Come in. Sit down."

"Oh! No, Ann. We wanted to stop by to see you, and didn't know you were sleeping."

"Don't be silly. Sit down. Would you like a cup of tea?"

"No! No! We won't be staying long."

"What are you talking about? You like tea. We always have a cup of tea together. Just because I'm in bed doesn't mean you can't have a cup of tea!" They gave in.

"Good. Now go make the tea, Donna." I turned to leave the room. "And," pausing to wait for me to turn around, "Don't forget the cookies! I made them myself!" She said proudly.

"You made them!" they gasped. "When?"

"Last week just before Donna arrived."

So Mom and her best friends had a bedside tea party. Laughter floated through the house with talk about neighborhood news. She told them about John's hospitalization and how wonderful it was that he was finally getting help. They complimented Mom on her cookies and thanked her for all her parties she hosted over the years, especially this past Christmas when 35 neighbors and friends came to her champagne-dessert party. Mom loved champagne on special occasions, and was glad to hear her friends would never forget their good times together.

As they were about to leave, she pointed and said, "Give me my book. I want to read something to you." It took a moment but she read from her Daily Word Devotional. Struggling with failing eyesight, Mom used the words in this chosen passage to help her convey her feelings with gentleness and calm:

"I pray for my loved ones with heartfelt faith, love, and assurance. I include all people who are near and dear to me in my prayers today for life, love, and wisdom.…God bless my loved ones with enthusiasm for life and living. Bless them with prosperity in matters large and small, and with strength of body and spirit…Protect and guide them every day of their lives. And, God, I thank you for the blessing of their companionship and friendship in my life."

Then she said, "There's one more thing." Turning to me she pointed to the Bible, but she choked up and couldn't speak. I said, "Do you want me to read something for you, Mom?" She nodded her head. "What do you want me to read?"

Her energy was draining, so she simply said, "You know."

"Psalm 103?" She nodded again, and I knew what she was doing. She wanted to use Scripture, God's words, to tell her friends how she was feeling and to give them a final message of encouragement.

"Bless the Lord, Oh my soul...And forget not all his benefits. He forgives all my sins and heals all my diseases; he redeems my life from the pit and crowns me with love and compassion. He satisfies my desires with good things so that my youth is renewed like the eagles....The Lord is compassionate and gracious, slow to anger, abounding in love...He knows how we are formed, he remembers that we are dust...The Lord's love is with those who fear him, and his righteousness with their children's children—with those who keep his covenant and remember to obey his precepts...Bless the Lord, you his angels, you mighty ones who do his bidding, who obey his word. Bless the Lord, all his heavenly hosts, you his servants who do his will...Bless the Lord, O my soul."

When I had finished, she was able to say, "Please remember that for the rest of your lives, and—remember me."

Her friends were on the verge of tears, but they held it together long enough to tell her that they would never forget her. After they kissed her good-bye, my very tired mother slept. Again, true to form, this strong-willed woman rallied again later that evening when, pushing back the covers, she asked to come to the table for dinner. With delight, we complied with her wishes; she did not want to be isolated from her family in the time she had left.

Dinner for Mom was raspberry-applesauce and mashed sweet potatoes. The spirit was willing but the body was weak. We had to keep reminding her to chew, swallow and drink. After dinner and dishes Mom seemed to have been touched by an angel when, with another burst of energy, she said in a commanding voice. "Well..., did you bake the cake yet?"

"Not yet," we sheepishly admitted.

"What are you waiting for? Tomorrow's Easter! You two are ridiculous! Bake the cake right now!" She demanded, and hastened to add, "And after that, we have to make the chocolate pie because Connie doesn't like coconut."

"You don't have to make a chocolate pie for me," said Connie.

And jealously I whined, "Yeah, and why do you always have to treat Connie or Roger so special anyway?"

She laughed and said, "Because Grandma taught me that you have to bend over backwards to be nice to your son- or daughter-in-law. They don't have to love me, but you do."

The Easter cake brigade went into action. Connie got the metal mold shaped like a lamb and the can of Crisco. Before you knew it, Mom grabbed the mold, stuck her hand into the Crisco and began greasing the pan while I got the cake mix, bowl and beaters and whipped up the batter. She was trying to take charge as usual. "Is the oven on?" She said.

"Yep, it's heating up," replying to the master chef. "Are you ready with the mold?"

"Yes." She handed it to me. "Pour it in." As Mom supervised, I started to fill the mold with batter. "More……a little more……You have to fill it to almost overflowing! If it rises you can level it off, but you have to fill it really full so it takes the shape of the mold," she instructed. Watching carefully, she finally pronounced, "That's good." Into the oven it went.

"Now! While the cake is baking, you have to make the Dutz's icing, and I'll tell you how to do it." I reached for a bowl, measured the flour and milk, and dumped it into a bowl. Just as I started to mix it, she yelled. "No. No. No. You aren't listening to me! You have to cook it!"

She startled me because I thought I was following her instructions. Maybe I didn't hear her say cook it, or maybe she thought she said it, but it didn't matter. Right now, I was looking down at my frustrated mother. And no wonder! She was sitting helplessly in a wheelchair—out of control in her own kitchen for the first time in her life! This was a big deal. She could barely hold a spoon let alone bake a cake, but she wanted her last Easter to be absolutely perfect. To myself I said, "Focus, Donna. Focus! Keep it moving."

In an attempt to diffuse her emotions and mine, I quickly apologized. "Sorry. I wasn't concentrating. Of course you cook it." And I dumped the mixture in the sauce pan and turned up the heat. "Okay, Mom, here we go. How long do I cook it?"

"You have to keep stirring. Don't stop stirring until it gets like a thick paste. I'll tell you when to stop. Just keep stirring." Mom stayed right next to me at the stove and I occasionally took the pot off the burner to show her how it was coming.

"Not done yet. It has to be really thick. Keep stirring."

Then finally, "Okay! That's good. Now put it in the refrigerator until the cake is done. It has to be cold." We eventually decided that we could ice it the next day, because it was getting late and the cake was still in the oven and had to be thoroughly cool before icing. "We can do it early tomorrow morning," she said. "The coconut is in the pantry and you have the jelly beans, right?"

"Yes, we do." I stooped down to hug her and said softly, "I know you would have had everything done by now, Mom, but with your help it's going to be great. We're your sous-chefs and with your directions we're glad to finally learn how to make the Lamb Cake. It's a tradition you started long ago and we'll be able to keep it up."

She said, "Good. Since Connie hates coconut, I want you to have the mold, Donna."

"Okay, but I don't want to think about that now because we have Easter eggs to dye. Where's Larry?" He came bounding in from the family room. "Come on, Lar. We're going to dye eggs."

"All right!" Larry said with the delight of an excited child. "Let me read the directions. Okay, we're going to do it the easy way, Mom, and I think you're gonna like it. All we have to do is put the sleeves on the hard boiled eggs that we made this morning and drop them in boiling water, and they'll be decorated with colorful pictures rather than bothering with vinegar and water."

When the water was boiled, Larry helped Mom hold the egg and guided her hand as she put on the first sleeve. I held the pot of water and we all watched as she dropped the egg in the water.

"Yeaaaaaa! You got it, Mom. Now do the rest while I get this one out of the water with a slotted spoon." So, with Larry's help, Mom was the one, as usual, who dyed the Easter eggs.

When we took the cake out of the oven, I was not able to keep up the front any longer. I slipped into the bedroom to have a cry, face in pillow. This was the last time Mom and I would ever work in the kitchen together. No more Sunday cooking marathons. No more menus to plan. No more Thanksgiving, Christmas and New Year's Day feasts like the ones we just had. I wanted to wake up from this nightmare! But no, this was reality, and after the blessing of tears gave me some relief, I went back to the kitchen and stopped dead in my tracks.

Mom was actually standing in front of the kitchen counter. Connie had lifted her out of the wheelchair, moved behind her and wrapped her arms around Mom's waist from the back to keep her steady. "What are you doing?" I asked nervously.

"Mom wanted to take the cake out of the mold herself, so I'm helping her stand so she can do it." It was an amazing sight! Slow and shaky, but she was actually doing it. Using a knife to loosen the edges, she turned it over by herself with a tea towel for an oven mitt. She positioned it onto the large cake platter where it would finish cooling until morning when we would finally ice it.

Proud of her accomplishment and smiling happily, Mom said, "There! That's done! Let's go over the menu one last time so you know where everything is for tomorrow, including the wine, and then we can relax." With help, she settled back into the wheelchair.

While Connie and I cleaned the kitchen, Larry moved Mom back to the living room. In a short while we all sat congratulating each other on an incredible day, grateful that our mother was living every moment of her life to its fullest just as she hoped to do. In one day, she had visited with her sister, entertained many friends, held a tea party, ate dinner, baked her Easter Lamb Cake, colored Easter eggs, and given us our marching orders for the next day.

It is true that, with God, all things are possible—how else could you live with ovarian cancer for two years without pain, until six days ago. Ah, the power of prayer and the gift of hospice! Life really *is* a big surprise!

Easter Sunday, April 15

Mom wanted to go to church this day, but it was impossible. I had to give her Oxyfast early in the morning, and that knocked her for a loop. It was only the smallest amount possible, but because she was so sensitive to drugs, it worked very quickly on her. That, added to the regular dose of pain medicine after breakfast, really slowed her down. She was the same mother with the same positive attitude and determined spirit, still fully with us—but drugged!

After following Mom's morning routine—wash, dress, food and drink, change of bed linens, conversation, and putting her back to bed for a nap, Connie and I set the table. We used Mom's yellow Easter table cloth and napkins, candles, her best china, crystal and silver then added the centerpiece of yellow and red tulips. More flowers, platters of Easter eggs, and the special chocolate candy we bought were dotted around the house.

Earlier in the week, I tried to arrange for her pastor to make an Easter visit with Mom because she couldn't go to church and we had no plans on leaving her alone. He was out of town and the other ministers in the area were fully committed to services and crises with their own congregations. It was disappointing, but then I thought of Gervis.

Gervis Black, a family friend and retired minister from Canada lived only an hour or so away with his wife Liane. I called and they offered to come Easter Monday and spend the day with us. In this way, we could extend our Easter celebration to include Roger who would be arriving Easter night.

When Mom awoke from her nap, she reminded us that we were to ice the cake, but she wanted to stay in bed to conserve her energy. I kept making trips back and forth from the bedroom to the kitchen to get her approval. "That looks good; now add the coconut." When that was done, she asked, "Where are the jelly bean eyes? And don't forget the nose and mouth." Then…"You forgot the grass!" Finally…"Perfect! I couldn't have done it better myself." High praise, indeed!

Satisfied everything was under control, she fell into a deep sleep for a long time. Connie verbalized what we were all thinking, "She's not going to be able to get out of bed and eat today is she?" We agreed, and talked about how symbolic it would be if she were to die on Easter Day. Resurrection Sunday! On the other hand, we knew she was determined to wait for Roger.

We took turns sitting with her while she slept. Larry and I happened to be together when she finally opened her eyes. Once she was able to focus, she managed a grin and said, "Did you ever get the feeling people are staring at you?" We laughed and knew her sense of humor was still intact, if not her body.

She could hardly keep her eyes open, but said, "Talk to me."

"What do you want us to talk about, Mom?"

"Anything."

"Would you like us to read to you?" She nodded her head.

Larry asked, "What's your favorite part of the Bible?"

She whispered, "Psalm 103." The same one she had me read to her lady friends the day before. Larry reached for the Bible on her nightstand and began. *"Bless the Lord, O my soul, and all that is within me…"* Mom listened and began mouthing the words along with him. Larry's face shone with love, happy to be able to comfort his mother with the word of God.

His voice, while steady throughout, sometimes tightened with emotion, and cracked slightly when he read Verse 14: *"For he knows how we are formed, he remembers that we are dust. As for man, his days are like grass, he flourishes like a flower of the field; the wind blows over it and it is gone, and its place remembers it no more."* He cleared his throat, and his face flushed knowing he would remember her forever. Larry continued in love and reverently finished the psalm as it began: *"Bless the Lord, O my soul."*

I left the room so Larry could talk to Mom alone, but not before looking back and locking the image of the two of them together. When she fell back to sleep, we continued taking turns walking with her as she continued the journey home, but she would have to make the final leg alone. We wondered when that would be. Later, we learned it would not be on Easter Day.

"What time is it? How long have I been sleeping? It must be time to eat. Gotta get up! When is Roger coming?" Back from the brink! We're going to make it through Easter together after all.

We helped her up, took care of "business," washed her face and combed her hair, even put a little blush on her cheeks and brought her into the dining room. She loved the way the table looked with the tulips and the attention we paid to every detail, using all her favorite things. The only problem we had was that it wasn't until Mom had mentioned dinner that we realized the ham was still in the oven. We had been so preoccupied with her that we didn't even pay attention to the smells of the baking ham and sweet potatoes that wafted through the house.

The ham was a little dry, but tasty. Mom let us feed her some baked sweet potato and peas we mashed for her and even some small bits of her special ham with pineapple. She loved the raspberry applesauce and washed it all down with water she could easily drink from a straw.

After dinner, Larry got her settled on the couch while Connie and I did the dishes as usual. It was still early evening when Aunt Angie appeared followed by Aunt Jennie, Frank, and her son, Cousin Ronnie, visiting from Pittsburgh with his daughter Carly. We all babbled on about Easter dinner, the weather, and generally caught up on all the family gossip. Mom's mind was sharp even though her movements were not, and everyone tried to pretend this was just another typical holiday at Aunt Annie's.

As we ran out of topics of conversation, ever the gracious host, Mom said, "Would you like some cake and coffee?" And then with a wave of her hand, Connie and I got the signal to begin resetting the table for dessert and presenting the "perfect" lamb cake. It was placed in the middle of the table along with the Easter chocolates, jelly beans, and colored eggs—all sitting on green plastic grass. We gathered round the dining table just like old times—except that Mom and her younger sister

Jennie were in wheelchairs. Mom had lost all interest in food by this time, something hospice told us would happen.

As the sun was setting and darkness began to fall, the inevitable good-byes had to be said. Trying not to cry and holding on to the last bit of hope, her sisters said, "We'll see you tomorrow, Annie." Aunt Angie stood and bent down to kiss Mom good-bye. Ronnie took some last minute photos of his mother and Mom, and Aunt Jennie twisted her body and leaned toward Mom as best she could from her own wheelchair and I stood close to both of them in case they might slip.

Suddenly, Mom lifted her arms and grabbed hold of Jennie's face, kissed her sister on both cheeks and whispered in her ear with a slight whimper, "Jen, I'm scared; I'm so scared."

With the softest, most comforting tone, Jennie said, "Don't be scared, Annie. It won't be so bad. Remember what you told me. There is nothing to be afraid of. It's part of life. It will be all right." She grabbed hold of Mom's hand and managed to smile.

As the two sisters looked into each other's eyes, Mom simply said, "Okay. I love you."

"I love you, too." Then slowly and awkwardly, Aunt Jennie drove her motorized wheelchair down the makeshift ramp Larry had fashioned out of some spare pieces of wood. Frank and Ronnie helped her into their car and Larry walked Aunt Angie to hers. She asked to be called if things got worse.

That farewell was another dip in the emotional roller coaster we were all riding. As soon as they left, all Mom could say was, "I want to go to bed." After Larry and Connie got her settled, they retired to the family room to watch television while I sat nervously with Mom.

Soon I mustered the courage to ask, "Are you going to wait for Roger to arrive?" She nodded affirmatively, but I wondered. I called Roger to discuss whether or not I should risk picking him up at the airport or call a limo service. We decided he would call a limo if I wasn't at the gate to meet him.

When it was time to go, I checked on Mom and she reassured me that she would be waiting when I returned with the son-in-law she loved so much. Just to be on the safe side, I gave her permission to go. "Okay, Mom, I'm going now, but if you change your mind and need to leave before I get back, it's okay with me. I'll see you later regardless." She knew what I meant and I left the house praying, "Father I abandon my mother into your hands…"

After our airport reunion, Roger and I drove back to Mom's and ran straight to her bedroom. It was empty. A split second of panic and then, "We're in here," Connie yelled. Our next sight was of Mom sitting in the family room with Larry and Connie eating potato chips and watching cartoons on TV! Merciful Lord, how good you are! Hugs and kisses galore were exchanged, and Mom said, "Donna, make him something to eat. Let's all go into the kitchen."

Knowing that Mom loved seeing photos of our trips, Roger came equipped with his pictures of his Habitat trip to the Dominican Republic already in an album. Unfortunately, she couldn't see them and asked that he just describe the highlights. Soon it was time for Mom's pain medicine and bed. "More tomorrow, dearest Roger. I'm so glad you're here."

Monday, April 16

This was the day I was dreading—the day we were scheduled to see John and his doctor. During the previous week, his social worker called to arrange the meeting and inform us that John was "nearly ready to be released." Larry was his Health Care Agent, and as his Power of Attorney, we were both required to be there. Roger would be moral support for all as we finalized the long-term housing and care arrangements for John. Thankfully, Gervis and his wife Liane were on their way, as promised, for our extended Easter celebration.

While we waited for their arrival, I grew more anxious about seeing John again after talking with him by phone a few days before. Had it been only one week since this nightmare began?

"Come and get me. They aren't helping me," John ordered. His social worker promised she would tell him of Mom's current condition, but he was incapable of asking even one question about Mom, his wife of 33 years.

"I'm so sorry, John, but you can't come home. Your bed has been replaced with a hospital bed for Mom. She can't take care of you any more because she's dying, and I can't take care of both of you. Please be patient. The doctors are trying to help you."

People with loved ones suffering from any form of mental illness know that it is next to impossible to reason with them, yet we persist. Slowly, like Chinese water torture, stress, anxiety, and frustration begins to eat away at caregivers. How much more emotionally and physically draining it must have been for Mom to care for him day in and day out, especially in recent weeks, and now it truly was impossible.

"Please, John. The specialists are still trying to get a handle on the right medication for you," I reasoned. "Don't leave while they're still observing you. Cooperate and give them a chance to help you. They haven't given up on you and want to find a solution to your pain."

His response evoked mixed feelings in me. Should I pity the man who seemed to have moved into a permanent state of denial, or despise him for being so self-absorbed and uncaring? It occurred to me that while the two-year process of dying was coming to an end for Mom, John's dying process began long before he ever met my mother. He started withdrawing from reality when he was young, moving in and out of the fantasy world he built for himself. His body was handsome and strong, but his spirit was tormented by alternating obsessions and his inability to accept the love he coveted but never received as a child.

For years we watched and listened to John's endless ruminations about his latest religious obsession, always delivered with an air of superiority to cover the problems that resulted, in part, from his sad and misguided past. No matter what Mom or anyone did to include him in normal activities, John would distance himself from the family, withdrawing more and more into his own mind. He often sat in the dark in his bedroom listening to sermon tapes, avoiding all contact with visitors or family members. Even when he was in the same room—in or out of the house—he seemed to be far away. When words failed to bring him back, a gentle touch often resulted in a pulling away. Mom told of the day he had wandered off when they were at the Mall then forgot where he was or how to find her again. While he panicked, John thankfully had the presence of mind to have her paged, like a little child separated from his mother. But now it was time for Mom to go home without him.

Mom stayed in bed while we waited for Gervis to arrive, and when we checked on her that morning, she was quietly talking to people none of us could see. She seemed to be between two worlds. There was no anxiety; her nightmares were gone, and all that remained was peace—asleep or awake. Every time she opened her eyes, she smiled with contentment. She was in heaven—well, almost.

Earlier she refused to use the bedside commode, but when she saw how hard Larry and Connie struggled to help her to the bathroom, she said angrily, "This is the last time my children are going to do this!" The effort required on her part to put one foot in front of the other or move her body in any direction was too great. We knew time was running out.

The transformation from independence to dependence was dramatic, happening swiftly in just one week! Still she packed in a lot of living with Easter cards, planning her last holiday dinner, spending quality time with her family and friends, enjoying a mother-daughter outing, watching movies, playing cards, doing lunch with her favorite nurse and volunteer, having a bedside tea party, baking a lamb cake and dying Easter eggs.

Happily, our visitors arrived bearing bags of fresh locally grown tomatoes, strawberries, and a new ice cream maker. As Connie and I laid the table, Liane put the berries in the freezer then spent time getting reacquainted with Mom. The open living-dining room was the perfect setting for enjoying our indoor picnic, we at the table and Mom propped up on the couch so she could be part of the conversation. Mom had no interest in food, but loved Liane's strawberry ice cream—her favorite flavor.

As Roger, Larry and I left for the hospital, we noticed Gervis had pulled up a chair to sit close to Mom, but as soon as we left, we learned she asked Connie to help her back to bed. Gervis remained by her side to read and pray with her. Mom asked to write out the poem he recited to her so she could share it with us because it spoke of her faith and hope.

> We can only see a little of the ocean,
> A few miles distant from the rocky shore.
> But out there, beyond our eyes' horizon,
> There's more. There's more.
>
> We can only see a little of God's loving,
> A few rich treasures from His mighty store.
> But out there, beyond our eyes' horizon,
> There's more. There's more.
>
> We come into this world all helpless and bare.
> We go through this world in struggle and care.
> We go out of this world, God only knows where.
> But if He lies in us here, we'll live with Him there.

In another part of the house, Liane helped Connie grieve, later swapping places with Gervis. Liane said Mom apologized for not being able to keep her eyes open, but she wanted to listen to her stories about her life and children. With Liane chattering away, Mom was able to conserve her energy, but she became animated when Liane mentioned her sons. "Oh, I have a son, and my son is wonderful, too. All my children are wonderful." Liane held her hand and continued to speak softly until Mom fell into a very deep sleep. Gervis and Liane were gone by the time we returned home.

On the way to the hospital, Roger and Larry were alarmed as I expressed a mixture of terror and anger at the prospect of being persuaded to bring John back home with us. Since John was always able to relate better to Larry, he would be the one to reason with him. My role would be to handle the doctor and social worker if it came to that, and Roger would pick up the pieces and ensure we handled the entire encounter with dignity and compassion.

Waves of sadness enveloped me as we walked into the psychiatric ward—another world. We were ushered into a plain, small office with a desk, computer and the doctor who was waiting for us. There was barely enough space for the extra chairs we had to squeeze into the room to accommodate us. John was not yet present.

The doctor, who had been away most of the previous week, began by saying he was ready to discharge John, and could not declare him legally incompetent at this early stage in his diagnosis. My blood suddenly ran cold as I remembered being told that I could be jailed if I abandoned John in the ER. But just as quickly, I was bolstered by last week's advice from the nurse at the VA clinic, "Once he is admitted, you do not have to take him back home. He will no longer be your responsibility. If your mother dies, they will consider him to be a sick, homeless veteran without a caregiver, and they must find him a place to live."

I responded to the doctor, "Doctor, as head of the department, your staff has been taking care of John while you were away. Have you been thoroughly briefed on his history and the current situation in our home?"

"Yes," he replied.

"Well you obviously need an update on the situation. Our being here should tell you that we have compassion and concern for John who has been a very sick man since the day he came into our lives. While you have observed him for only a week, we have lived with him for 33 years and can tell you his condition has dramatically worsened since my mother's diagnosis. Now his wife, and only caregiver, is dying. She called for my help, and when I arrived I discovered that she had been depriving herself of pain medicine so she could be alert enough to care for him. John had been screaming in her face for days to take him to the hospital, and I brought him here last week in a heightened state of anxiety and pain.

"This poor, demented man will only go back to his former home over my dead body. Nightmares of his returning home have robbed my mother of her peace, and it has taken an entire week to reassure her that you will see to it that he will have the professional care he needs when she's gone. I pity John, but he has tormented my mother for the last time. I won't let him stand at her death bed. Not once has he asked about her condition since he's been here.

"We cannot divide our time and attention between the two of them. There is nobody who will watch him, give him pills, or listen to his constant mutterings about pain and anxiety or deal with his panic attacks while my mother is dying. And when she dies, my husband and I are going back to New York and my brother and his wife will return to their home and jobs in Orlando. The house, which is in my name, will be placed on the market.

"My brother and his wife have already visited the VA Domiciliary in Lake City. We have talked to them, know that they have vacancies, and have shared this information with John's social worker. I have worked very hard to apply for and get approval for a VA non-service related pension for 100% aid and attendance. When my mother dies—assuming she is still with us when we get home—we do not plan to pick up her cross.

"I don't know what you think the purpose of this meeting is, but we came to be reassured in person that you will transfer him to an appropriate assisted living facility so he will have care for the rest of his life. Please tell us what you plan to do—for his sake and my mother's peace of mind."

He did not answer, but the social worker offered a brochure of the Lake City facility. I would have asked the doctor if he was bluffing or testing us when he suggested we take him home, but the door to his office abruptly opened. It was John. When I saw him I was flooded with emotions of fear, pity, anger, compassion, which added to my disappointment and confusion with the doctor. My heart grieved for what could have been in the life of this poor man. His illness robbed Mom of the husband she could have had and the stepfather we longed for.

What would it have been like if someone had been able to reach him in his youth? Stories of his apathetic family came to mind—his mother, father, brother and sisters. Why could he not receive forgiveness, forgive in return, and accept love and affection? How sad and unfortunate for all of us. I felt sick. Mental illness infects everyone!

John was wearing a brown jumpsuit provided by the hospital, and he looked thinner and frailer in only one week. He was obviously on medication; his movements were slow, and after the first awkward moments, we asked how he was. He responded meekly, "Not very well."

The doctor reassured him and suggested patience saying, "The new drug you are taking will help you, John, but it takes a little more time to see the effect."

John turned to us and said, "I need to get out of here."

It was Larry's turn. "We can't take you home because Mom is very sick, and we can't take care of you as well. We wanted to make sure you are getting the help you need and the right medication. You have been in pain for quite a long time. Give the doctors a chance. It's only been a week."

Silence filled the room, and after a long pause, John asked Larry for the first time, "How is she?"

Softly, tenderly and with great respect, Larry answered. "She's dying, John."

Without missing a beat, he quickly replied. "Well, I guess it's time for me to plan on getting on with my own life." You could hear a pin drop.

John reached into his pocket and held up another VA domiciliary brochure. "This is the place I'm thinking of going to," he said.

I should have kept my mouth shut, but I didn't. "Yes, we have seen the brochure. In fact, Larry and Connie went there to see it in person just to make sure it was nice, John. They liked it very much."

"What?!" he said, wide-eyed. "You've been there? When? How long ago? Did you know about this?" Paranoia was setting in. It was obvious by his reaction that he thought we were in collusion with the doctors. To him, we were implementing a plan to confirm that he was crazy and must be locked up.

Larry gently described the place. "It's beautiful, John. There's a lake where the men go fishing; they take you to ball games; there's transportation to take you into town or to the Mall. They have lots of activities and two large screen TV's, one specializing in sports which you love. You can do as much as you want or as little as you want. You can stay in your room and lay around all day, or you can make friends and get out." John listened but glared at me.

After a prolonged silence, I said, "If there is nothing more we can do today, we had better be getting back to Mom."

The social worker asked whether or not John could come to the funeral. Her question did not appear to even register with him, but she thought it would be a way for him to come to closure. We said yes, and we would call with the logistics when the time came. Thanking the doctor and social worker, we walked to the door with John. We hugged good-bye and said, "We're glad you're getting help, John, and we're so sorry it has to be like this. Please be patient. We'll see you soon."

Praying we had done the right thing, no one spoke again until we began the drive home.

Mom was sleeping when we arrived, but later we brought the picture brochure where John would live to her bedside and told her all about it. She smiled, nodded approvingly, and whispered, "Good." We thought she would never get out of bed again. We were wrong.

Late that afternoon, Larry and Roger decided to go and buy a pizza, and Connie said she would make a salad. Mom was up and in her wheelchair again in the living room with me. The boys left the front door open for some fresh air, and since it was a beautiful day, I said, "Mom, would you like to go for a walk?"

She raised her eyebrows and softly said, "Yes."

"We'll be back, Connie. Mom and I are going for a walk." From behind, I maneuvered her wheelchair down the makeshift ramp—and away we went. Funny, but nobody was out in the open or even on their screened-in porches. Whenever we walked together, people would inevitably wave and stop us to chat, but not today. The outdoors was ours.

As I pushed the wheelchair in front of me, Mom tilted her head toward the sun. She took a deep breath and looked at the sky and wispy white clouds. There was a breeze, and a gentle gust of air brushed her hair. "I can't see your face, Mom, but I can hear what you are thinking. 'My kind of day—blue sky, low humidity, and perfect temperature.' That's what you always say on a day like this, isn't it?"

I slowed to a near stop so I could peek around to look at her sideways. She turned, smiled, reached for my hand, nodded in agreement, and murmured, "My kind of day."

We went around the block and when we got to the corner, a car drove toward us. "Look, Mom. It's Larry and Roger coming back with the pizza." As they approached I could see their mouths open, eyes wide, hardly able to believe what they were seeing—me and Mom "taking a walk." She waved at them, and I said, "See you in a little while."

In a minute or two, I asked if she wanted to walk around the lake. She said, "Yes, but we'd better not. They'll be worried. We probably should go back." I took my time going home. As we approached the front door, Mom held up her hand to tell me to stop. Little did I know that another indelible picture would soon be etched on my mind.

There were two soft evergreen shrubs John had planted years before on either side of her front walk near the house. Now slightly overgrown, their foliage was easy to touch with an outstretched arm, even in a wheelchair. Mom grabbed one of the plants with both hands and gently ran her fingers through the greenery, feeling the sensation on the palms and back of her hands. Then in one spontaneous movement, she buried her face in her hands full of fragrant greens. She nuzzled them to feel the texture on her soft, clear skin and to breathe in the sweet smell of spring. This was the last opportunity she would have to commune with nature, but there was no smell of death in her house; only the promise of new life, new growth.

When her hands returned to her lap, I asked if she wanted to sit on the porch for a while longer. She said, "No, we'd better go in." Mom wanted to join us at the table, but she had no energy left to chew anything, let alone pizza. However, we found one thing that gave her a taste treat—Liane's remaining homemade strawberry ice cream, really a refreshing sorbet.

Connie and I took turns feeding Mom and laughing with her. On the first bite, her heavy eyes opened in surprise and she said, "Mmmm, delicious!" The second, third and subsequent tastes elicited much the same response. She let the frozen fruit melt in her mouth ever so slowly to savor the flavor, and raised her eyebrows with delight even though her eyes were closed. Then she said, "That's enough, let's sit on the couch."

Larry sat on the couch with her while the rest of us quickly cleaned the kitchen before settling down for the evening. Connie went into the family room to watch television while Larry sat at one end of the couch reading to Mom, her feet on his lap. Roger and I decided to take a stroll around the block and when we told Mom we were leaving she dreamily said, "Good; you two go for a nice walk." As we walked past her on the way to the front door, she reached out and grabbed Roger. With a sense of urgency in her voice, she said, "Roger, make sure you take a sweater or a jacket!"

"We don't need a jacket, Mom, it's warm."

"No, no! You must wear something!" She was adamant. He asked why and bent closer to her to hear the response. As if she were telling him a secret, she said, "You need it for the bull rushes."

"The bull rushes? What do you mean, Mom?"

Still whispering, "It's Moses. They put Moses in the bull rushes. You have to be very careful. Don't tell anybody. But they put Moses in the bull rushes—in a basket. Be careful." She put her finger to her lips, "Shhh."

The three of us looked at each other, realizing that she really was between worlds. "Okay, Mom. We'll be careful. Enjoy Larry's reading, and we'll see you in a little bit." She nestled back into the pillow when we kissed her goodbye. Larry smiled as we left Mom in a puddle of love. When we returned, Larry was still reading aloud while Mom continued her travels without ever leaving her living room. She stirred with every change in her beloved son's voice and with our announcement, "We're back!"

Mom shifted her body slightly, smiled sweetly, and quietly repeated, "We're back."

"Wow! Larry's still reading to you, Mom." I stopped short of saying, "You must be nearly at the end by now." Those prophetic words caught in my throat and my eyes filled with tears.

Without opening her eyes, she responded to my comment. "Yes, he's a good reader." With a giggle she added, "Hey, Lar, did you ever think of getting a job as a reader. You'd be so good at that."

Connie joined us and as we sat together, Mom asked for a piece of chocolate, so we peeled the foil off one of the small milk chocolate Easter eggs and watched her swoon as it melted in her mouth. Sips of water kept her hydrated and helped her swallow. She had a wonderful Easter holiday, and now it was time for pain medicine and bed.

We all participated in the process, hugs and kisses, wishes for sweet dreams, and assurances that we were right outside her room if she needed us. Connie turned on the angel night light and I started Nigel's CD so he could pray her to sleep. Another day with Mom had come to an end, and the four of us were emotionally exhausted. It had been a long Monday.

He said to them, "Come with me by yourselves
to a quiet place and get some rest."
(Mark 6:31)

Tuesday, April 17

Mom never woke up, really. She barely opened her eyes all day. Neither food nor water were wanted or needed. She had only enough energy left to breathe, and all we could do was hope she sensed our presence. Even swallowing a pain pill was impossible. Any care would be strictly "hands on." With tentative confidence that Mom would stay alive for a few more days, Connie left for work saying, "I'll be back tomorrow, and she'd better not die on my birthday!"

The hospice home aide arrived to give Mom a bed bath, change the bedding, and use the adult diapers for the very first time. We slit another clean night gown up the back so it could easily be slipped over her head without bothering her. On this day, Mom had no energy to move on her own, and appeared not to be able to speak or swallow. Throughout the day we moistened her lips with a swab, wiped her eyes with warm water if they looked crusty, held her hand, or stroked her hair or arm to let her know she was not alone.

The day nurse taught us how to administer pain medicine to Mom since she could no longer swallow. Larry and I looked at each other in shock! But if Mom was in pain, we had to get over our squeamishness and learn how to administer a suppository. This was our Mother and it was a privilege to help her remain pain free. We learned another lesson that day: you never know what you are capable of doing until you have to do it.

I looked at Larry and said, "My fingers are thinner."

He said, "But mine are longer." I love my brother.

This Tuesday Larry donned the rubber gloves and took the top off the K-Y. I held Mom's hand and told her we were going to give her pain medicine and how we had to do it. Then I placed the pill on the tip of Larry's finger. After rolling Mom toward me, I held her close while Larry did what he had to do. She winced. "Sorry, Mom. We're so sorry. But you can't swallow, so this suppository will keep you out of pain. We love you, Mom."

"Okay," Larry said, "it's done." We both were nervous wrecks and gently repositioned her. Mom tried unsuccessfully to open her eyes, but she managed to whisper "thank you" before drifting off again.

I telephone Mom's sister. "Hi, Aunt Angie, you wanted me to call if there was any change in Mom's condition. Well, there is and I think if you want to see her again, you had better come soon, and please tell Aunt Jennie, too. It's not good." She said she would come after lunch and pass the word onto the others.

Before they came, her neighbor Sue who helped me ready the room for the hospital bed came to the door. I guided her to the doorway of Mom's room. She stood silent, saddened and shocked. Nobody thought Mom would ever really go. She always rallied. I asked Sue to tell the neighbors that we were no longer receiving visitors. From now on, only the family would hold a vigil and I asked her to pray for Mom and all of us. She left in tears.

Mom slept all day, even when Aunt Angie and Aunt Jennie and Frank came to visit. We transferred Aunt Jennie into Mom's smaller wheelchair to more easily get her into Mom's bedroom. Both sisters spent the afternoon reminiscing and talking to Mom, but there was no response from her. They just sat there holding back tears, as they read from Mom's Bible and her favorite devotionals. "Would you like to hear the CD that Mom listens to every night before she goes to bed?"

They were agreeable, and soon Nigel began leading my aunts through relaxation exercises and healing prayers. It was just what they needed to hear.

Since Mom had Larry and her two sisters with her, Roger and I decided to visit the minister at the church we had selected for her Florida memorial service. The pastor was a big teddy bear of a minister, very warm, welcoming, and had a sense of humor. He agreed to allow us to use his church for Mom's service since most of her lady friends attended All Saints Lutheran. He welcomed the participation of Mom's own pastor who only did memorial services in the evening, too late for the frail elderly. He also honored the hospice chaplain's request to say a few words; after all, he had been her spiritual counselor since November.

We summarized Mom's life and walk with God for the pastor and talked about the many roles she filled. All we had to do when Mom passed away was to simply call him and pick the date for the service. Roger would lead the music; Mom loved to listen to him play and was so proud when he was asked to be the substitute organist at Mom's own church for her last Christmas.

When we returned home, it was nearing dinner time and after sitting by Mom's bedside all afternoon, her elderly sisters and brother-in-law needed a break to rest their own weary bones. They kissed Mom and said good-bye over her sleeping body, planning to return the next day.

After dinner, Ronnie and Carly came alone to sit with Aunt Annie. Ronnie talked with her, hoping she would hear. He told her how much he loved her and how he was always going to remember her and all the family parties she hosted through the years. Carly cried, not only because she loved her great-aunt, but also because this was her first experience with the death of someone so close.

Connie called many times that day to check on Mom, saying hopefully, "I know Mom's going to still be there when I come tomorrow." When Larry called that night to let her know Mom made it through the day, she said, "Don't call me in the morning. I'm going to make a quick stop at work, and then I'll be on the road. If she dies before I get there and you tell me, I won't be able to see to drive." He honored her wishes.

The three of us took turns sitting with Mom the rest of the evening. During one of my shifts, I noticed Mom's eyes looked as if they were glued shut. After soaking a washcloth in warm water, I carefully wiped the sticky moisture from her lids and lashes. She felt warm, so with a cool cloth I refreshed her face, hairline, neck and arms. She uttered her second "thank you" of the day.

"You're welcome, Mom, and thank you for all the times you wiped my brow. I'm so glad we are all here for you. Larry and Roger are watching TV. Do you want to see them?"

She nodded.

Running through the dining area, I yelled through the kitchen slider into the family room, "Quick! Roger. Larry. Mom wants to see you." They leapt to their feet and were at her bedside in a flash. They greeted her with big smiles and kisses. Larry sat down so his face could be close to hers. Roger stood at his shoulder.

She struggled to get the next three words out because her mouth was dry and her tongue thick with medication. Her body was shutting down. All she could manage was, "I love you," before she drifted peacefully off to sleep. Those were her precious last words, most likely the first words our tiny ears heard her say when we were born.

Around 10:30 before we went to bed, Larry administered her last pain pill, and I gave her a tiny bit of Oxyfast to be safe. We went to bed, with Larry sleeping just outside her room.

Wednesday, April 18

About 1:15 a.m., I woke up with a sudden urge to check on Mom. I didn't like the way she sounded. Larry was awake as well and said that while he had heard the change in her breathing, it was steady, very consistent. Looking closer, I noticed her furrowed brows in the glow of the angel night light.

"I don't like the way she looks. I think she may be in pain," I said, and quickly grabbed for the Oxyfast on her night stand. I opened her mouth with my fingers and gave her a small dose under her tongue before I called the hospice. After describing what I saw, I said to the person on call, "I just need some reassurance that I'm doing the right thing, and I was wondering if someone could tell if 'this is it' or not."

"Why don't we send Mary-Ellen the night nurse to the house to check on her?" I was relieved, and in a few minutes we saw Mary-Ellen's shadowy figure through the frosted glass panels on either side of the front door.

Mary-Ellen told us we were doing everything correctly, and gave Mom another tiny dose of Oxyfast to make sure she was out of pain. It was comforting to have the nurse come in the middle of the night and tell us her vital signs were still pretty good. "She could be like this for a few more days."

I worried that we were giving her too much pain medicine, but Mary-Ellen told me that some patients get much more. Mom never needed very much. Only the slightest amount knocked out the pain in a matter of seconds from the first time she took it. Mary-Ellen left about 2:15 a.m., and we went back to bed.

Something woke me with a start at 6:30 a.m. and I ran to Mom's room. Her lips were now parted and her teeth clenched. She was taking such hard breaths of air that her chest heaved up and down unnaturally. Now on the exhale there were gurgling noises emanating from her throat. *Is this Mom's death rattle?* When I turned on the bedside light, I could see more clearly. She was fighting for every breath. *Had she been waiting for us? Was she in pain?* I felt guilty and helpless.

My thoughts turned to my friend Kathy who asked her hospital nurse when she was in pain on her deathbed, "What would you do for me right now if I was the wife of the Head of Oncology?"

"I would give you a large dose of Ativan combined with morphine."

"Then do it!" Kathy demanded.

With that in mind, I picked up the Oxyfast and began talking to her as I filled the dropper. "I'm here, Mom. I know you can't speak to me because you are concentrating on breathing. I think you may be in pain with all this work you're doing, so I'm going to give you some Oxyfast to help you." Her jaw was locked. I tried to pry her mouth open, but couldn't. My eyes filled with tears.

I struggled to hold onto the dropper as I used the fingers on both hands to separate her teeth. Finally, I squeezed the rubber top several times to make sure the Oxyfast was administered onto the soft tissue by her tongue.

As I screwed the dropper back on the jar, Larry walked in. He took my place on the left side of her bed, lowered the guard rails so we could get closer, and sat on the chair next to the night stand with the light and clock. Moving the chair on right side of the bed closer, I called to Roger. He was already in the doorway. When he saw Mom was struggling for every breath, he dashed into the other room to get the Prayer Book. Returning in seconds, and unable to find his own words at this moment of time, he began to read aloud for all of us to hear:

"Almighty God, look on this your servant, lying in great weakness, and comfort her with the promise of life everlasting, given in the resurrection of your Son Jesus Christ our Lord. Deliver your servant Anna, O Sovereign Lord Christ, from all earthly bonds and may she rest in her eternal home with the Father and the Holy Spirit. Into your hands, O merciful Savior, we commend our mother Anna to you. Acknowledge her, a sheep of your own fold, a lamb of your own flock, a sinner of your own redeeming. Receive her into the arms of your mercy, into the blessed rest of everlasting peace, and into the glorious company of the saints in light. Amen."

Then there was nothing but silence.

All we heard was my beautiful mother's labored breathing. Maybe it was my imagination, but the effects of the Oxyfast seemed to help, but just a little. Was it only hours before that the nurse told us she could be like this for a few days? I knew she was wrong, but the last thing I wanted to do was break down, because it would upset Mom. *What do I do now? Is hearing really the last sense to go? What does she need to abandon herself into God's hands? Is it permission, reassurance from us?*

I began to speak for all of us, especially for Larry whose eyes were fixed on her, grave with incomprehensible sorrow. He was only able to talk to her with his heart and his eyes. I could hear Mom's voice in my head saying, "Be strong. There will be time to grieve."

I began, "Mom, we're here. We're all here. Larry, Roger and me, just like you wanted. You said we would always be together, and you were right. We're the Team! You, me and Larry. We know you can't talk to us because you're working on breathing, but we know you can hear us.

"We love you so much, and we always will. We'll never forget you or the lessons you taught us. And we will always be together. Larry and I love each other, Mom, and we will stay close. We'll take care of each other and we'll both make sure John is in a safe place. He will have all the help and care he needs. We promise there will be no discord. No discord, Mom.

"Your God will be our God until the day we die. But right now, your work is finished here on earth and it's getting close to the time when you have to go. We want you to know that we're okay, and we are ready to let you go. It's time for your promotion! It's time for you to hear the words: Well done, good and faithful servant.

"This is not good-bye because we'll see you later. You just happen to be going before us. But for now, we're going to stay right here with you. We are not going to leave you. We'll sit here quietly and watch and wait with you until you and God decide when it's time for you to go. We love you, Mom, and know you love us with your whole heart. God bless you, my precious, beautiful Mother."

The world stood still. We sat motionless, just listening and holding her hands, Larry to the left and me to the right. We never took our eyes off her except to glance at one another with trepidation. Then her breathing began to change, yet again.

She still struggled, but there seemed to be a growing pause between each exhalation. As her breathing slowed, so did the gurgling sounds made when air passed through the back of her throat. We were brought to the edge of our seats several times when it stopped, only to start again after a second or two. Then it finally happened. With one long and slow release of her breath—she left.

Without taking his eyes off Mom, my baby brother, Mom's Gentle Giant, waited and then stretched out his long arm attached to his 6′4″ frame and placed his large hand gently across Mom's throat to check her pulse. He kept it there for a while, trying to sense a distant heart beat. Looking past his solemn face, I noticed the digital clock next to him on the night stand. It read 7:09 a.m., just three minutes after giving her permission to go.

When Larry took his hand away, we sighed with relief, but sat for a while secretly wondering if she would wake up. My body tingled as I shook off what felt like a protective bubble that had engulfed me for two years. The reality set in and tears filled our eyes. Dazed, we just looked at each other as if to say, "What do we do now?"

"The hospice nurse told me that when Mom dies, we don't have to do anything. We can just sit here for as long as we like, and call them when we want to. There's no rush."

It's a bit of a blur now. We were in shock even though this was the moment we had been anticipating. We began pacing in and out of the bedroom, feeling lost, not knowing whether we should sit or stand—alternating from hugging each other to just sitting and gazing at Mom. She was lovely. Cancer did not ravage her exterior. As always, she still had good color and her skin was so smooth, like a much younger woman.

Larry said, "Connie is going to be so upset. Today is her birthday."

We all agreed not to call so she could drive safely. Those were her instructions. I prayed the seed I planted the day before would sprout: "Remember, Connie, if she does die tomorrow, the two of you will have the same birthday—you in this world, and she as she enters her new life for all eternity." *Would she remember?*

When we were ready, I called hospice. As we waited, I wondered if I should fix something to eat for Roger and Larry. Then the doorbell rang.

A neighbor lady whom I had never met, and whose name I can no longer remember, stood in front of me when I opened the door. She was holding a plate of freshly baked cranberry muffins. "The Lord woke me up this morning and told me to bake these," she said.

"Why, thank you. Who are you?"

I'm your mother's neighbor. We live just down the street and we go to the same church."

"Oh, how nice."

"Is there anything I can do."

"Well, there's nothing to do now. I'm sorry to have to tell you like this, but my mother just passed away and we are waiting for someone to come."

"Oh, dear. Oh, dear. I'm so sorry. I knew she was ill, but I saw her in church less than two weeks ago and she looked so good. Now I understand why I felt I had to get up and bake. I'm so sorry. Are you sure there is nothing I can do?"

"Well, there is one thing. Could you please call Pastor Jim and tell him?"

"Oh, yes. I'll do it right away." She hurriedly turned to go.

"Thank you." And I thanked the Lord for the cranberry muffins.

And do not worry about what you will eat or drink;
Your Father knows…But seek his kingdom,
and these things will be given to you as well.
(Luke 12:29-31)

It took about 15 minutes for the hospice nurse to arrive; it was Mary Ellen, still on duty. Larry and Roger said they would take turns showering, and I followed the nurse into Mom's room. She looked like she was sleeping. Mary-Ellen approached Mom's body very tenderly, and checked her vital signs to officially note the date and time of death. She then called the funeral home which we had prearranged to handle Mom's transfer from Florida to Pittsburgh for burial.

After that, she asked if I would mind leaving the room so she could get her ready to go, and I asked, "Do you need any help?"

She looked shocked and said, "Oh! No. You don't have to do that."

"Why not? What are you going to do?"

"I'm going to wash her and make sure she is ready when the funeral director comes."

"Wouldn't it be easier for you if I helped? I don't mind. This is not my mother. It's just the house she used to live in, and I would consider it a privilege."

She nodded and I closed the door. We went to work. The nurse rolled her body toward me. I could see her face and feel her softness while holding her close. The nurse did what she had to do and, surprisingly, everything was fine. There was no mess, no odor. I heard no noise or saw no change in Mom's appearance. The unpleasant stories about people's bowels and bladder emptying right after they die did not happen with my mother.

Mom's body was still warm, and it felt just like it did the day before when Larry and I washed her ourselves and changed her clothes. I knew where my mother was, and it wasn't in this bed.

Mom died a holy death—a death set apart for a special purpose. She used the more than two years of living with a terminal illness to teach us how to respond to Faith's call to action in times of crisis, especially when someone you love is dying. With the help of the Holy Spirit she modeled how to continue living until you take your last breath.

We were not with John when he passed away. Mom died three days after Easter and he died the following Good Friday, free at last. After a rapid decline in his mental condition and not long after Mom's funeral, he was moved to a secure Alzheimer's wing of an assisted living facility. God used this disease to end his years of mental torment, and he was not even aware that he was diagnosed with an aggressive, inoperable cancer which caused his ultimate death. John was surrounded by angels, seen and unseen, at the end of his life, and he was buried with military honors.

In hindsight, the positive lessons learned from John's life are many, and I asked to be forgiven for my anger and lack of self control during the years he was part of our family. Forgiving and receiving forgiveness were integral to my personal healing and ability to move forward with my life.

Grief can be debilitating, and Mom knew that all too well. She protected us from the experience and replaced our fear of losing her by creating new memories throughout her illness, while together or apart, including the last nine days of her life. Mom was a model of grace, forgiveness, and compassion to the end. Remembering what we learned from her and recalling the love and laughter we shared in the simple pleasures of life places a protective cover on the hole in our hearts.

In my mind's eye, I can see Mom experiencing the reality of a dream God gave me over four years before she died—a vision of what happens when we are instantly thrust into the presence of God. I prayed then to remember the dream forever, especially when someone I love dies before me. He answered my prayer.

Today you will be with me in Paradise.
(Luke 23:43)

The Dream

Listen to this dream I had. . .
(Genesis 37:6)

It began at a World War II Veterans Conference. There were rows of booths displaying the latest in military technology, from hand guns to bombs. Information centers were crowded with people trying to locate friends and relatives who served in various branches of the armed services. As I approached a display used to search for the names of those still missing in action, I noticed a man who looked as if he was waiting for someone. Suddenly, I recognized him. *Could it really be my father?*

"Daddy, daddy! It's me, your daughter Donna. You're alive! We thought you were dead!" I began to cry and reached out to touch him.

He no longer looked like his pictures, but I was positive it was my father. As he turned to face me, I could see he was scarred from shrapnel wounds, and his eyes revealed a faintly vacant look. "Don't you recognize me, Daddy? Of course you don't; I was only a year old when you went away."

Just as he was about to speak, I noticed a blue beam of light with a red tip pointed at his chest. I turned and saw another man holding a new high-tech rifle in the booth next to us. "Nooooo!" I screamed and lunged at him, pushing the weapon upwards. The force of our impact knocked the rifle from his hands, and it went off as it fell to the floor.

Shocked, the man exclaimed, "Oh, my God, it was loaded!"

I pounded on his chest as I yelled, "You fool! You almost killed my father. I just found him after all these years, and you nearly killed him!"

His response incensed me even more. "I'm sorry, lady. It didn't hit him; and even if it did, it would have been an accident."

"An accident! An accident! How could you even think like that?"

Just then, there was a tremendous flash of light—an explosion—and everyone was instantly thrust into the presence of God!

There was no pain or damage to our bodies, but all of my senses were heightened. I felt a sudden release of all negative emotions and was aware of, by contrast to the blast, the sound of utter silence. But we were not alone. Surreal figures seemed to stretch throughout a starlit infinity. Wonderfully weightless, I slowly turned toward a single Source of Light that seemed to flood the heavens and begin to envelop everyone. It was too bright to see anything or anyone at the center of it, but there was no doubt—it was God.

We stood still and speechless, until our knees collapsed. Awestruck, we sucked in the air around us. Everyone was being filled with the new Breath of Eternal Life!

The next thing I remember was hearing something nearly indistinguishable. Then, as if someone was turning up the volume on a radio, I heard an indescribable blend of voices, a variety and combination unlike any the human ear has ever experienced. My head lowered to my bent knees in humility and gratitude until my own voice surfaced from deep within me, adding to the cacophony of sounds coming from the innermost part of every being in the Light.

Tens upon tens of thousands were spontaneously praising The Creator of the Universe, adoring Our Heavenly Father. The volume and rhythms of what must have been music to God's ears ebbed and flowed without ceasing. Lost in the wonder of it all, I was no longer able to distinguish any features of those around me. It was as if we beings were simply melded together—old souls and new ones like mine and my dad's—glorifying the King of Kings.

Then it happened. I was completely absorbed by The Light and became one with God with legions of angels surrounding us.

When we see something marvelous on earth, we normally turn to those around us and invite them into our experience saying, "Isn't it beautiful, incredible, spectacular!" There was none of that because we were all transfixed. The only word to describe what it feels like to receive this outrageous display of affection from the Living God is "breathless."

I gasped for air and awoke from my dream—not that I wanted to.

"Roger, Roger!" I reached for my husband and said, "I can't breath. A dream—I just had a dream." He listened drowsily as I spouted disjointed phrases and he drifted back to sleep. But I prayed. "Dear God, thank you for this dream, and please let me never forget it so when someone I love goes before me, I'll know where they are and be able to rejoice with them." God answered my prayer the morning my mother died. I remembered. I grieved. But it was good grief.

Elements of my dream are not inconsistent with the accounts of people who claim to have had near-death experiences. They do not want to come back. They say the bright light was like a magnet, too wonderful for words. The peace. The freedom you feel. The total acceptance. I'll never forget the sounds of praise.

If that's what it's like when we die, I wonder what happens next. Do we stay in that suspended state of adoration for eternity? The Bible tells us that we will be at rest with God until the dead will be raised when Christ returns to earth. I don't know about you, but it is impossible for me to comprehend the things God has in store for us during this period of rest or what being reunited with our bodies will be like when the earth is renewed.

While my puny mind has difficulty comprehending eternity, I do believe my dream gave me a glimpse into what happened to my mother as she released her last breath on earth. She was instantly thrust into the presence of God, and immediately filled with the Breath of Eternal Life.

Our sacred walk through the pages of this book is now ending, but I pray, dear reader, that your real life walks through the valley of the shadow of death will forever more be filled with light. Whether it is you or someone else holding the candle, look to the Light of the World and trust in God's promises. He is true to his word and you will never be alone.

For God so loved the world that he gave his one and only Son, that whoever believes in him shall not perish but have eternal life. (John 3:16)

About the Author

Donna Authers has a passion for applying her natural caregiving skills to help bring hope and healing to hurting people. These skills have been honed through use and her leadership in Stephen Ministry and Community Bible Study. She is a gifted teacher and, as such, has trained and mentored many other volunteers to develop their own caregiving skills to serve others.

Over the years, Donna has been invited regularly into the homes of families learning to accept death and has walked with them throughout the grieving process. She has worked closely with hospice organizations, counselors, social workers and clergy, and has been an advocate for individuals dealing with the medical system and government agencies.

After earning a B.S. degree from the University of Pittsburgh in Social Science and Business Education, the author enjoyed a successful business career in sales and management for thirty years, mostly with the IBM Corporation. She retired after meeting her husband on a business trip to Paris in 1991 and has never looked back. It seems as if God had a bigger plan for her life, and what she thought was her career she now views as her training ground.

She moved from the business world to full-time volunteer work in 1993, and today continues to devote much of her time to caring ministries. Helping others, young and old, cope with new chapters in their lives and finding renewed enthusiasm for the future is a key element of her work.

Donna values feedback from her readers and appreciates when they take time to share their own experiences with her. She can be contacted through her website where you can also order a *Discussion Guide* for use by small groups studying *A Sacred Walk* in community.

www.asacredwalk.com